CU CENTURY®

100 YEARS OF COLORADO UNIVERSITY FOOTBALL

a pictorial and entertaining commentary on 100 years of growth and development of the University of Colorado football program - 1890 to 1990.

by **Fred Casotti**

Published by
Original Publications, Inc.
1738 Blake St.
Denver, Colorado 80202

ISBN: 0-926714-90-2

PHOTO CREDITS

The photographers who took the color pictures are designated by their initials, as follows: CG-Cliff Grassmick; EK-Ed Kosmicki; BB-Bill Brittain; MB-Mark Brodie; FC-Fred Casotti. All the black-and-white photos are from three CU sources: athletic department files, the CU Heritage Center and the CU Archives. The cover photo of Darian Hagan scoring against Kansas is by Grassmick. The back cover is a pair of shots by Brodie from the Texas opener with the post-game fireworks superimposed on a scene from the game which was played on Labor Day night.

The photos of the All-Century and 1961 Reunion teams were by Dan Madden.

D E D I C A T I O N

This book is dedicated to all Buffaloes, past and present, whose efforts made the first CU century not only possible but, for the most part, exciting and entertaining. And in particular we salute the 1989 squad whose superb performance wrote such a spectacular finish to the first hundred years.

Introduction

The sensational finish to the first CU century was a fitting conclusion to a Colorado University football program which was consistently a winner during that period.

A look at the record indicates the quality of CU football over those first 100 years. The school ranked 24th in the nation (among 106 Division I NCAA schools) in victories with a 521-338-22 record following the end of the regular 1989 campaign.

During that time, Colorado squads won or tied for 22 conference championships, finished second 16 times and third 20.

For the record, let it be known that neither the author, the publishers nor anyone else even remotely connected with the birth of this book utilized special visionary qualities to deliver it during the high mark of a hundred seasons.

The idea was hatched by David Plati and Bill Marolt as simply one of many pieces of the celebration of the end of the first century. So the credit goes to them and in particular to Plati, the latest and the brightest in a succession of CU sports information directors which includes the author.

Many others also were important in producing this work, among them the following:

Sports editor Dan Creedon of the Boulder Daily Camera, the best in the business, and his ace photographer Cliff Grassmick, whose outstanding shots dominate the color section;

Other contributing photographers Ed Kosmicki of the current CU staff; former CU camera men Floyd Walters, Myron Harding and George Kupfner, whose work spanned nearly half of the first century; and free lancers Bill Brittain and Mark Brodie;

Cartoonist Drew Litton of the Rocky Mountain News, whose nimble brain and adept pen portrayed so vividly the "game of the century" against Nebraska in 1989; Mike Baier and Jon Burianek who supplied the vital figures concerning Folsom Field capacities and costs;

Nancy Markham, who rules over the CU Heritage Center, and her assistant, Karie Darrow, who allowed me to literally rip important historical pictures off the center's walls;

Cassandra Volpe, CU's diligent guardian of western history and archives, and her assistant David Hays who were so valuable in helping me dig into the past;

Franklin and Fred Folsom, Jr., sons of the CU immortal, for their help in picturing the past.

A pair of real old-timers, Jack Healy and Hatfield Chilson of the great 1923-24 teams, whose moral and pictorial support were real inspirations;

And last but not least, the sports information trio of Dave Plati, Becky Yahn and Tom Petersen who permitted me to rummage unchecked through their hallways, offices and files.

There are more but these were the main ones and they deserve the gratitude of everyone who labored on this history or who has enjoyed reading it.

As to the sequence, it was ripped out of its intended chronological pattern by the excitingly exquisite and certainly surprising 1989 season.

It begins with the 1989 season, finest of the first century, where it belongs: up front.

Then comes the national championship Orange Bowl meeting with Notre Dame for the ultimate bragging rights of 1989.

And then the first 99 years and their scores of heroes, sung and unsung, who have etched their feats and the records of their teams into CU's gridiron history. You'll find most of them present as you meander through those first hundred years.

At the back of the book you'll find the culmination of 100 years of records and statistics.

May your journey bring happy memories.

The goal posts come down as a jubilant crowd covers Folsom Field at the end of the Nebraska game.

A FANTASTIC FALL 1989

A strange atmosphere was settled over the CU football scene as fall practice opened in mid-August of 1989. On the positive side was a veteran, talented squad returning, one which had almost reached the heights against Oklahoma and Nebraska the year before only to fall short by the narrowest of margins then capsize against BYU in the Freedom Bowl. On the negative side was the almost-constant turmoil which had clouded the picture, beginning with grumblings about the bowl performance and continuing almost uninterruptedly until early summer with repeated charges and counter-charges concerning incidents involving CU players and local police. Compounding the problem was a continual barrage of publicity and criticism from local then national media.

So the fall began with high hopes and nervous forebodings. Which CU squad would emerge - a talented, veteran crew ready to resume its quest for the Big Eight title, or one dominated by the over-aggressiveness off the gridiron which had begun the year with such an adverse climate?

1989

Texas figured to be a perfect opening opponent for the Buffaloes. The Longhorns were in a rare "down" period, coming off a 4-7-0 season and still in a rebuilding stage after a controversial coaching change in 1987. But Texas nevertheless carried a big-time label. The Longhorns traditionally are one of the top programs in the nation. By 1989 they were definitely on the way back and would provide a solid opening test for the Buffaloes who were still being questioned, despite excellent returning personnel from 1988's 8-4-0 team, because of the disappointing finish in the Freedom Bowl.

That 1988 windup and the constant turmoil which clouded the CU situation almost continually following the BYU aerial ambush at Anaheim produced an air of uncertainty about the Buffaloes even though they had the nucleus for a fine team.

But things had settled down considerably by mid-summer although McCartney added one more disciplinary bombshell just before the start of the August workouts when he suspended regular defensive backs Deon Figures and Keith Pontiflet, the top two left corners, because of off-campus incidents involving their presence at downtown Boulder confrontations which produced no violence but which incurred Mac's wrath. Figures had been named the Big Eight's defensive newcomer of the year after a fine frosh performance in 1988.

The loss of those two veterans to an already suspect secondary added to some nagging worries about the CU situation. Sal Aunese was battling cancer courageously. But he was losing a hopeless battle. His obvious physical deterioration was casting a pall over the CU campus. Compounding the negatives was the by-now public knowledge that the stricken CU star had fathered a son to McCartney's daughter and there would in all likelihood be no marriage. A Boulder throwaway newspaper trumpeted this story with an account that would have embarrassed even the National Enquirer.

Mac never flinched. He plowed steadily ahead with his 1989 game plan, making no public pleas for understanding about his personal problems while preparing for the season which would present the biggest-by-far challenge in his 8-year tenure at CU.

Greeting him for the beginning of fall practice would be 37 lettermen including nine offensive and seven defensive regulars (Figures would have made it eight.) There was no doubt in anyone's mind that the 1989 Buffaloes were almost, if not quite, up to the standards of an Oklahoma or Nebraska physically. With that fact established, the pressure would be on Mac. He now had the pieces in the puzzle to contend for a Big Eight title. Now it would be up to him to make them fit.

There was one key problem, one of major magnitude. Without Aunese the Buffs would be forced to go with sophomore Hagan, a youngster who had flashed signs of brilliance as a late-game replacement for Aunese the year before. But he had failed miserably under pressure in the Freedom Bowl when he was sent into the game in the third period to rescue a faltering Sal. Had a year of inactivity and disappointment dulled the edge of this promising youngster? That was the big question which had to be answered favorably beginning with the opening game against a Texas team which would be as physical as ever though not as skilled as previous Longhorn elevens.

Privately, the CU offensive staff wasn't as concerned as the public might have suspected. Hagan had had a fine spring. He was a quick and strong runner who had operated the option in April much more effectively than his two predecessors, Aunese and Mark Hatcher. And just as importantly he appeared to have a better arm than either of those two men. The CU coaches felt he had great physical tools. The big question mark was: was he ready to face the likes of Texas, Illinois and Washington in September? If he could handle his early assignments the Buffaloes would be a force. If he failed, as he had at Anaheim, the Buffs would be in serious trouble - there were no backup quarterbacks who could cushion that shock.

Only two non-freshmen were even available. Both had emerged from limbo. Only one, Marc Walters, had any experience and his career had apparently been ended after the 1986 campaign when he underwent surgery on one knee then injured the other in spring drills. The other was sophomore Charlie Johnson, who had been in for only one play late in the 1988 opener against Fresno State and who had not even been on the opening spring practice roster because of financial problems which jeopardized his college career.

Walters had decided to give his mended knees a try but only as a desperation replacement in case both Hagan and Johnson, who had clarified his status with the university in time to get in the final half of spring drills, went down.

That was the situation entering the Texas opener. It was a seasoned and talented starting CU cast with the exception of quarterback, which was merely the most important piece in the CU puzzle. The stubby (5-10, 185) Hagan had been just as impressive in fall practice as he had been during the spring. But the 1989 opener would be the biggest test of his career.

27 Texas 6

The Texas game was one of the greatest spectacles in CU history. It had been moved ahead three weeks to Labor Day so it could be on national television. In addition, it would be a night game, again because of TV. A near-capacity crowd in a holiday mood was on hand. All the pressure would be on the highly-favored Buffaloes and, in particular, on Hagan who would be on center stage for the time.

That was the situation at the kickoff. The suspense did not last long. The Buffaloes destroyed Texas quickly and the little quarterback was even more brilliant than the wildest CU supporters could have wished.

CU's "Houston Connection" - tackle Arthur Walker and ends Albert Williams and Kanavis McGhee - spearheaded a defense which completely shackled Texas, which had gone into the game hoping they could puncture the Buff secondary with a pass-oriented offense. They didn't. Williams pulled the plug on the Longhorns when he almost beheaded quarterback Mark Murdock with a vicious sack on the first

Tight end John Perak heads downfield with a pass for a key 13-yard gain in the Texas opener.   DAILY CAMERA

play of their second possession. The Texas thrower wobbled off the field and returned a series later but was never the same.

The final score was 27-6. Texas got only field goals in the second and third periods and needed a fumble recovery and a penalty to move into position for them. Hagan, meanwhile, wasted no time taking command. On the second play of the game he raced 75 yards to the Texas two. Two plays later, Bieniemy dove over and the Buffaloes were on the scoreboard with just 1:15 gone in the season.

If there was any doubt about Hagan's play under pressure it ended two series later. The Buffaloes drove 80 yards in 14 plays. Darian produced 66 of those yards, carrying three times for 19 and hitting all four of his passes for 47 more, the last good for a 5-yard TD to burly fullback George Hemingway. It was 14-0 at the quarter and 17-3 at the half as M.J. Nelson's 47-yard kickoff return following the Longhorn field goal and a 23-yard Hagan-Mark Henry completion set up a short Ken Culbertson 3-pointer.

It was no contest after the rest period as CU reserves played much of the last quarter. CU's ground domination - the Buffaloes outgained the losers 310-115 - was paced by Hagan's 116 yards in 14 carries and solid support

from Bieniemy (66 yards) and Flannigan (51 yards). Hagan added 95 yards on 7-12 passing for a dynamic debut of 215 total yards. The little Buffalo was off and running and so were the Buffaloes. And the 47,269 fans who watched the evening fireworks on a balmy September evening went home happy. So did Mac and his staff. Hagan was for real and so were the Buffaloes. Nobody in the crowd was happier than Aunese, who watched the game from a private area, his face pale and drawn from his six-month ordeal. His teammates saluted him from the field after each big play and he returned them with joyous waves of that right arm which had propelled the Buffaloes to those great come-from-behind victories over Iowa and CSU less than 12 months before. Happy times were ahead for the Buffaloes after this impressive getaway. But time was running out for their gallant comrade.

45 CSU 20

A football staff's worries never end. If there are no real problems facing them these men are adept at manufacturing some. But there was no need for artificial motivation the following Saturday despite the less-than-awesome challenge of a Colorado State team which was under the new leadership of Earle Bruce after going 2-21-0 the previous two seasons. Bruce was no stranger to CU fans. During five years at Iowa State a decade earlier he had proven to be a formidable foe before moving on to Ohio State.

But the factor which produced sleepless nights for McCartney and his men was the jam-up in the schedule created by the advancement of the Texas date. The CSU game would be less than five days later, meaning the Buffaloes at most would have only two days of full practice. CSU had produced cause for anxiety itself with a most impressive opening performance of its own, battling heavily-favored Tennessee to the wire at Knoxville before finally yielding, 17-14. Most of the current CU players hadn't been on hand three years earlier when the Rams had upended the Buffs in Boulder, 23-7. But Mac and his coaches remembered and were understandably apprehensive as the game drew near. But nobody else was concerned. The Buffs were a cinch to breeze in this one, figured the fans.

They did, but not before a nightmarish start. On the first scrimmage play of the game, CSU fumbled the snap then ran 59 yards to the end zone. With only 10 seconds gone, the Buffs trailed, 7-0. But before the CU nightmare could develop, Hagan darted into an opening inside left end and sped 71 yards to tie the score in less than two minutes. Still, CSU persisted, driving to the CU 26 before linebacker Michael Jones, who would be one of the biggest defensive Buffaloes in 1989, stopped the Rams with an interception.

CSU came right back with a flawless 75-yard drive to go in front 14-7 and send more shivers down CU spines. Bieniemy countered 44 yards for a halftime tie. The Rams had one more shot left as they kicked a field goal early in the third period for their third lead of the game, 17-14. Ken Culbertson matched it on the next series and it was all CU thereafter as the Buffaloes took command and won going away, 45-20, as reserves again played most of the final period. The backup Buffs were also impressive as little Johnson directed a 61-yard scoring drive in which he displayed some nifty option moves.

Hagan again had an impressive game, running for 103 yards and hitting two of three passes for 28 yards. But it was Bieniemy who supplied the major fireworks, hammering out 156 yards and three touchdowns. The CU offense rolled up 505 yards. But the game was definitely not a Buff defensive gem as CSU netted 444 yards. In retrospect, the quick followup game had obviously dulled the Buffaloes. But Mac's forces still had enough poise and power to handle a CSU team overflowing with incentive with relative ease once midgame had been reached. Now they would face their third test, this one the stiffest thus far, in 12 days as Illinois, paced by the Big Ten's finest passer in Jeff George, prepared still another Folsom Field invasion.

38 Illinois 7

It would be the first meeting ever with Illinois and it would be against an excellent team which would be helped by the presence of assistant coaches Lou Tepper and Steve Bernstein, McCartney's top two defensive aides who had joined the Illini staff a year earlier. After a crushing 44-6 defeat in their 1988 opening game against Washington State, Tepper had rallied the Illinois defense as the Illini went on to become the surprise team in the Big Ten, finishing third with a 5-2-1 league mark.

The presence of George, an out-

Ace receiver M.J. Nelson makes a fingertip reception of Eric Bieniemy's pass for CU's second touchdown against Illinois.
DAILY CAMERA

standing passer who had transferred from Purdue when that school hired a ground-oriented coach, had been the principle reason for the rejuvenation of Illinois football. He would present CU's secondary with its most difficult test to date.

But he didn't. As he did against Texas, Williams took care of the Illini ace quickly and effectively whiplashing George for a 16-yard loss on the sixth play of the second period and shaking him up so that he had to leave the game temporarily. George's pinpoint passing had led the Illini on an 80-yard scoring drive on their first possession of the game. But he was never a serious factor after that as the combination of a ferocious CU rush and good secondary coverage handled his aerial threat effectively.

Hagan, meanwhile, again detonated a lightning scoring thrust on the opening series of the game, hitting Jeff Campbell deep for a 74-yard gain to the Illinois 15 on the third play. Bieniemy scored from there in three tries and the Buffs were off and running for the third

straight game.

Bieniemy then displayed passing ability of his own the next time CU got the ball, nailing Nelson for a 48-yard scoring bomb. When Flannigan took a pitch from Hagan and fled 45 yards to score, the Buffs took a 21-7 lead into halftime and the game, for all intents and purposes, was over. The Buffs upped their lead to 31-7 after three periods and the reserves again played most of the fourth as the game ended, 38-7. Bieniemy's 100 rushing yards followed by 98 from Flannigan sparked CU. Hagan netted but 20 yards on the ground but had his finest passing day of the young season, connecting on six of eight for 175 yards.

And so the Buffaloes completed their hectic opening cram course with three sparkling victories. Mac's marauders gave impressive performances each time out, unleashing solid defensive muscle and sparkling skills on offense. The start was almost too good to be true. In particular, Hagan's performances were far above expectations. The stubby sophomore had not only run and passed with more ability than any previous CU quarterback, he had displayed tremendous instincts, almost always making the right move at the right time.

45 Washington 28

But the Buffaloes still hadn't left friendly Folsom Field. Their first road test would be at Seattle in two weeks - there was an open date created by the advancement of the Texas game - against a solid Washington team coached by ex-CU assistant Don James, one of the top head men in the nation. His Huskies had switched to a wide-open passing game with which they had humbled Texas A&M and Purdue in their first two starts. CU fans would know whether or not their Buffaloes were for real after this game.

But tragedy was to strike first. Aunese, who had attended the first three CU games but in a wheel chair for the last one, died on the open date Saturday. His death was a tremendous blow to the CU squad and coaches and everyone else who had known him or watched him play. In late spring when he had rallied after undergoing chemotherapy, the popular Samoan had seemed indestructible. But cancer is a merciless killer and it reduced Sal to almost a shadow before his body finally gave in on September 23.

There followed an extremely emotional week with more than 2000 people crowding Macky Auditorium for a memorial service on Monday followed by a week-long period of mourning. It all added up to a tremendously distracting week of preparation for the Washington challenge. No one knew how the loss of their erstwhile leader would affect the Buffaloes. Certainly, anticipating them to be keyed up for the game was too much to expect. The death of a peer is a traumatic experience for young people. There was good rea-

DAILY CAMERA

Seven of Sal Aunese's classmates carried their dead leader's coffin. *L-R,* O.C. Oliver *(partially hidden),* Joe Garten, Bruce Young, Jeff Campbell, Okland Salavea *(partially hidden),* Erich Kissick and J.J. Flannigan.

Sal, and other CU tragedies

Colorado's first century ended with more than its share of tragedy involving CU players.

The sad sequence began in 1974 when sophomore defensive back Polie Poitier died suddenly of sickle-cell anemia during preseason practice.

In the next five years three ex-Buffs who were playing regularly in the NFL followed: Melvin Johnson (Kansas City Chiefs) during a seemingly routine surgical procedure; J.V. Cain (St. Louis Cardinals) of an unsuspected heart condition; and Troy Archer (New York Giants) in a one-car accident.

Another superb young Buffalo, junior Derek Singleton, died on New Year's Day, 1982 after apparently recovering from an attack of meningitis which came during the football season.

Then came the tragic brain injury to one of 1984's brightest stars, Ed Reinhardt, who suffered a crippling injury in the second game of the season at Oregon.

But the most poignant tragedy of all came during the school's 100th season when quarterback Sal Aunese, the team's offensive leader for the past two years, developed inoperable stomach cancer in late March and fought valiantly but in vain before dying September 23, 1989.

His illness and death were devastating to his teammates, coaches and legions of fans who had watched him lead the Buffaloes back from gridiron oblivion in 1987-8. He was the acknowledged leader of the CU team. His performance under fire had lifted the Buffaloes to almost-

unbelievable comebacks against Iowa and CSU the preceding fall. It was almost incomprehensible that he would be gone in less than 12 months.

But in sickness and death he proved to be even more of an inspiration to the CU program than he had been in life if that were possible. Instead of sinking in grief, his teammates dedicated the season to him and carried his memory proudly and importantly as they reached the greatest heights ever achieved by a CU squad.

1989 became a "Crusade for Sal." The Buffaloes wore his number on their uniforms and his name on their sleeves. His empty locker became almost a shrine to remind his CU teammates of his presence and of his important place in their lives.

More than 2000 persons jammed Macky Auditorium for memorial services. Hundreds more stood outside the building, listening to the tributes via a loudspeaker system.

In Seattle the following Saturday for a critical non-conference game against a strong Washington team, the CU players and coaches, 75-strong, knelt as one in midfield before the kickoff in silent tribute to their fallen mate.

Then they squared their shoulders and hammered the Huskies into total submission as Sal would have wanted. And onward they continued to march, to a truly story book season in the crusade for their comrade.

Sal was gone. But his spirit remained. And most certainly his memory will remain so long as Golden Buffaloes battle for gridiron glory.

son to assume that the Buffs wouldn't be ready for the Huskies. But somehow they were, and the resilience and stability they displayed in their Seattle performance was the tipoff that this might be an unusual group of young men now on a mission to play the season for their departed teammate.

The game began with a touching tribute to Aunese as the entire CU traveling squad, 60-strong, knelt at midfield before the opening toss. Almost a morbid silence gripped the packed 70,000-capacity stadium. Then the Buffaloes put their grief on a backburner and turned to the task ahead. The challenge was Washington. The Buffaloes answered it.

CU's coaches had kept their fingers crossed all fall, hoping the inexperienced Hagan wouldn't have a sophomorish bad day and disrupt the Buffalo offense. To the astonishment of nearly everyone, Darian had performed like a fifth-year senior in the first three games, getting CU out of the starting gate quickly in each one. Now, on a gloomy, drizzly Seattle afternoon, he opened the game with signs of the shakes. He lost two yards on the Buffs' first play, then barely got back to the line of scrimmage on the next one, getting manhandled by the Husky defense both times. On third down his off-balance pass was intercepted and suddenly Washington was at the CU 32.

But free safety Tim James promptly got the Buffs out of the hole as he picked off a first down pass at the nine. Hagan got no respite from the home team defense. After a short gain on a well-covered option, he tried another third-down pass and was lucky to avoid a safety, getting buried at the six for an 8-yard loss. And, once again, another new Buff came to the rescue as CSU transfer Tom Rouen knifed a punt through the drizzle which died at the Husky 44, a 50-yard lifesaver with no return.

Washington quarterback Cary Conklin now settled down into a short passing game and took the Huskies to a field goal and 3-0 lead. But the Buffaloes had recovered from the sputtering, untypical beginning and took control of the game which was never really a contest after that as McCartney turned the game over to the reserves early in the fourth period which began with the Buffaloes far in front, 38-3. Washington outscored the Buffaloes, 22-7, in the final 15 minutes to make the score respectable, 45-28. But it was an eye-popping rout all the way after the first period.

The Buffs had retaliated ferociously after falling behind in the opening minutes, covering 70 yards in five plays with their two power men, Bieniemy and fullback George Hemingway, leading the way. Hemingway woke up the CU offense with a bulldozing 17-yard charge to the Husky 35 in which he carried a defender for the last 10 yards. Then, on the next play, Bieniemy broke loose to score.

Washington had one last gasp as the Huskies pulled to within 7-6 early in the second period. The Buffaloes then broke it open in the final minutes of the first half, scoring twice after an excellent defensive stand which forced an errant Husky field goal attempt at the 23.

The Buffs took over at that point with 6:41 remaining and promptly went 77 yards in 11 plays with the biggest one, a variation of the "Flea-Flicker" which CU called the "Hook and Ladder", for 25 yards when Campbell took a short pass from Hagan and quickly lateralled to Pritchard who covered the final 10 yards. Hagan then cut into the open for 14 yards to the two from where Bieniemy scored.

When Washington went to the air after the kickoff, linebacker Michael Jones intercepted promptly at midfield and Hagan, on the first play, drilled Pritchard 40 yards downfield at the seven and three plays later the Buffs took a 21-6 lead into the rest period.

It was "no contest" in the third quarter. CU scored on each of its three possessions. Culbertson started it with a 43-yard field goal, Hagan darted in from the three after Flannigan's 39-yard dash set it up, and Campbell applied the clincher with his special reverse for 56 yards.

And so the Buffaloes had passed their final non-conference test with relative ease. Hagan's September play was almost flawless and, to say the least, sensational. In particular, his passing had been a most pleasant surprise. He had thrown short, long, with strength and with excellent touch. His quickness and running ability out of the option had been a well-established fact when he started the season. But no one could have anticipated his tremendous poise and playmaking ability, not to mention his accurate passing. Veteran observers quickly labeled him the best quarterback in CU history. Accolades such as that might have seemed premature. After all, he'd only played four games.

But the record doesn't lie and Hagan's September marks were A-plus.

His leadership pulled everything into place. The Buffaloes had been tough on the ground but inconsistent through the air under the direction of Aunese. Now they had a complete arsenal: a huge offensive line, fine receivers, speed and power at running backs, hard-running fullbacks who could block well and a fine kick return game. All this blended perfectly with Hagan's running, passing and ballhandling abilities.

The defense had been solid and, in particular, the secondary had absorbed the loss of Figures and Pontiflet without any obvious loss in effectiveness. The savage charges of Williams, Walker and McGhee kept constant pressure on opposing passers to give considerable comfort to the youngsters manning the secondary. Up front, the Buffaloes were potent.

So McCartney had his ducks (or buffaloes) in order as the Big Eight campaign loomed on the immediate horizon. Conference teams would be more physical than the pre-season foes. There were few question marks about this CU team. But one big one was how would they stand up to run-oriented power offenses such as the two Oklahoma schools and Nebraska featured. But that was still down the road a month and, in the meantime, the next three foes - Missouri, Iowa State and Kansas - would continue to probe the CU secondary. Thus far there had been no serious leaks back there.

49 Missouri 3

Missouri, regrouping under a new coach after several uncharacteristically bad seasons, got struck by CU lightning. The Tigers never knew what hit them as Hagan hit Campbell for 58 yards on the first play of the game and scored from nine yards out on the second. It was 7-0 with only 28 seconds gone.

Before the first quarter was finished, so were the Tigers. Hagan was the one-man assassin, scoring two more times with ease on short option runs to cap 90 and 37-yard drives to make the score after 15 minutes, 21-0. The Buffaloes kept up the pressure in the second period to take a 35-0 halftime lead. McCartney, possibly showing mercy on his alma mater, did not use his starters in the second half as the CU reserves kept control and got some valuable experience. The final score was 49-3. It wasn't that close. The Buffaloes, playing before the first non-Nebraska sellout in more than a decade, ripped out 439 rushing yards and added 156 more by passing for a 595-225 total offense advantage over the toothless Tigers. Hagan accounted for 262 yards during his 30-minute workout, 106 rushing and 156 passing, for his finest afternoon of the young season.

52 Iowa State 17

Iowa State was next at Ames, in recent seasons a difficult road stop for Buffalo teams. The Cyclones had been stubborn in Boulder the previous year, forcing the Buffaloes to score twice in the final period for a closer-than-expected 24-12 triumph. The Iowans were led by a wily ex-Wyoming Cowboy quarterback named Jim Walden, who had built a reputation for knocking off favorites during a successful tour of duty at Washington State. His strong suit was preparing an underdog for an upset. He'd be ready for the Buffaloes after a frustrating September in which his Cyclones had outplayed Iowa but lost to the Hawkeyes in their big intrastate rivalry.

The Iowa State test turned out to be a laugher although the Cyclones actually led briefly before CU turned loose an awesome 35-point second quarter barrage which destroyed the Iowans and their homecoming partisans.

After an opening Culbertson field goal, Iowa State drove impressively 77 yards on its opening possession to send a chill through the CU fans who were there. But that only served to arouse the Buffs who scored on their next six possessions to set up a second straight Saturday in which the regulars sat out the second half which began with CU in front by an astonishing 49-3.

In that adding machine attack, Hagan & Co almost blew a fuse on the scoreboard. The onslaught went like this: Hagan for 18 to cap a 7l-play, 44-yard drive after the Buffs recovered an onside kick; Hagan to Pritchard for one yard after the CU signal caller had hit the same receiver for 28 yards after running 28; Hagan for 12 after Bieniemy had run for 23 and Campbell had caught a 23-yard pass; Hagan to Pritchard for 39 after Tim James' interception; Flannigan for 23 after a fumble recovery; and, finally, with 1:38 remaining, Flannigan from the four after Hagan had optioned for 15 and thrown to M.J. Nelson for 36. CU piled up an awesome 662 yards of total offense. The Cyclones, who would lose by only 46-40 to Oklahoma a week later, left the

stadium knowing what someone buried by an avalanche felt like.

But it was a costly victory for the Buffaloes as Bieniemy suffered a broken fibula. It was the first serious injury of the season to a CU regular and it couldn't have come at a worse time for the Buffaloes who would need their stubby power man in two weeks when they faced showdown contests with Oklahoma then Nebraska. Even though the fracture was to a non-weight-carrying bone, it would still hobble the ringleader of CU's straight-ahead running attack. Bieniemy vowed he'd be back in time for those games but it was likely he'd be unable to run effectively for at least a month, if then.

49 Kansas 17

The Buffaloes didn't need him for the homecoming game against Kansas as they sputtered through most of the first three periods but managed a worry-free 49-17 victory. Flannigan, getting a rare start because of Bieniemy's injury, took advantage of his opportunity, scoring three touchdowns on a pair of short plunges plus a 41-yarder in which he broke free after a perfect last-second pitch from Hagan.

CU fans, suddenly accustomed to topheavy wins, watched quietly for much of the second half as the reserves again came on for the fourth period. The score was 21-3 at the half and 35-3 after three periods. The highlight of the second half was an impressive 54-yard scoring drive engineered by reserve QB Johnson who got the TD with a nifty 8-yard cutback.

20 Oklahoma 3

By now the Buffaloes had caught the eye of the entire nation and were firmly locked in third place in the national rankings, trailing only perennial powerhouses Notre Dame and Miami. Sportswriters came from each coast to marvel at the CU crusade, singing the praises of the team's on-field ability. It was a sharp contrast to six months earlier when countless columns were filled with comments and criticisms about the personal problems of several Buffaloes. If ever a team rose from the ashes it was this 1989 Colorado crew. Beginning with the bad night against BYU in Anaheim and extending through the January-February problems with the Boulder police then hitting bottom with Aunese's terminal illness and adding one more distraction with the McCartney maternity before Aunese's Sep-

CU's defense was never far from the ball as shown by this swarming stop of a Kansas runner by Joel Steed (93), Michael Jones (59), Terry Johnson (48) and Okland Salavea (99).

DAILY CAMERA

Defensive backs Bruce Young (7) and Dave McCloughan (12) celebrate after stopping an Oklahoma threat.

DAILY CAMERA

one runner at the Norman shootout. Once again, there was a new problem for CU fans to fret about. Oklahoma would be the first power running offense the Buffs faced in 1989. Thus far, every CU foe had passed first and run second. Oklahoma teams did not pass. They lined up and came straight at you. Would CU's front defenders be up to that challenge?

The Buffaloes were more than up to the Oklahoma assault to the delight of more than 3000 fans who traveled to Norman for the game. After a scoreless first period in which the Sooners had the upper hand in a fierce physical stand-off, the Buffaloes broke through in the final five minutes of the half, driving 50 yards to set up a 30-yard Culbertson field goal with 5:13 left.

The defense, which met the Sooners head on and dominated the second half, forced a quick OU punt after the 3-pointer and Hagan, who had been contained to that point by a Sooner defense obviously set up to stop his option sprints, broke free for 40 yards to the 13 on the next play. Four plays later he flipped a perfect pitchout to Flannigan as he was diving off balance into the line and J.J. stepped into the end zone with no Sooner within 10 feet of him.

That gave the Buffs a sudden 10-0 lead and when they got the ball back right away it appeared as though they might make a serious bid for a third score. Campbell returned a short Sooner punt to midfield but a clipping penalty moved the ball back to the 33 and the Buffs elected to run out the final 1:30 rather than risk an interception.

A pair of roughness penalties as the third quarter began got the Sooners out of deep holes and gave them two opportunities to score. But Jones knocked down the OU quarterback a yard short of a first down at the Buff 24 to stymie the first attempt and the Sooners had to settle for a field goal from the 16 after reaching a first down at the 23.

CU promptly answered with another Culbertson field goal to make it 13-3 midway through the final period and the teams slugged it out on the ground the rest of the way with the Buffs icing it late on an 8-yard keeper by Hagan following reserve nose guard Garry Howe's recovery of a bobbled reverse at the Sooner nine.

27 Nebraska 21

And so the Buffaloes became the first CU team since the 1937 Whizzer White group to win eight straight

tember death wrote the closing chapter, the Buffaloes appeared doomed for destruction.

Instead, they headed for Oklahoma wearing the unexpected robes of favorites. The two teams had slugged it out a year earlier in Boulder with the Sooners coming away with a field goal triumph on the strength of a long fourth-period drive which the Buffaloes couldn't

match. But the Sooners had had 1989 problems of their own after a series of late winter and spring incidents which cost them their superb quarterback Charles Thompson. And on the same afternoon that Bieniemy was injured, Oklahoma's standout sophomore running back Mike Gaddis was lost for the season with a knee injury. So both teams would be minus their number

games. But the big one with Nebraska was dead ahead and it would be for all the Big Eight marbles and a probable Orange Bowl national championship meeting with No. 1 ranked Notre Dame. It would be the most important game for CU in the first century of competition. Suddenly, the entire state was afire with enthusiasm about this team which had overcome so much adversity to become destiny's darlings. The entire nation awaited the struggle with tremendous interest.

No game in 1989 had matched such high-ranking rivals. The Cornhuskers were rated No. 3, just one notch behind the Buffaloes. CU was a slight favorite, less than a touchdown, chiefly on the strength of its home field advantage and a tougher non-conference schedule. CBS-TV was on hand to televise the game nationally. Scalpers were having a field day. Amazingly, the Buffaloes were the toast of the state and the nation. Mac's men for one of the few times in history had pushed the Denver Broncos out of the spotlight. Would the Buffs continue their sensational 1989 story? Or would always-powerful Nebraska once again spoil the CU party?

The week-long media buildup for the game was overwhelming. Denver newspapers, radio and television stations flooded the metropolitan area with hype of all types. Media members from coast to coast invaded Boulder to send their reams of analyses and prognostications back to their home bases in such scattered cities as Los Angeles, Dallas, New York, Washington D.C. and Miami. In addition, national wire services sent correspondents to the CU encampment. There were semi-unpleasant aspects to the week, too. Some over-zealous metropolitan radio stations belittled the neighbors to the east with a flood of "Nebraska jokes" lifted almost word-for-word from the famous (or infamous) Texas Aggie one-liners which had been a popular part of Lone Star folklore for decades.

And Nebraska coach Tom Osborn fueled the fire with publicly stated concerns that CU's crowd might treat the visiting Cornhusker fans rudely. What sort of violence Osborn feared was unrevealed. CU football was in its 100th year and to the best of anyone's knowledge no visiting fan had been murdered or maimed. Aside from an occasional flurry of snowballs when mother nature had supplied that type of ammunition for rebellious fans suffering through still another Cornhusker thumping of the Buffaloes, there had never been serious incidents during Nebraska, or any other games. And Boulder's famed Chinook winds had completely evaporated a 4-inch snowfall which had fallen on Monday thus removing any possibility of a white barrage during the game.

And so the big day arrived and it was a perfect football afternoon featuring 65-degree temperatures and mostly sunny skies and, importantly, no snow anywhere except to outline the Flatirons and the Front Range to remind the 52,877 fans who jammed Folsom that fall and the football season was coming to a close.

As for the game itself, it was a shoot-out completely worthy of its pre-game buildup. The two teams slugged it out with an entertaining mixture of sensational plays and old-fashioned power football with no quarter given. The attending network TV moguls who ask of a game only that it stretch its tension to the last second if possible left the stadium with smiles wider than McCartney's. For it was a classic confrontation which featured a long touchdown on the first scrimmage play and a potentially-game-winning touchdown pass batted down in the end zone in the last second.

The final score was CU 27, Nebraska 21 and it was even closer than that but needn't have been had the Buffaloes been able to cash in on a great opportunity to ice it with five minutes left in the game. At the frantic finish with the Cornhuskers trying desperately to get into the end zone for a one-point win, everyone whether in gold or red was limp with nervous exhaustion, overworked enthusiasm, prolonged hangovers or whatever other stadium activities drain a person's energies. And, undoubtedly to the great surprise of that superb football teacher but less effective appraiser of football crowds, Osborn, no Nebraskans had to be carried away from the battle scene on litters.

The game began as a nightmare for the nearly 50,000 CU fans in the crowd. Cornhusker pressure forced an errant Hagan pass on CU's first possession with the visitors getting an interception at midfield and exploding a seemingly innocuous screen pass into a 51-yard touchdown on their very first scrimmage play. Shades of the CSU opening seven Saturdays earlier. But as they had done all fall, the Buffaloes kept their cool and retaliated just as spectacularly five minutes later when Hagan optioned left and slid into the secondary to sprint 30 yards before lateraling to Flannigan who streaked the rest of the way for a 70-yard tying TD.

As it turned out, that was the only touchdown generated by the CU offense. But the Buffaloes again unleashed their "Cornhusker Killer" Jeff Campbell whose reverse had started the Nebraskans to defeat in the 1986 shocker. Campbell set up CU's other two TDs in this one with spectacular punt returns of 47 and 55 yards to keep

Michael Jones (59), Dave McCloughan (12) and Alfred Williams (94) zero in on Nebraska's Ken Clark.
DAILY CAMERA

the Buffs in front despite impressive Nebraska statistics which saw the Big Red forces build margins of 19-13 in first downs and 397-227 in total offense. Campbell's 102 punt return yards, however, more than evened up the figures which some legendary gridiron expert had once proclaimed "were for losers." Certainly, the Cornhuskers owned the statistics in this game. But CU left Folsom with the most important number: the final score.

The fleet feet of Hagan, Flannigan and Campbell plus the continued deadly-accurate right leg of Ken Culbertson, who booted a 49-yard field goal into the wind as the half ended, gave the Buffaloes a 17-14 intermission lead. They stretched it to 24-14 midway through the third quarter on another nifty Hagan-Flannigan pitchout following Campbell's second escape act with a Husker punt. But the Cornhuskers, as always unemotional, unshaken and efficient, countered with a long TD pass in the opening minute of the fourth period.

The Buffaloes then squandered their golden opportunity to wrap it up after Hagan's heroics had taken them to a first down at the two. The little lightning bug broke back-to-back 17-yard option thrusts to get to that point. But, mysteriously, CU's brain trust shunned the straight-ahead route and sandwiched three Hagan efforts around a motion penalty and had to settle for a 28-yard 3-pointer by Culbertson thus keeping Nebraska's hopes alive and setting up the Huskers' furious but futile finish.

The first critical long-yardage effort the Cornhuskers missed all afternoon -they'd converted five straight similar third down situations to that point - halted their bid for a winning touchdown at the CU 26 with 3:58 left when quarterback Gerry Gdowski's hurried pass went low and wide.

After CU's national-leading punter Tom Rouen boomed a 63-yard lifesaver dead at the 12, the Cornhuskers still had one last shot left. This time Gdowski completed a fourth-down pass for 14 yards then a 20-yarder to midfield. He missed three straight times but on fourth down appeared to have hit an open receiver in the end zone. However, CU's Dave McLoughan knocked it away and the game was over. It turned out that Gdowski had crossed the line of scrimmage before the pass so the play was dead. But hardly anyone in the stands noticed the yellow flag so the end

Mike Pritchard, an unsung but highly productive Buffalo, speeds downfield with a Darian Hagan pass for a 32-yard gain to set up an early touchdown at Kansas State.
DAILY CAMERA

seemed even more dramatic than it was.

As the ball bounced harmlessly on the end zone Astroturf, the playing field suddenly was jammed with a golden celebration as CU fans marched through the ranks with parts of the goalposts held high. But CU authorities had the potentially-dangerous situation under control. They had installed hinges at the bottoms of the uprights earlier in the week and attached ropes to the metal poles with which stadium workers had pulled them to the ground to prevent injury.

So the day and the game and the week were finished gloriously and McCartney had the most appropriate post-game comment. "It wasn't pretty but it was beautiful," he smiled to a friend who congratulated him in the

Buff dressing room. As the CU celebration wound down in the early hours of Sunday morning, Mac and his staff began fretting about the seemingly-smooth path ahead to the Big Eight throne room and the automatic Orange Bowl bid. The big two hurdles, Oklahoma and Nebraska, were behind. Ahead were only Oklahoma State, struggling following the loss of most of the top hands from the 1988 team which had manhandled the Buffaloes in Boulder, and ever-struggling Kansas State. But both games would be on the road. And OSU still had Mike Gundy, the Big Eight's best quarterback for the past two years and just beginning to return to form after early season injuries. And no longtime CU fan could forget the heartbreaks at the hands of

9

the Cowboys suffered by undefeated CU teams in 1967 and 1972. It would not be a week without worry even though the Buffaloes rightfully figured to be heavy favorites in the two closing tests.

41 Oklahoma State 17

Oklahoma State turned out to be almost anti-climactic. There were fears that the Buffaloes would be down, emotionally and physically. After all, it had been a long, tough trail since Labor Day night and the team had reached the heights in dumping arch-rivals Oklahoma and Nebraska on successive weekends. It was not likely that the Buffs would be keyed up for the Cowboys. And they weren't. They promptly got into early trouble before they settled down. When they did, what then happened was an old fashioned, unemotional, walloping of a team that CU didn't particularly care about, mainly because the Cowboys had whacked them around quite brutally the past two seasons.

OSU came out smoking and put 10 quick points on the board to send the Buffs into their deepest hole of the fall. But Mac's men were battle-hardened by this time and if they had shown one characteristic in 1989 it was poise under pressure. This team simply didn't come unglued and, more importantly, it didn't kill itself with mistakes and turnovers. When they decided it was time to go to work, the game quickly developed into a rout and the scene was much like a beach bully kicking sand into the face of a 90-pound weakling.

What the Buffaloes did was unleash a Stillwater slaughter, scoring 41 straight points after the 10-0 deficit at the first quarter turn. And it was a multi-faceted surgical job which totally decapitated the upset-minded hosts. There was no particular ringleader to this flogging although Hagan again triggered the attack and the Houston Connection of Williams, McGhee and Walker brutalized the Cowpoke offense. But there were lots of heroes to go around. Hagan and Campbell teamed up on a pair of key second period connections for 18 and 38 yards to move the Buffs to the OSU nine and set up the first TD as Flannigan went in standing up in two carries. If the Cowboys thought they had the answer to the CU offense they had received a quick lesson. The Buffaloes went 75 yards in seven plays requiring barely more than three minutes.

Now they pulled out the plug, scoring in their next three possessions to take a 24-10 halftime lead. Flannigan's 25-yard burst started it and he carried the ball four times for a total of 28 of the 49-yard, 6-play drive. Hagan dove over for the first of his two touchdowns.

The backbreaker was supplied by M.J. Nelson who made a sensational diving catch in the end zone of a 26-yard pass from Hagan to make the score 21-10. CU receivers made many great catches in 1989. None were better than Nelson's stretching dive to scrape up the ball just inches from the playing surface.

Culbertson ended the first half carnage with a 40-yard field goal made possible by Mike Pritchard's leaping reception good for 29 yards to the 25.

The Buffs pounded it out on the ground after intermission with big full-back George Hemingway ripping for big gains behind the huge CU line which had taken control of the line of scrimmage in the second period. As in every game except the preceding two big ones, the reserves mopped up for much of the fourth period. The final score was 41-17.

And so the Buffaloes had a lock on the Orange Bowl invitation. Only a road game with lowly Kansas State stood between them and an almost unbelievable perfect 11-0 record. They were solidly locked into second place in the national rankings. All signs pointed to a national championship meeting in Miami with No. 1 Notre Dame. The Irish still had two tough tests remaining, with Penn State and Miami. But they would be favored to win both games. And even if they stumbled in one they would still probably get the invitation. After all, Notre Dame was a magic name

Darian Hagan cuts toward the end zone for the 14-yard TD at Kansas State which sent him over the 1000-yard rushing mark.

DAILY CAMERA

in college football. And CU with an almost inevitable win at K-State would be either an undefeated No. 2 playing undefeated No. 1 Notre Dame if the Irish went 11-0. Or the Buffaloes would be an undefeated No. 1 playing a once-defeated Notre Dame or Miami if the Irish stumbled once. Whatever the results, a CU-Notre Dame meeting seemed almost certain. It would be an almost unbelievable climax to a totally unbelievable season for the Buffaloes!

59 Kansas State 11

If there was one opponent in the world a team would like to play to insure a perfect season it was Kansas State. The lowly Wildcats, locked in to their cellar position as almost always, were 42-point underdogs to CU. And they wasted no time proving the point spread was correct.

Mike Pritchard returned the opening kickoff 32 yards to the 41. On the first play, Flannigan sped 57 yards to the two and scored on the next play and the Buffs were in front with just 21

seconds played. With the exception of a brief Wildcat spurt for a touchdown at the beginning of the second half it was a totally one-sided game from start to finish.

CU led at the half, 31-0. During the first 30 minutes, the Buff defense held their hosts to eight yards of total offense and no first downs. Their perfect 11-0 regular season safely tucked away after a 14-0 first period lead, the Buffaloes concentrated on boosting the season records of Flannigan and Hagan, both shooting for high personal marks.

Flannigan needed 59 yards to reach the 1000 yard rushing mark for the year. He got them in less than a half-minute then continued on to his greatest day as a Buffalo, winding up with 246 and tossing in four touchdowns for good measure.

Hagan's game figures weren't quite that imposing but he still ran for 156 yards and passed for 69 more and scored three touchdowns. But the little ringleader of the CU attack reached the 1000 yard mark in both offensive cate-

gories (1004 yards rushing and 1002 passing) to become only the fifth player in college history to accomplish that double. And, amazingly, he reached those totals despite sitting out two third quarters and eight fourth quarters, the equivalent of two-and-one-half games, because of big CU leads.

The final score was almost an afterthought, 59-11, as the Buff reserves played almost the entire second half. And so the regular season finished on the highest of high notes. The Buffaloes had overcome adversity and tragedy to record the finest season of the first century and set the stage for a national championship meeting with defending title-holder Notre Dame in the Orange Bowl.

The Buffs were one step away from a national title. They would undoubtedly enter the New Year's night game as underdogs. But this was a squad accustomed to adversity. McCartney assured CU fans his team would be ready for the test. And the entire nation awaited the confrontation.

THE NATIONAL CHAMPIONSHIP GAME
CU vs. NOTRE DAME
ORANGE BOWL

January 1, 1990

The Buffaloes, who had rolled past 11 straight 1989 foes with the cold' competence of a surgeon, ran into not one but two teams who finally conquered them on New Year's night in the Orange Bowl: themselves in the first half and Notre Dame in the second.

As 81,191 fans watched, the Buffs' dream of a national championship evaporated into the cool Miami night in an old-fashioned slugfest which had threatened to become a CU rout in the first 30 minutes.

The Buffs opened the evening savagely, pounding through big holes for three major penetrations: to the Irish 19, 5 and 1. But their own errors and a bristling Irish goal line defense produced only a scoreless halftime tie which left the Buffs totally frustrated and the Irish elated at having dodged so many Buffalo bullets.

CU could easily have scored 17, and possibly 21, points in those first 28 minutes. Instead they got none as they continually shot themselves in their collective feet on an Eric Bieniemy open field fumble at the 19, a shocking scuff of a chip shot field goal attempt by usually reliable Ken Culbertson and, finally, with four futile stabs into the line after reaching a first down at the one.

As it turned out, there was no second chance in the second half as the Irish struck swiftly for TDs on their first two possessions.

The CU nightmare began as Bieniemy, seeing his first action since breaking a leg in mid-October, squirted into the open from the Irish 35 and seemed headed inside the 10 if not the end zone when he dropped the ball while trying to move it to his right hand.

Notre Dame covered the fumble at the 19. End of threat one! But that disappointment didn't stop the Buffs. They came back immediately to drive 77 yards in 11 plays, the biggest a 28-yard pass from Darian Hagan to Erich Kissick.

The drive stalled at the five. Ring up three cinch points from the accurate leg of Culbertson who had converted 59 straight PATs in 1989. But he duck-

hooked this one, sending it skidding harmlessly into the end zone. That should have told the Buffs it wasn't their night. But still they roared back.

This time a TD was a cinch as Bieniemy roared nine yards to a first down at the one after a steady 60-yard march. But hold the phone! Bieniemy's apparent TD leap was ruled short on a questionable call. Hagan failed with a sneak. Notre Dame stacked up an option to the short side, burying Bieniemy for a 2-yard loss. On a fake field goal, CU failed to execute well and Campbell's desperate dive when he couldn't pass failed by a yard.

Still the Buffs were in good shape. Notre Dame faced third down at the six. Alfred Williams almost sacked QB Tony Rice in the end zone but Rice got away for 18 yards and the Irish moved quickly to the CU 10 where nose guard Garry Howe blocked a field goal try on the last play of the half. Noboby realized it but the tide had turned.

Notre Dame took command with the third quarter kickoff, driving 69 yards in seven plays. When Hagan's hurried pass was tipped by John Perak into an interception, the Irish promptly went 59 more as fleet Raghib Ismail broke inside Kanavis McGhee's near-miss tackle for 35 yards on a third down reverse. That one put CU into a deep 14-0 hole from which they never escaped.

But there were still frustrations to come. The first followed Hagan's brilliant 39-yard TD scamper late in the third period. (The little leader rang up 171 yards of total offense, tops in the game, despite being hounded relentlessly by the strong Notre Dame defense.) Again Culbertson failed, hitting the upright on his PAT kick to erase much of the luster from Hagan's score.

Then Notre Dame finished off the Buffs with a brutally efficient 17-play (all runs) 82-yard drive to score the final touchdown and, more importantly, eat up nine of the remaining 10 minutes of the game.

There was still more frustration early in this march. CU got its only penalty of the night, a 5-yard face mask on a first down play at the Irish 39 in which the Buffs buried Ismail for a 2-yard loss. But the penalty enabled the Irish to keep moving and prevent CU from getting the ball back with lots of time left.

And so 1989 was history and the second century loomed dead ahead. What lies in store for Buffalo football? A seemingly bright future, that's what! Now firmly established as a legitimate Big Eight force, CU would undoubtedly be a co-favorite (with Nebraska) for the 1990 Big Eight title and a return to Miami.

The dynamic Hagan's presence plus 40 other lettermen (12 of them returning starters), guaranteed CU excellence in the immediate future. And the recruiting skills of McCartney and his staff, honed to a high-tech pitch by CU's charge at the end of the decade, seemed certain to keep the quality of CU's athletes at a national contending level.

So a century which began with that 103-0 drubbing in CU's first home game, back on Nov. 22, 1890 and concluded with the national championship battle on January 1, 1990 left CU fans not only looking back on 100 years of achievement but forward to a future which seemed as bright as a beacon.

Hopefully, a Buffalo Beacon which would spotlight CU for many seasons to come!

Ralphie leads the Buffalo Stampede onto Folsom Field.

(CU)

UNIVERSITY OF COLORADO

PHOTO BY BILL BRITTAIN - Zemi Photograph

TOP ROW (L to R): Scott Phillips, Leonard Renfro, Ron Woolfork, Chuck Snowden, Mike Freeman, Jack Keys, Andy Renfroe, Ross Ronan, Aaron Shaw, Cam Brown, Ollie Williams, Doug Wolanske, Doug Van Horn, Ken Windham.

2nd Row: Ron Bradford, Scott Brunner, Bryan Campbell, Dennis Collier, Dwayne Davis, Brian Dyet, Marcellous Elder, Sean Embree, Richard Fisher, James Hill, Roger Ivey, John Katovsich, Greg Lindsey, Greg Loest.

3rd Row: Jason Perkins, Tate Nelson, Doug Adkins, Greg Bierkert, Kyle Cummings, Chad Brown, Eric Hamilton, Julian Hayward, Clint Moles, Jim Hansen, Rick Grunden, Darren Muller, Scott Martinson, Scott Starr, Terrance Britt.

4th Row: Russ Heasley, Chris Bloomstran, J.C. Orvis, Brent Branch, Robbie James, Mark Henry, Tony Senna, Joel Steed, Pat Blottiaux, Jay Leeuwenburg, David Arterberry, Chris O'Donnell, Roger Yago.

5th Row: Kanavis McGhee, Tom Rouen, Neil Schlesener, George Hemingway, Jon Boman, Eric Bieniemy, Darian Hagan, Charles Johnson, Scott DeGoler, Garry Howe, Jim Dadiotis, Alfred Williams, Mike Pritchard, Mike Motley.

6th Row: Michael Simmons, David Brown, Rob Hutchins, Ariel Solomon, Joe Garten, O.C. Oliver, Tim James, Dave McCloughan, David Gibbs, Paul Rose, Lamarr Gray, Terry Johnson, Mark Vander Poel, David Ellis.

7th Row: Ken Culbertson, Scott Hanna, Okland Salavea, Arthur Walker, Jeff Campbell, J.J. Flannigan, Darrin Muilenburg, Michael Jones, M.J. Nelson, Bill Coleman, Greg Gould, Erich Kissick, Bruce Young, John Perak, Jeff Cantrell.

Bottom Row: Mike McCartney, Brian Cabral, Jeff Madden, Joe Rizzo, Zaven Yaralian, Gerry DiNardo, Bill McCartney, Mike Hankwitz, Gary Barnett, Ron Vanderlinden, Mike Barry, Don Frease, Greg Schammel, Bob Simmons, Oliver Lucas, Tom Whelihan, Chris Symington.

1989
BIG 8 CHAMPIONS

Tackle Bill Coleman, one of CU's captains, gives an enthusiastic "touchdown" signal. (CU)

Mac applies some body english in a tight situation at Oklahoma. (CG)

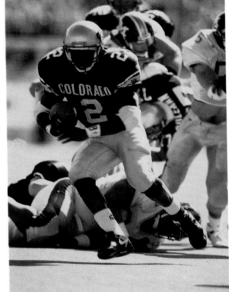

J.J. Flannigan races into the open against Missouri. (CG)

Sal Aunese looks for Jeff Campbell as he prepares to throw the long completion which launched CU's winning touchdown drive against Iowa in 1988. (CU)

Mac and his men await the signal from Ralphie's handlers to make their pre-game entrance. (CU)

Eric Bieniemy and J.J. Flannigan leave the field after a CU touchdown against Missouri. (CG)

Fullback George Hemingway blasts through a big hole against CSU. (CU)

The "Houston Connection" - Arthur Walker, Kanavis McGhee and Alfred Williams - celebrate after a defensive stand against Illinois. (CU)

Eric Bieniemy, though hurt much of the '89 season cheered the team on proclaiming "Things have Changed". (CG)

Eric Bieniemy bursts through a big hole to score against Illinois. (CU)

One of the turning points in the Illinois game came when Arthur Walker sacked Illini quarterback Jeff George early in the second quarter. (CG)

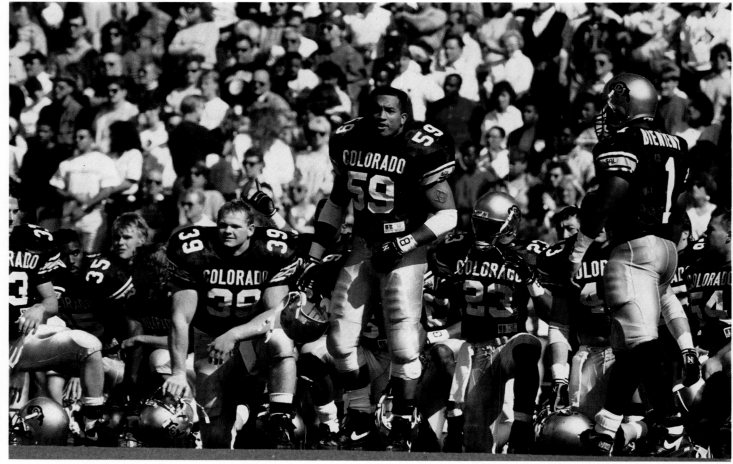

Alfred Williams, Arthur Walker, Bruce Young and Michael Jones, among others, celebrate the opening victory over Texas. (CG)

These two unheralded Buffaloes, punter Tom Rouen (left) and placekicker Ken Culbertson, played important roles for CU in 1989. (CG)

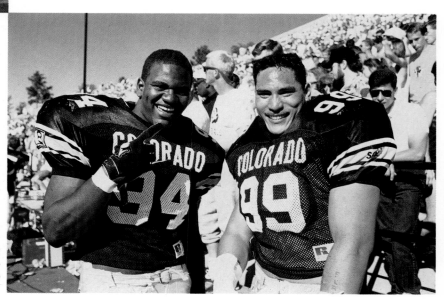

Alfred Williams (94) and Okland Salavea (99) let off steam after the win over CSU. (CG)

A disconsolate Sal Aunese slumps in the CU locker room after the 1988 near-miss against Oklahoma. (CG)

The CU squad kneels at mid-field before the Missouri kickoff in silent tribute to the memory of Sal Aunese. (EK)

CU's captains (l-4) Bill Coleman, Erick Kissick, Bruce Young and Michael Jones head to midfield for the coin toss.

(EK)

Darian Hagan follows up Campbell's punt return with this vault into the end zone to give CU a 14-7 lead over Nebraska.

(CG)

One of the turning points in the Illinois game came when Alfred Williams sacked Illinois quarterback Jeff George early in the second quarter.

(CG)

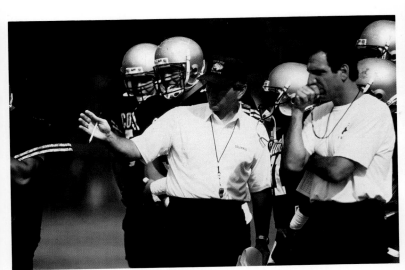

Bill McCartney and offensive co-ordinator Gerry DiNardo during a serious moment during practice. (EK)

Jeff Campbell leaves a Nebraska tackler behind as he races 49 yards to set up CU's second touchdown. (CG)

Defensive co-ordinator Mike Hankwitz gets a ride off the field after the Texas game on the shoulders of Kanavis McGhee (l) and Tim James (r) after his men kept the Longhorns out of the end zone. (CG)

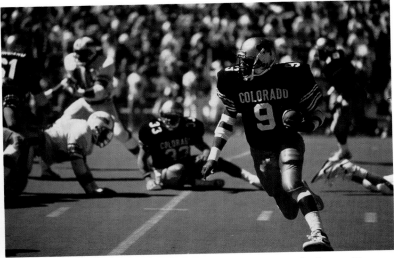

Versatile Mike Pritchard found the open field often on kickoff returns, with pass receptions and on wingback reverses. (EK)

The CU sideline is tense during a critical moment against Nebraska.

Erich Kissick leads Eric Bieniemy into the end zone against Missouri.

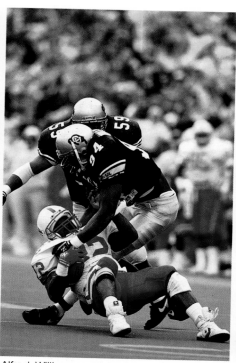

Alfred Williams and Michael Jones hammer Nebraska's Ken Clark to the ground in the opening moments of the big game in Boulder.

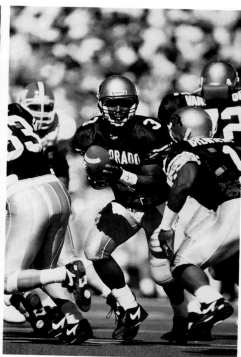

Coolness under pressure was a Darian Hagan trademark in 1989. He starts a play against Illinois as Erich Kissick, Eric Bieniemy and Mark Vander Poel prepare to execute.

Alfred Williams, Arthur Walker, Bruce Young and Michael Jones, among others, celebrate the opening victory over Texas. (CU)

The scoreboard tells the story and jubilant CU fans carry a section of the goal posts after the 1986 breakthrough victory over Nebraska. (CU)

And here comes Ralphie! (EK)

Athletic director Bill Marolt and CU vice president Dick Tharp count the crowd before the Oklahoma game. (CG)

As CU's dramatic win over Nebraska wound to a close, the student section flashed this symbolic sign. (EK)

These are the only three men in CU's first century whose jersey numbers were retired: Bobby Anderson (11), Byron White (24) and Joe Romig (67). (FC)

Mac looks away but listens to some advice from his biggest fan, CU president Gordon Gee. (CG)

CU's most famous athlete and graduate, Byron "Whizzer" White prepares for his introduction during halftime ceremonies honoring CU's All-Century team. CU recruiting co-ordinator Rick George co-ordinated the ceremony. (EK)

Drew Litton's vivid Rocky Mountain News cartoon captured the feeling of CU's dramatic victory over Nebraska which paved the way to the Big Eight championship and Orange Bowl bid for the Buffaloes.

Coaches Bill McCartney and Lou Holtz discuss how to stop a potential confrontation between their two squads before the coin toss of their Orange Bowl meeting. (CG)

The Buffaloes got to the beach in a hurry after they arrived in Miami for the Orange Bowl. (L-R): Tom Rouen, Dave McCloughan, Pat Blottiaux, Chris O'Donnell, Scott Hanna, Tony Senna, Jeff Campbell and David Gibbs! (CG)

Okland Salavea checks out his pursuit form at Miami Beach. (CG)

Darian Hagan poses for Boulder Daily Camera photographer Cliff Grassmick as the CU quarterback and several teammates romp in the Miami Beach surf. (CG)

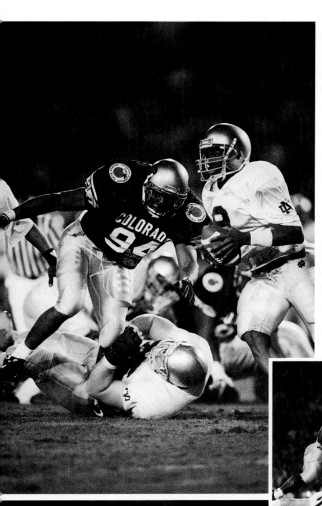

Alfred Williams hones in on Notre Dame quarterback Tony Rice to throw the Irish star for a loss. (CG)

Mark Vander Poel helps Eric Bieniemy tear loose from a Notre Dame tackler as the Buff tailback rips 16 yards to the Irish 19 before fumbling. (CG)

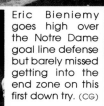

Eric Bieniemy goes high over the Notre Dame goal line defense but barely missed getting into the end zone on this first down try. (CG)

The look on Darian Hagan's face tells the story at the finish of the Orange Bowl game. (CG)

Darian Hagan explodes between two Notre Dame defenders en route to his brilliant 39-yard touchdown run in the third quarter at the Orange Bowl. (CG)

Here are two CU quarterbacks of the future. Darian Hagan, Jr. with his father (top) and Tim McCartney with his grandfather (left). Watch for them. They're likely to be wearing the Silver, Black and Gold in CU's next century!

(CG)

Former CU linebacking star Brian Cabral, now a Buff graduate assistant, consoles a dejected Michael Jones near the end of the Orange Bowl game.

(CG)

This photo of the 1891 squad is the earliest team picture on record. *L-R, standing:* Howell Givens, Pat Carney, Bert Kennedy, Harry Gamble, Wesley Putnam, Ed Newcomb, Jim Garrett, Conrad Bluhn; *sitting,* Homer James, Bill McIntosh, V.R. Pennock, Clarence Perry, Charlie Easley, Harry Layton. In the center is CU president Horace Hale.

FROM THE BEGINNING - 1890 - 1990

1890

CU's football debut was, putting it mildly, inauspicious.

In fact, it might be fair to say that no American university started more unimpressively.

Without a coach, without a following and, obviously, without much talent, that first squad opened out of town, losing in Denver to the Denver Athletic Club, 20-0, on November 15, 1890.

A week later the team introduced Boulder to college football and did it in record-setting fashion, establishing a negative mark which still stands. The CU novices were overwhelmed by the reigning power of the state, Colorado Mines, 103-0.

It's unlikely that that record will ever fall although Chuck Fairbanks' Buffaloes made a strong run at it for 30 minutes in 1989, trailing 56-0 at the half to UCLA in Los Angeles. But neither team could maintain that historic pace and CU turned a table, but not the tables, by outscoring UCLA 14-0 in the final half.

And in 1946, a CU team traveled to Texas and took a 76-0 pounding. However, Texas divided its scoring almost equally throughout the game so that the record was never really in danger.

But unlike that 1890 team, those later ones were well-backgrounded, well-trained and fairly cohesive though almost equally inept.

The initial CU team was built around its quarterback and chief organizer, Tom Edmundson who, with a medical student named William Hosford, assembled the first squad.

Before 1890, students played European-style football, soccer. In 1890 the sport was basically rugby which then gradually evolved into today's game.

That 20-0 loss to DAC was actually a very impressive beginning. The CU team Edmundson captained used only 12 players but it was a costly defeat.

Edmundson was injured and lost for the season. His replacement was Pat Carney who led the team for the next three seasons. But he wasn't ready for a powerful Mines team which ran roughshod over the Buffs.

Conrad Bluhm, who stepped into the starting fullback job in the second game, shared the same fate as Edmundson. He took such a battering that he never played again.

"We had a big problem," he explained years later. "We had practiced soccer most of the pre-season and didn't know much about rugby. We sort of learned the game as it went along. Considering that, we really didn't feel we had done too badly. But our line simply could not stop them. My defensive position was what you would call a linebacker today and on every play it looked like an army of Mines players was coming right at me. By the end of the game I looked like a rolled beefsteak."

CU got some unexpected help from its president, Horace Hale. Seeing Bluhm buried by Mines tacklers one more time, was too much for the tiny (he barely weighed 100 pounds) president to endure and he leaped over the sideline ropes and began groping for Bluhm. (Presidents too, were hardy men in those pioneer days.)

The CU men then nursed their wounds with the help of an open date then a storm which disrupted their train schedule to cause cancellation of a game at Colorado College. The game was played a week later and CU tumbled for the third straight time, 44-0. But the Boulder squad was beginning to show the benefits of its trial by fire. In particular, the offense displayed the first signs of cohesion that afternoon despite the third straight shutout.

The final game of the first season produced another clubbing from Mines but CU broke its scoreless string. The score was 50-4 (that's what touchdowns were worth in those days - a successful conversion counted two points) but the highlight of the game for CU was its first score.

Ironically, it came from the defense when tackle George Darley caught a Mines fumble and thundered 65 yards into the end zone. The name "Darley" has been prominent throughout CU history. Dr. Ward Darley carried the family colors to the top in 1953 when he became the school's seventh president.

That Darley touchdown let the team finish its first season on a note of hope. Despite the only winless season in the school's history, the team had made considerable progress. From a squad which had been described by an onlooker as "knowing no more about football than a bunch of jackrabbits" it convinced its tiny group of supporters that better times were ahead.

The young team continued to take its lumps in the second season but it served notice in its first game of 1891 that it would soon be a force. With a season's experience behind him, Carney became an able leader for the offense.

Then, as now, defensive play put a premium on toughness and aggressiveness without the discipline required of an offense which required 11 men playing in unison. There was never any question about the CU players' toughness. Their problem had been picking up the fine points of a game about which they were almost totally ignorant going into the 1890 season.

1891

The first game of 1891 was against Colorado Mines in Boulder. CU's first gridiron was a nondescript rectangle of dirt, rocks and occasional blades of grass tucked away in a northeast corner

The 1892 squad finished 3-2-0 to become the first CU team to win more games than it lost. *L-R, back row:* Howell Givens, Bob Shafer, Harry Gamble, Fred Carroll, Wesley Putnam; *middle row:* Charlie Easley, Bill Arnett, B.M. Webster, Bill McIntosh, George Darley; *front row,* Harry Layton, Jim Garrett, Capt. Pat Carney, Ed Newcombe. Gamble was a player-coach and CU's first campus football field was named after him. Darley scored the first points in CU history that year when he returned a fumble 65 yards against Colorado Mines.

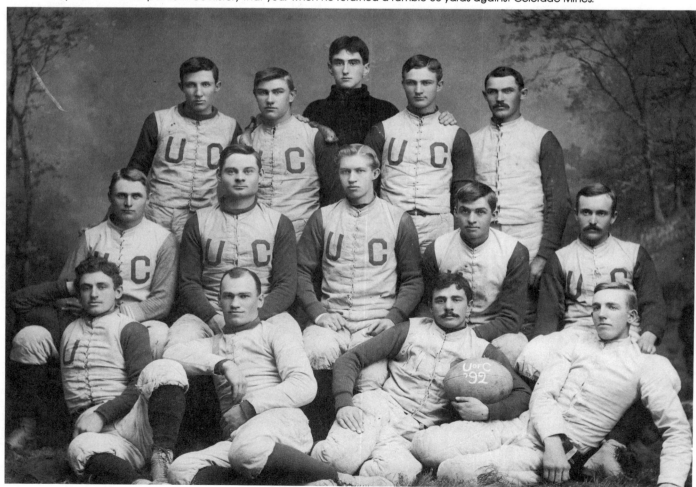

of a campus which contained only five buildings (Old Main, two cottages which served as dormitories for girls and medical students, a small hospital and brand new Woodbury Hall which was the men's dorm.)

The opponent was the same Mines team which had outscored CU 153-4 in two games the previous year. But times had changed. The Boulder bunch was no longer an inexperienced, bewildered team. The result was the school's first "moral victory", a 10-6 defeat which in effect, signaled the arrival of CU as a budding state power.

A very elementary addition played an important role in the CU team's dramatic improvement. It got a coach, if only a part-timer whose primary role in life was as minister of Boulder's Episcopal Church. The man was Dr. Frederick F. Kramer, an easterner with brief collegiate experience, who volunteered to guide the team's uncertain destiny.

Kramer's most public achievements in football came as an official. He was considered the top referee in the state for several years. However, his contribution to CU football was as the man who introduced order and 1890's-type organization to the program.

With Carney captaining the team as quarterback, CU fans happily anticipated the remainder of the season after that auspicious beginning. Like many CU fans in many future years, they got disappointment instead.

The next two games were with Denver AC and they were nightmares for CU. DAC won in Boulder 42-0, and repeated by 44-0 in Denver the following week.

But Kramer and company got things turned around in the fourth game, taking Colorado Mines to the wire again before bowing, 6-0. That set the stage for the next landmark in CU gridiron history.

The date was November 26, the site Colorado Springs, the opponent Colorado Springs Athletic Association, a team composed primarily of Colorado College students.

Carney was brilliant, directing the team to the school's first victory with a double-figured attack, 24-4.

The game marked the end of the beginning for CU football and the beginning of good times which saw its teams fashion winning seasons in 20 of the next 23 years, four of them undefeated.

The Original Starters

This was the starting lineup when CU took the field for the first time, against Denver Athletic Club in Denver on November 15, 1890:

E:	Ed Ingram, Boulder
E:	John Nixon, Greeley
T:	George Darley, Alamosa
T:	Delos Holden, Boulder
G:	Howell Givens, Denver
G:	Harry Layton, New York City
C:	Charles McConnell, Unknown
QB:	Tom Edmundson, Bisbee, Arizona
HB:	Homer James, Estes Park
HB:	Wesley Putman, Denver
FB:	Bert Kennedy, Denver

1892

CU got over the .500 mark for the first time in 1892 with Carney continuing to lead the way as a talented, and more importantly, durable quarterback. CU victimized Denver University in the first two games, 26-0 and 46-0.

It was close again with Mines but still a losing 10-6 effort, and when DAC, which had supplanted Mines as the top team in the state, hammered CU 42-6, the team was 2-2 at the conclusion of the fall season.

But a rivalry which has burned fiercely, smouldered, lay dormant and flared up again through the years since, was conceived during the winter and delivered in a February 10, 1893 game in Ft. Collins with Colorado A&M. This time it was the CU players who were more polished and proficient and they poured it on their upstate rivals, 70-6.

The win produced the first winning season for CU even though it spanned parts of two calendar years.

Following that 1892 season, the state's first conference was organized. Named the Colorado Inter-Collegiate Athletic Association it included five schools; CU, Denver University, Colorado College, Colorado Mines and Colorado A&M.

1893

The 1893 team, featuring an adept punter and placekicker in George Wailes, who had already played three years in the east, slipped slightly to a 2-3 record, bowing to DAC twice and defeating Highland School (the ancestor of Boulder High) in non-conference games, then breaking even in its first league encounter to finish third. CU lost to Mines for the sixth straight time, 24-10, after clubbing A&M again, 44-6.

Football was now a fixture among campus activities and it was time the school got a full-time coach. It did, in 1894.

1894

It must be remembered that football at CU during those first four years was a very loosely organized sport with no eligibility rules, not much supervision, no financial support from the fledgling university and no coaching. In more modern times it would have had trouble qualifying as a club sport.

These facts of life were quickly recognized and as the 1894 season approached, a search ("probe" might be a better word) for a coach began.

HELLER

At this point a young student athlete named Harry Gamble, who had captained the 1893 team, took the initiative and recommended a friend and fellow gridder named Harry Heller at Baker University. He agreed to coach CU. Whatever stipend he received was raised by contributions from the players and fans. He was also a student, but with at least some experience in coaching.

Before his arrival, a primitive dressing room featuring shower facilities was constructed in the basement of Woodbury Hall, then a men's dormitory. It may have been the first campus shower built for athletes in the region.

Upon Heller's arrival, a search for a new playing field began. The crude campus area was deemed unsatisfactory.

The 1894 squad was CU's first conference champion, finishing with an 8-1-0 record. Coach Harry Heller is at the far right and his player-assistant Harry Gamble is at the far left.

A field was scraped into shape on a hill approximately one mile north of the campus known as "Lover's Hill." Following World War II that area was developed into home sites and called "Panorama Heights."

Heller also established some rules of diet for the players, working with the cooks at the regular dining hall to give a semblance of order to the team's eating schedule.

Though small by later standards, Heller's improvements produced dramatic results. But there were still formidable obstacles to be overcome. His top priorities as he prepared his first, and only, CU team for the 1894 season, were teaching his team his system of play and, just as importantly, finding enough men for a second unit.

It wasn't easy to build up the squad. The sport was rough to the point of being brutal and there was no protective equipment for the players. Injuries were numerous. The newspapers of the day emphasized the roughness of the game. Consequently, the average able-bodied student was not enthusiastic about subjecting himself to such risks. But Heller and Capt. Gamble finally enticed extra men and the team was ready for the season.

1894 proved to be a real eye-opener for CU fans, but not before an incident which almost killed the sport in infancy. Going into the most ambitious schedule in the school's 5-year history, eight games plus an opening practice affair with Denver's East high, everything seemed under control.

Heller's team, as expected, rolled over East 46-0. But on the last play of the game a CU player received a severe head injury in a scrimmage melee. He was unconscious for several minutes but not seriously injured. The morale of the squad was, however. On the following Monday barely enough players showed up to field a team. The new additions obviously decided they'd made a mistake and that the game was not for them. Again, Heller and Gamble coaxed them back.

Their bad times behind them, the CU squad promptly knocked off DAC for the first time, 12-4, then ran its winning streak to seven straight before losing the rematch to DAC in Denver 20-6.

The final record for 1894 was 8-1-0 (the East game was considered official) and the school had its very first conference championship with a perfect 5-0-0 mark.

Heller was a popular figure in Boulder. The future was bright. The school had a firmly established grid program with an obviously competent coach. But Heller declined to continue, electing to concentrate on his studies. He did however, agree to stay on as a player. But he was only a part-time participant the following year and did not even earn a letter.

One last comment about that early

time and its lack of eligibility rules. Gamble was a regular for six years, from 1891 through 1896. If there was ever a key rock in the early CU foundation, it was him. It figured that when the first official gridiron was built on the campus two years after the conclusion of his career, it was named Gamble field.

1895

Heller had yielded his coaching whistle. CU fans were perplexed at this sudden turn of fortune. Could the school find another leader of his quality? It did, and in doing so, found the man who became renowned as "the father of CU football."

FOLSOM

Waiting in the wings at Dartmouth College near his native Maine was Fred Gorham Folsom, a 21-year-old pre-law graduate who had been an outstanding football and baseball player at the eastern school. Labeled as the finest end ever to play at Dartmouth to that point, he had led the school to two straight championships. More importantly, he had acquired valuable coaching experience while playing. Player-coaches were not uncommon in that early time when coaching was not yet a field to attract a large following.

Folsom's name came up quickly in a search for a replacement to Heller. A group spearheaded by CU's captain, Bill Caley, quickly established him as the man for the job.

Folsom's primary interest, however, was in obtaining a law degree and to that end he was planning to enroll in Michigan University's law school that fall. But when CU assured him he could attend law school in Boulder while coaching football he accepted the job. That decision was the turning point for CU football and the school immediately became a regional power. But even more significantly, the slender (5-11, 170) young easterner would become a leader in athletic, university, legal, civic and state affairs for the next half-century.

In truth, a man to match Colorado's mountains. A man who, in the following two decades, 15 of them as CU's coach, would establish marks which would hold up for the school's first century of football: most years coached (15) and most games won (77) in a career capped by having CU's stadium named after him. Not to mention a law degree from CU, a chair on CU's faculty and a distinguished career as a jurist.

But football was his primary objective when he arrived in Boulder in October, 1895. CU officials got their first sight of him when he stepped off the train in Boulder. They were not overly enthusiastic about that first impression. Charles Southard, who managed the CU athletic association, said Folsom was "slight of build and sway backed with a hand shake which felt like a bag of bones." Quick to spot that dismay at his appearance, Folsom never let Southard forget that first impressions are not necessarily accurate.

A keen sense of humor was a Folsom trademark throughout his life. But on the field he was a stern disciplinarian who installed his system quickly and constantly added innovations and new plays from an always-active and creative mind.

If Folsom had a coaching "weakness" it was his failure to remember his players' names during practices. Instead, he referred to everyone as "Bill" in those busy sessions. As a result, his players, in turn, called him "Bill." Player-coach relationships obviously were relaxed in those early days, a situation which did not always exist in later years. Folsom's real nickname, however, was always "P.I." to his friends. A native of Prince Edward Island, Maine (the town was Oldham) where the islanders were called "PEIs" after the initials, Folsom got that tag when he enrolled at Dartmouth. The middle letter was slurred by eastern accents and evolved into "PI." He carried that label proudly as a mark of his native state.

CU's football fortunes moved quickly forward as Folsom's playing and coaching background took effect. His first team went 5-1-0 and repeated as conference champion. (Folsom had actually arrived on campus too late for the opening game, a 36-0 victory over Denver's Manual high.) Then his team defeated Denver Wheel Club (32-0) and Denver U. (28-0).

Folsom's first loss, 10-22 to DAC, had extenuating circumstances. The referee, another Episcopalian minister named Frank Spalding, was a member of the DAC and had been a former fullback for the club. Most of the calls that day understandably went against CU and not even the presence of Kramer as umpire neutralized the situation. But that was only a temporary roadblock and CU bounced back to overpower Colorado College (38-10) and Colorado Mines (14-0) to take the title.

Incidentally, CU's uniforms those days consisted of red jerseys, tight-fitting canvas jackets, canvas or moleskin pants, red stockings and regulation shoes. Equipment was an occasional rubber noseguard and padded shin guards. There were no helmets. If a player wanted extra protection for his skull he let his hair grow.

Fred Gorham Folsom
Hanover, New Hampshire, about 1904

1896

For an encore in 1896, Folsom delivered CU's first undefeated team, one of four he would coach. Gamble, a special protege of Folsom, who was also a law student and like his coach would become a prominent Colorado attorney, captained the team for the third straight year.

This was Fred Folsom's first CU squad in 1895 and it won the first of nine championships during his 15 years as head coach. Harry Gamble, who continued to play and help coach is in the middle of the front row and Harry Heller, who coached the previous season and played in this one, is at the far right of the front row. Folsom's coaching trademark was his Dartmouth letter sweater and he wears it in this picture. (Note the only items of protective equipment these men used: nose guards and legging-type stockings.)

The key game of 1896 was a rematch with DAC at Denver in the final game. Hard feelings had carried over from the disputed game the previous year. CU insisted on, and got, a different officiating crew even though there weren't that many qualified persons available. The November day produced a blizzard, almost cancelling the state's first "really big game."

More than 400 CU students and Boulderites rode a special football train to Denver where the game was played on what is now the site of East high. The CU team rode the school's first chartered vehicle, a horse-drawn vehicle known as a "tally-ho." CU's now proficient forces ground out an 8-6 upset, the first win ever over DAC. And despite the terrible weather conditions, the first victory parade from playing field to downtown Denver erupted, a scene which was later to become a tradition following victories at Denver University's stadium. The jubilant students cut the horses loose from the CU team's tally-ho and carried the players on their shoulders to the DAC club building. Football fever had arrived at CU!

1897

However, a cloud passed over the campus in 1897 when the young conference passed its first eligibility rule, limiting a player to four seasons of competition and ending the possibility of a star like Gamble playing for as long as he was in school or someone like Wailes playing three years at one college then moving to another for an equal length of time.

CU protested strenuously about the new rule and played the 1897 season under the threat of leaving the league which it did just before the championship game with Mines. However, an ineligibility problem between the two schools was resolved and CU won a convincing 36-2 victory and the championship. Before that game, CU had unofficially resigned from the conference but that matter was also cleared up during the off-season and the school entered the 1898 season in good standing after the 7-1-0 record the year before.

1898

The new rule took its toll on Fol-som's team as captain-to-be and quarterback Harry Chase, a 4-year regular, and center Bob Shafer, a 5-year starter, had their playing careers ended by it. As a result of losing key men like these, CU slipped to a 4-4-0 mark and fourth place. However, 1898 was a landmark year in that it produced the first intersectional game in the school's history (and a herald of big games to come) against Nebraska.

Actually, there were two landmarks. A new playing field on campus was ready for use and it was called Gamble Field after its 6-year stalwart who was now two years into his gridiron retirement. The new field featured another big first for CU -real grass on the playing surface. (This innovation would endure for the next 73 years until synthetic grass was layered onto the Folsom Field surface.)

The Nebraska game had been delayed a year when that school's faculty ruled that Boulder was too far for the team to travel. But that distance problem was resolved a year later and the Nebraskans promptly established a precedent by defeating CU 23-10, as the Boulder men fought fiercely but were physically overpowered.

1899

Firmly entrenched in only four seasons as the top coach in the region, Folsom, who had now obtained his law degree, dropped a bombshell just before the 1899 season when he announced he would resign at the end of the season to enter private practice in Denver. His team promptly went 7-2-0 to make his departure even more painful. His 5-year record was an imposing 28-8-0.

MORTIMER
1900

Coaching was in Folsom's blood however, as he found time away from his new profession to help coach the Denver Wheel Club team in 1900. One of that team's wins was an 11-0 shutout of CU to add to the Boulder fans unhappiness.

T.C. Mortimer, who had been an outstanding tackle at Simpson College in Iowa then at Chicago University and then a successful high school coach in Chicago, was named to succeed Folsom. Possibly his greatest contribution to CU's young tradition was the establishment of letter sweaters which were awarded to the players for the first time. There was a slight catch, however. The players had to buy them. But as a concession, they were permitted to select their own colors, so despite the fact that the official school colors were Silver & Gold, most of the players chose a maroon sweater with a white "C" on it.

FOLSOM II

Despite the 6-4 record, Mortimer's coaching job was deemed satisfactory and the big Iowan was set for his second season. However, Folsom changed all that quickly. Disenchanted with a life limited almost entirely to his legal desk, he announced, just as surprisingly as he had done two years earlier, that he would be interested in returning to CU. CU officials accepted enthusiastically, Mortimer yielded gracefully and the Folsom career was back in bloom. Understandably, the CU players were overjoyed at getting their old coach back. His coaching ability, his compassion for his men, and his wry wit on and off the field had already made him an unforgettable leader.

Fred Folsom was always an athletic activist. He's shown here when he was head judge of the finish at a CU track meet.

1901

Folsom wasted no time getting CU back in the groove. His 1901 squad lost only its last game, to DAC, to finish 5-1-1 and regain the championship.

1902

1902 was almost a duplicate, CU going 5-1-0 and repeating as champion. The highlight of that season was a CU team's first game outside the state as the Folsom forces traveled to Lincoln to meet a nationally-ranked Nebraska team. The Coloradoans played mightily but once again were out-muscled by Nebraska, 0-10.

Interestingly, even though it would be nearly half a century before it happened, CU people were already talking about the school looking eastward for a new conference affiliation. A commentary in the 1903 yearbook stated that "the season of 1902 will have a far-reaching effect on our football history. Our magnificent showing against Nebraska has done wonders for our reputation. It showed conclusively that we should someday enter into a league with Nebraska, Iowa, Kansas, Missouri and, perhaps Ohio." Strong words for those times, but prophetic ones. Although including Ohio in the scheme was perhaps stretching the boundaries of potential alliance more than somewhat.

But now the topsy-turviness of the Folsom years returned and the now-you-have-him-now-you-don't coach exited again, this time for his alma mater, Dartmouth, where he would become head coach and a member of the law faculty. That prestigious move was understandable. Folsom had a strong feeling about his New England roots and, in particular, for Dartmouth. He wore his Dartmouth letter sweater constantly during his early CU coaching days and returned to New Hampshire quickly when the call came.

CROPP
1903

So he returned to his native northeast and for the second time in four years CU replaced him with a mid-westerner, Dave Cropp, who had played at Lenox College (Iowa) and Wisconsin and coached at Cornell (Iowa) and South Dakota. Cropp proved to be an able replacement just as versatile and energetic as his predecessor. Certainly, CU got its salary's worth from Cropp who signed on as the school's first official athletic director in addition to being business manager for athletics and coaching football, baseball and track. (The record does not reveal what Cropp did in his spare time.)

During that first year Cropp managed to coach CU's gridders to an impressive 8-2 record, finishing as undefeated conference champions and losing only to midwestern foes Nebraska and Kansas. At the same time, he was busy as CU's first athletic fundraiser, coaxing $387 from Boulder merchants which, coupled with increased gate receipts, erased a $1500 athletics deficit.

1904

A year later, he introduced spring football practice to the campus. The game which had somewhat resembled an hour-long tug of war to this time was now becoming more sophisticated as coaches throughout the country added new concepts, formations and techniques to the game. Cropp felt that improvements such as these required more learning than the customary few weeks before the fall season and scheduled six weeks beginning in April to improve the skills of his charges. The game was opening up and Cropp was wise enough to recognize the need to be ready.

There was great enthusiasm in Boulder for the Nebraska game as 6000 fans packed Gamble Field despite a chilly, rainy afternoon. The sideline bleachers were full and spectators packed in 4-deep completely around the campus gridiron. An early CU scoring thrust plus some fine goal line stands produced a 6-0 upset.

Nebraska was bigger (with a 190-169 weight advantage in the line) and better. But CU was tougher on this wet afternoon.

Cropp's men scored after a short drive on a 3-yard plunge by fullback

UNIFORM COLORS

Uniform colors have almost always caused controversy among CU fans because of the lack of contrast between the official school colors, silver and gold.

The grumbling began as far back as 1921 when the following editorial appeared in the campus newspaper, The Silver & Gold:

"CU teams always look poorer than any other conference schools because of the bad combination of colors. At best, silver can only be represented by gray, which usually shows up as a dirty oxford color in wool. The gold is commonly a dark yellow. The gray sweaters of the team resemble camouflaged armor, especially when mud and perspiration are added.

"Although radical views are sometimes understated and often attended with much unpleasantness, we venture to suggest that it would not be amiss in the future to suggest to change the colors of the University for football. We suggest black and red or blue and red as combinations perfectly possible and plausible."

End of editorial.

In the beginning, maroon and white had been used but silver and gold prevailed until 1959 with the exception of an aborted attempt to change to a blue jersey in 1946. But the first time out wearing that color, CU absorbed a horrendous 76-0 beating at Texas. Upon the return to Boulder, the jerseys were put away and never used again, except for practices.

With the arrival of Sonny Grandelius as coach in 1959, black jerseys with silver helmets, pants and numbers were introduced. The only gold was the trim of the numbers and a stripe on the pants. Not exactly a dynamic combination, either, but with much more contrast than before. A very modernistic "buffalo horn" on the helmet was the most distinctive feature of the new outfit. Traditionalists roared their disapproval but black has been the basic Buffalo color ever since.

Briefly, in 1962, the basic color was changed to something called "Sunflower Gold" but it was more like bright yellow and when that team suffered a disastrous season, those outfits, like 1946's navy blue ones, were quietly shelved and even the traditionalists failed to complain.

Eddie Crowder quickly went back to black when he took over in 1963. But he brightened the uniforms with gold helmets and pants and white numbers. Now there was contrast with plenty of gold and white showing. Many old-timers continued to growl quietly but the color combination stuck.

There was one more experiment from 1981 through 1985 when a movement led by regent Jack Anderson replaced the black with a medium blue. Hardly anyone, old or new, was happy with this change and when the worst drought in the school's history descended on the last teams of Chuck Fairbanks and the first ones of Bill McCartney, the latest shade of blue was discarded with no mourners. Obviously, CU fans reasoned, a live program dressed in black was better than a dead one dressed in blue.

And so the first century ended with black jerseys and gold and white trimmings.

Elwin Caley with 8:30 played in the first period. From then on Caley, who doubled at linebacker, and guard Charles Karnopp sparked a gritty defense which stopped Nebraska inside the 5-yard line three times in the first half and once more after the rest period. End John Salberg and halfback Ray Roberts also stood out for CU. But the real ringleader of the upset was Caley, who did all the scoring with an extra point after his TD, punted, kicked off, carried the ball most of the time and was one of the outstanding defenders on the field.

Cropp's preparations paid big dividends in the fall of 1904 despite a 6-2-1 record which wasn't considered up to CU's recent standards. In particular, a 33-0 disaster at Stanford in the final game of the season left everyone with bad memories of the campaign.

KEINHOLZ
1905

Cropp moved on after the 1904 season and was replaced by a Minnesota University graduate, Willis Keinholz, who kept CU on pace with a fine 8-1-0 record in 1905 despite more school problems with the CIAA which resulted in CU's withdrawal from the state conference before the season. All games with state foes were cancelled and Keinholz' team played primarily against regional teams, defeating among others, Wyoming, Kansas and Utah while losing only to Nebraska. Loose academic requirements in the CIAA caused CU's one-year absence. When the conference added a rule that required all athletes to be passing a minimum of 10 hours per semester, CU came back into the fold for the 1905 season.

CASTLEMAN
1906

Kienholz returned to the midwest after his only season and was succeeded by an easterner, Frank Castleman of Colgate. Castleman's first squad, in 1906, bogged down by offensive rules changes which required great adjustments for all college teams, slipped to the school's first losing record in 12 years. Forward passing had been legalized to open up the offense but the first down requirement had been increased from three downs to make five yards to 10 yards with the same number of downs.

Castleman's first CU team, blanked State Prep 22-0 in its opener then scored only six points the remainder of the season. Indicative of the problems teams had with the new first down rule, four of the nine games ended in scoreless ties. The forward pass had arrived but mastery of it had obviously not reached the west.

game with Mines by the baseball-ish score of 5-4, an extra point making the difference.

FOLSOM III

Folsom had re-surfaced in Boulder the year before, rejoining the CU law faculty where he would serve continu-

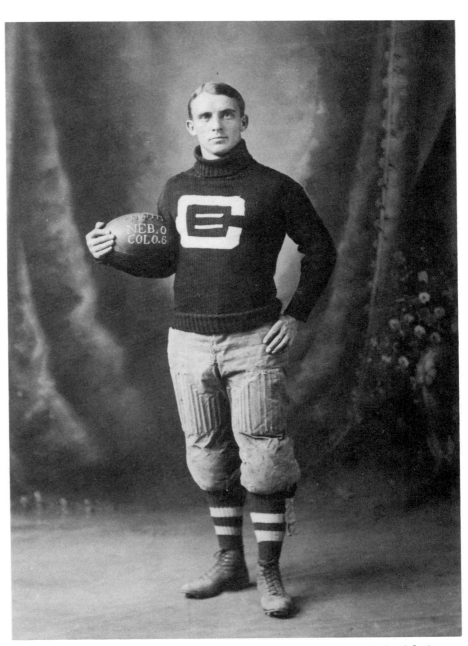

Quarterback Everett Owens, the 1904 captain, holds the game ball used in the 6-0 win over Nebraska that year.

1907

Castleman's second, and last, squad got untracked, with the unexpected help of Folsom, in 1907, going 5-3-0 and losing the conference championship

ously from 1906 until his retirement in 1942. Boulder was in Folsom's blood and so was CU football. A constant practice visitor upon his return to the mountain country, his advice was quickly sought out by Castleman who, no fool, named Folsom as his unofficial assistant for the 1907 season.

1908

When Folsom indicated he would take the head job in 1908, Castleman wisely stepped aside. He had plenty to do anyway, directing the athletic program and coaching basketball, baseball and track. Additionally he would assist Folsom in football at both CU and State Prep where Folsom's contract also called upon him to coach. For his dual coaching role, Folsom was paid $1,000.

His return to the head job in 1908 was marked by a typically fine 5-2-0 record, but a 14-10 loss to Denver cost CU the conference championship. The afternoon was additionally marred by a post-game brawl between the student bodies which caused the two schools to cancel their series for the next five years.

To add insult to injury, the Pioneers used a favorite Folsom play to win the game. A year earlier, the rules had been changed to permit any member of the punting team except the punter to re-cover a kick once it had touched the ground. Folsom drilled his punters to kick into the open areas and devised a formation which enabled the other 10 men to converge quickly onto that spot. (Recovered punts were an important part of CU's ball control game that fall.) Injuries to key men made CU a heavy underdog going into the DU game but the team outplayed the Pioneers and led late in the game. Denver turned the tables on Folsom however, by recovering a punt of its own to set up the winning touchdown.

The significant thing about 1908 was that Folsom was back and so was CU football. Colorado would carve out perfect 6-0-0 records for the next three years going unscored upon in 1909 and winning 18 straight games. CU yielded only eight points during this longest streak in their history, and went 21 games without allowing a touchdown. In that dynamic 3-year span, Folsom established records which would last a century and earn him the title, "Father of Colorado Football."

1909

Early in 1909, CU's Athletic Board Chairman, Dr. George Norlin, a professor of Greek, led a movement which resulted in a new alignment called the Colorado Faculty Athletic Conference. Charter members included CU, Colo-

rado A&M, Colorado College and, later that year, Colorado Mines. A year later the name was changed to Rocky Mountain Faculty Athletic Conference as the league expanded geographically and numerically to include Utah and Denver, and later, Utah State (1914), Montana State (1917), Brigham Young (1918), Wyoming (1921), and Western State and Colorado Teachers College (1924). The new league, built on a foundation of faculty control of athletics, lasted until 1937.

Norlin was a great faculty leader for CU athletics. A slight, sprightly Greek scholar, his interests and priorities meshed closely with Folsom's and the two formed a formidable alliance for collegiate sports. Norlin constantly praised athletics, and football in particular, as an important activity for both participants and spectators, something behind which a student body and entire community could rally.

"So long as contests are held we shall win if we can," he stated. "But we

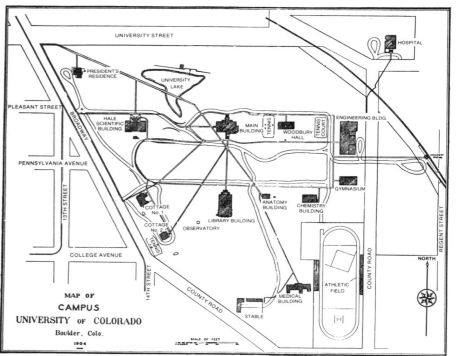

with compliments of J. W. Broxon

Map of the CU campus in 1904 showing the newly completed Gamble Field football, track and baseball complex.

will win honorably, regarding an unfair victory as far worse than a fair defeat." The tiny professor, so important in CU's formative athletic years, became the school's fifth president in 1919 and served for 20 years and if Folsom was the father of CU football, Norlin was, at the least, an important member of the family.

With the beginning of the new conference came Folsom's and CU's finest hours in football. No CU team during the first century reached those again. In 1909, William Bull Stirrett captained the team to a perfect season as CU outscored its opponents by 141-0 in the six games. Included were 53-0 and 57-0 thrashings of Colorado A&M and New Mexico. For the record, CU's toughest game that season was a 3-0 opener over State Prep, the Boulder team coached by (who else) Fred Folsom. It was a case of a Folsom team playing a Folsom team in a tight, tough football game. And one of the few known cases in college annals where two teams coached by the same man met.

A familiar campus tennis team through the years was Folsom (r) and Frank Wolcott, who played for him and later served on CU coaching staffs.

1910

There was not much CU could do for an encore in 1910 though Folsom's men came close, matching the perfect record but yielding three points on a Wyoming field goal.

1911

Another field goal by Wyoming and a safety by Colorado College were the only blemishes on the 6-0-0 record in 1911.

1912

But CU's win streak was snapped by a 21-0 Colorado A&M victory in the third game of 1912 and that defeat cost CU the championship.

Still it was a fine (6-3-0) campaign, one which finished on a high note with a 14-12 upset of Oklahoma at Norman in the first meeting between the two schools who were to become fierce rivals in the 1950's.

1913

His busy schedule between athletics, faculty and community was extracting its toll from Folsom and he began to think of giving up coaching. His team had reached the mountain top, had established itself as king of the Rockies and for Folsom there were no more heights left to conquer. The possibility of retiring didn't affect his coaching

though. In 1913 his team bounced back with a 5-1-1 record and his ninth, and final, conference title in 13 seasons.

1914

In 1914, CU was as formidable as ever with a 5-1-0 record but lost the championship in a bitter 6-2 loss to Colorado Mines. That was the beginning of the end for Folsom who, although only 40, was worn down physically by his long playing and coaching career.

1915

A series of illnesses sidelined him for much of the 1915 season and his team went 1-6-0, the worst record for him as either a player or coach. But, in fairness to him, he was unable to be on the field for much of that fall.

At the end of the season, he announced his retirement from coaching. Thus ended CU's golden period. Fred Folsom concentrated on teaching law until his retirement in 1942. He was acting dean of the college of law in 1927-28 and always remained active in athletics and chaired the athletic board until 1927. During that time he led the campaign for a new football stadium on campus and drafted the financial plan which enabled the school to build it.

Working closely with president Norlin, Folsom was one of the men most instrumental for the new stadium which was called Colorado Field at the beginning.

It is only fitting that the present CU stadium has borne the names of the two men so instrumental in its creation. Known simply as Colorado Field, its name was later changed to Norlin Field. And when Folsom died November 11, 1944, two days following his 71st birthday, the CU board of regents officially named the stadium, "Folsom Field" before the month was out. The additions made in 1956 and 1968 elevated the capacity to 52,000 and it is now known as Folsom Stadium.

No one ever did more to create the tradition of CU football than Frederick Gorham Folsom. In his 15 seasons he became a lasting legend, a symbol of kinder, gentler times in which football was a rough, tough and un-subsidized sport. Times changed, the sport became more polished and expert, the crowds increased and so did the costs, and the coaching pressures became deadly. But the game which Folsom had helped nurture has continued to be important on the CU scene and the memory of this slender, handsome young man from the state of Maine who became such an

An early CU team lines up during a practice session. (How about that 5-man backfield?)

important figure in CU athletics will always remain.

1916 - 17 - 18 - 19

By the time of Folsom's retirement, World War I occupied center stage everywhere. The world situation did not kill CU football but the teams barely stayed alive in 1916-17-18-19, covering those four seasons with a composite 11-13-2 record. Bob Evans, a high school coach from Owensboro, Kentucky, took over in 1916 and barely bettered the 1915 record with a 1-5-1 mark which included a 58-0 shellacking by CC. The following year he improved it to 6-2-0 and, with that impressive turnaround, moved to Stanford as head coach.

MILLS

The war hit the program hard in 1918 when Eddie Evans, the team's fine quarterback in 1915-16 was killed in action in France. Joe Mills, who had signed on in 1918 primarily as basketball coach, a job he held for six years, was named interim football coach and guided CU teams to a 2-3-0 record in

his first season. One of the wins was over a team called "The Lieutenants," undoubtedly a military group from a nearby army camp. Unfortunately, Mills could not schedule any other service teams and CU's 33-0 rout of Mines was the only win over collegians.

Those war years were basically unproductive ones for CU teams but two of its finest athletes came along in that period. Lee Willard, a Denver West high graduate who was rejected for naval duty because of thyroid problems, weighed in at 155 pounds in 1918 to launch a career which won him 16 letters, four each in football, baseball, basketball and track to become the only 16-letterman in the century. Willard was a fine halfback with sprinter's speed and, despite his size, was the offensive workhorse for the team during his time.

A year earlier, Walter Franklin had come to CU from Ft. Morgan to become a 4-year regular center and end, earning all-conference honors at both positions in separate seasons. Like Willard, Franklin also was versatile, a regular in both baseball and golf and a good enough boxer to win the conference heavyweight title. But these two men

had little support and spent most of their collegiate careers trying to rally losing causes. After the 1919 season and a 2-3-1 record, Mills stepped down as football coach to concentrate on his basketball job. CU needed another Folsom to regroup the football forces. Professor Folsom, now chairman of the athletic board, had a protege ready. And like so many of his coaching decisions, this one was dramatic and decisive.

WITHAM
1920

The man Folsom recommended was Myron Witham who may not have turned out to be another Folsom but who came awfully close during a 12-year career, lifting CU football to still new heights which included post-season play as well as another perfect season. A slender, studious athlete, Witham had played for Folsom at Dartmouth in 1903-04, earning All-American honors in 1904 and serving as a player-coach during his senior season. He was head coach at Purdue in 1906 then dropped out of sight for the next 14 years while working in his field of engineering.

Because he had been away from coaching for so long, Witham's only hope in getting the job was Folsom's recommendation. It was enough and he came to Boulder for the 1920 season. The Folsom influence would continue and prosper through his one-time pupil. Once again, the old coach had come through for CU. A new era was ready to begin.

If CU officials were unimpressed at first sight with Folsom, they suffered the same doubts when they met the second Dartmouth man at the same railroad station. Witham resembled a college professor more than an athlete-coach. But fortunately for CU, Witham's accents, like Folsom's, were on brains not brawn and the Dartmouth connection continued to click for CU.

Witham's first squad, in 1920, was impressive, compiling a 4-1-2 record, finishing in a tie for third in conference play and losing only to Utah. But that hard-fought 7-0 loss in Boulder was a harbinger of bad things to come for the little leader. The Salt Lake City school would always be his nemesis and even-

tually be the major reason for his departure. In 12 seasons, Witham's CU teams would manage only a 2-9-1 record against the Utes.

Even with that fine beginning, Witham's real early progress came off the playing field. He looked and acted like a well-organized man and he was. In his first fall on campus he established a training table of sorts for the varsity players, the first one at CU. Unlike later ones, this was basically a co-operative affair. The only outside help was a cook with the players taking turns at serving the food and cleaning up. Witham also toyed with the idea of starting a football dorm but felt that it might be pushing his luck, so he abandoned his idea of putting beds in the Armory for his charges.

He also guided the student body into forming a campus booster club of 60 underclassmen who helped in such important areas as high school relations (translate that "recruiting"), scholarship (tutoring), publicity and ways and means (anything the first three areas didn't cover.)

A year later, in 1921, he continued to plow new ground in athletic organization. The first big road game of the fall, and the biggest intersectional ever, would be against midwestern power-house Chicago. A pre-season training camp was Witham's brainstorm to prepare his team. The booster club made it possible, raising funds to pay for the rent and food at a facility near Eldora. The team worked there for two weeks before moving onto the campus.

When they got back, they in fact, found an "athletic dorm" awaiting them. The boosters, with a $1000 contribution coupled with another $2000 from Boulder businessmen and smaller contributions from campus groups, such as the women's auxilliary, and fraternities, purchased a 14-room house at 1016-14th street for $10,500. It contained eating, sleeping and study facilities for 30 men.

1921

Witham also saw that CU home games were filmed on a regular basis.

Football was, at least before the kickoff, a friendly sport in the early 1900's. CU's team, at left, and an opponent pose for a pre-game photo.

The first movies of a game had been taken in 1919 of the October 11 game between CU and Colorado Aggies. All in all, he had things well in order as the 1921 season began. Hopes were high even though the mighty Chicago team of Amos Alonzo Stagg, already a legend, lurked ominously as the second game of the schedule.

CU did improve to second place in the conference but any hopes of national prominence were dashed at Chicago as the Boulder men were humbled, 35-0. But still another precedent had been established. A special train carried 300 boosters and the band to Chicago for the game. They had a great time despite their team's rude introduction to the big time.

When CU recovered quickly from that disaster to go undefeated the rest of the season (only a 0-0 tie at Utah marred the last month), Witham had the complete confidence of everyone following the 4-1-1 campaign.

1922

Prosperity was just around the corner. But it was still a year away. The 1922 record was a disappointing 4-4-1 and there were poundings from Denver

(16-0), CC (21-10) and Kansas (39-6) in addition to the annual heartbreaker by Utah (3-0).

1923

But Witham, with the help of his boosters, had assembled an excellent freshman group, one which consistently outplayed the varsity in practices. Only three regulars returned in 1923 so there was no great public optimism because of the 1922 mark. CU was picked for the second division. Too many rookies and not enough seasoned talent, proclaimed the press.

Witham had other ideas and, typically, kept them low key. He knew he had fine sophomores in ends Dick Handy and Jack Healy, tackle Paul Steward, guards Bill McGlone and Ken Sawyer, center Bill McNary, fullback Bill Bohn and quarterback Hatfield Chilson. These youngsters stepped right into the breach and followed the lead of veterans quarterback-captain Art Quinlan, fullback Earl Loser, tackle Don McLean and halfback Fred Hartshorn.

The team was young. And tough. And smart. And ready to roll. By any comparison it would rank as one of the finest combinations of football-and

subsequent-career-talent in CU history. All would become leaders in their fields: lawyers Healy, McGlone and Chilson; physicians Sawyer and Hartshorn; engineers McLean and Loser; career army officer Handy; and businessmen McNary, Steward, Quinlan and Bohn.

The rookies played like veterans and the veterans played like 1922 had never existed as the team started quickly then gained momentum each time out. The result was an epic 9-0-0 record, the finest unblemished achievement of the first 100 years. Only the 1937 team compared favorably, going 8-0-0 in regular season play before losing a bowl finale. The 1961 (9-2-0), 1967 (9-2-0), 1971 (10-2-0) and 1975 (9-3-0) teams won more games but none was perfect like the 1923 group.

With the combination of old and new players blending quickly, CU mauled its first three foes - Western State, Colorado Teachers and BYU -by a combined score of 152-0. But these were weak teams and CU fans held their breath as the same Denver team which had manhandled Witham's squad a year earlier came next.

A week-long siege of rain and snow

Gamble Field during a game. Note the horse-drawn carriages along the sideline.

This squad picture of the 1914 team is probably the most unique one ever taken by a CU photographer. *L-R, atop the ball:* Wayne Ivers, Pete Nelson, John Donovan, W.C. Hamilton, W.H. Cooper, Phil McCary, Fred Walter; *circled:* Pat McKee (mgr.), Virgil Sells; *in front:* Ed Glendenning, Paul Guthrie, Frank Allen, Harry Gammon, Frank Powers, Roscoe Healy, Walt Ziegler, Bill Sloan, C.W. Bessee, Paul McBride, Ed Knowles, Kirk Huber, *Missing,* Fred Folsom (coach).

added to CU's worries because Witham had alertly built his single wing offense around the accurate arm of tailback Quinlan. The muddy field and slippery ball caused Witham to keep the aerial game under wraps in the first quarter which ended scoreless. But midway in the second period he gave Quinlan the green light and the CU captain passed as though the conditions were perfect, hitting an unbelievable 15 of 30 for 206 yards to lead CU to an awesome statistical advantage over the favored Pioneers: 356-41 in total offense and 23-3 in first downs. Despite the relatively close score (21-7) it was a statistical slaughter. Now everybody in the west became believers. CU and Witham were the toast of the Rockies.

Quinlan followed up a week later, again in bad weather conditions and a muddy field, with 13-of-16 accuracy good for 162 aerial yards in a 17-7 win over CC. The CU captain was in almost-perfect form during an afternoon which saw nine fumbles, none by him.

Misfortune struck a week later however, when during a 47-0 laugher

against Colorado Mines, Quinlan broke his right hand. There would be no more passing from the CU star for the remainder of the season as his contributions were thereafter restricted to place-kicking and kick returns. To compound the crisis, formidable Utah was immediately ahead and the game was at Salt Lake City. The honeymoon appeared over. Even Witham was pessimistic as the game approached.

Quinlan's replacement was Chilson, a tiny (5-8, 130 pound) rookie without great speed and hardly any prime time experience. The wiry Pueblan had gotten in on the assault against Mines with a 73-yard kickoff return. But he was still a big question mark because of his size and inexperience.

In his favor, he was a smart runner who had great ability to dart through the holes. And despite his size, he was fearless when charging into the line. But his forte was his passing. To overcome his height disadvantage, he had developed a jumping style in which he leaped into the air to get the ball over the onrushing linemen. It was an ability which would gain him national recogni-

tion as a senior.

He was an untested sophomore this day against Utah. But what a debut as a starter as his running, passing and signal-calling sparked CU to a 17-7 victory. Quinlan helped too, kicking for five of those points. (Fourteen years almost to the day later another CU back named White would scale the same heights in leading his team to an identical 17-7 victory on the same field.) But this day belonged to Chilson and the little guy from Pueblo was the big man on campus for this and the next two seasons.

The reserves played most of the way in a methodical 20-3 win over Wyoming but CU had to rally to edge Colorado Aggies in the finale. With his right hand still in a cast, Quinlan kicked a field goal to tie the score 3-3 then returned a punt 63 yards to the Aggie 25 with time running out to set up another kick.

The Buffs pounded down to the three yard line with less than a minute left. Quinlan came in for the winning field goal only to have it blocked. He recovered and CU was still alive.

Myron Witham, like Fred Folsom before him, was a scholar-coach.

Wyoming (21-0), the team returned home for the official dedication of the new stadium and, once again, the opponent on such an important occasion was Utah. Chilson was brilliant on this day, November 1, 1924, with 13-of-16 passing. But six fumbles plagued CU and it took a dramatic late 35-yard field goal by Loser to produce a nerve wracking 3-0 win. A 38-0 win over Mines a week later set up another crucial game at Denver. Sloppy ballhandling again bogged down the CU offense and the finish was a disappointing 0-0 tie. But Chilson got things going a week later to lead his team to a convincing 36-0 rout over Colorado Aggies and a second straight conference title.

There was more to come though, in the unexpected addition of two post-season games in Honolulu thanks to the

Joe Mills coached for only two seasons (1918-19) but he may have set a sartorial standard for CU coaches which has never been equalled.

Witham had wisely ordered the try on third down, Quinlan would have another chance. This time he made it and the 6-3 triumph sealed the perfect season. Bedlam reigned in Boulder as the team and its fans made an exultant return from Ft. Collins.

1924

Following that perfect season there was great clamor for a badly needed new stadium. Gamble Field had been swelled to the seams by overflow crowds which set a record season's total of 42,480, over five times the capacity of the field's bleacher seats. There was unanimous agreement for a new stadium.

Engineering professor Whitney Huntington came up with an ideal location, a ravine near the site of the new men's gymnasium. With proper drainage and the construction of seats on the sides of the ravine, a new stadium could be built quickly and economically. Into the football scene stepped Folsom again. He was now a full-time law professor and chairman of the athletic board. He enthusiastically approved of Huntington's location and, at president Norlin's request, came up with a financing plan. The stadium was built in eight months at a cost of under $70,000. Prosperity and progress marched hand in hand on the Boulder campus.

The field wasn't ready for the first game, a 29-0 shutout over Western State as football said farewell to Gamble Field. CU raised the curtain on the new field with a 39-0 massacre of Mines. The 1923 team had compiled a record impossible to better. But the 1924 crew almost did it, playing one more game and finishing 8-1-1.

After two more relatively easy victories at Colorado College (26-0) and

Witham's coaching staff included (l-r) Frank Wolcott, Ed Knowles, Jack Johnson, Witham, Walt Franklin and Alva Noggle.

efforts of several enthusiastic fans in Hawaii. Funds were raised and an 18-man squad plus coaches sailed to the islands for a holiday treat of paradise and post-season play. CU celebrated Christmas day with a 43-0 victory over a navy all-star team. Then they basked in reflected glory, enjoying life and forgetting about football for a week. The vacation cost them dearly as they were upset by an unheralded Hawaii University team, 13-0.

It had been a great season and there was no reason to believe the successes would not continue. Witham's system was working well. He had seemingly conquered the Utah jinx. His offense was as open and exciting as any in the west. Like Folsom, he had the ability to stay a step ahead of his rival coaches. A constant innovator, he had more new ideas in store for CU opponents as 1925 approached. Unfortunately, his coaching career had reached its peak in 1923-24. Success did continue. But not

in the same amounts.

For some reason, probably because of his long period out of football before taking the CU job, Witham had never been accepted enthusiastically by the school's followers. Quite possibly, they felt he looked, and acted, more like a professor than a typical football coach. It's obvious he did because he was well-educated, intelligent - and professorial. However, the magnificent seasons of 1923 and 1924 elevated his standing in the football community considerably. Unfortunately, his tenure at the top did not last long. His final seven years at CU, though all but two were winners, found him constantly subjected to criticism. To his credit, he endured quietly and efficiently despite the pressures of a non-approving public. His only glaring deficiency was his record against Utah. It proved to be fatal.

1925

His problems began in the first game

following that peak campaign of 1924. Always searching for new ways to move the ball, he came up with a new formation for the 1925 season. He called it an "indirect pass" system in which the quarterback lined up directly behind the center and handled the ball on every play, either keeping it or handing off to another back. Witham was merely 15 years ahead of his time: the "T-formation" would not be popularized until 1939 when Stanford's Clark Shaughnessy electrified the football world with it.

Withan's experiment was too much of an adjustment for his team to absorb. In the first game of 1925, a "breather" against Chadron State, the new offense floundered and so did CU. The result was a crushing 3-0 defeat at the hands of the upstarts from the Nebraska panhandle. The CU coach promptly junked his new formation, went back to the trustworthy single wing and moved on to a final 6-3 record, losing only at Utah

Lee Willard *(l)* and Walt Franklin *(r)* were a pair of all-time CU greats in the post-World War I period.

Fullback Bill Bohn gets outside as his teammates come up for support in the 41-0 win over BYU in 1923.

Quarterback Art Quinlan hands off to Earl Loser as Bill Bohn leads the way behind the CU line charge in a 17-7 victory over Colorado College in 1923.

Quarterback Hatfield Chilson dives over the line for a key gain in the key 17-7 win over Utah at Salt Lake City in 1924.

Hatfield Chilson passes to Jack Healy in the 21-7 win over DU in 1924.

(12-7) and at Colorado Aggies (12-0) while toppling Montana State (23-3), Creighton (14-6) and Colorado Mines (14-3).

The Utah loss was particularly galling, coming after CU's snapping of the Redskin jinx with its win the previous fall, the only one Witham managed over that school. When after building a 4-2 mark, Witham's men were upset at Ft. Collins, the grumbling began again. Those losses overshadowed a brilliant performance by Chilson in a 14-6 victory at Creighton which was observed by famed Chicago sportswriter Walter Eckersall who called the tiny Pueblo tiger the best ballhandler he'd ever seen, adding that Chilson's cutting ability was as good if not better than that of the legendary Red Grange. Praise, indeed, coming from an Illinois football writer. Eckersall, regarded as one of the top football writers in the nation, also had praise for McGlone who was on his way to being an all-conference guard for the third straight season.

1926

Witham had passed his peak in Colorado opinions. It would be downhill from now on, although the descent would not be steep. Witham's problems began quickly as his 1926 team skidded to a 3-5-1 record, including a humiliating 37-3 clubbing from Utah to spoil CU's homecoming. CU was beset with injuries for that game: 11 of the team's top hands were hobbled. As a result, CU was unable to scrimmage that week and the team was physically and psychologically unprepared for the game. Utah gave no mercy. Neither did CU fans after the homecoming horror. No matter the condition of the team, they wanted results not reasons for failure. (If the sport was still not as polished and professional as it would be in later years, the fans obviously had already learned to require victory at any cost and to harass the coach who couldn't produce that kind of results.) Witham was the first CU coach to feel the fury of the fans. But he continued in his calm, implacable style.

1927

Things didn't get any better in 1927

32

as CU fell below .500 for the second straight year, crashing and burning to lose the last three games in boxcar figures: Southern California (46-7), Colorado Aggies (39-7) and Denver (48-0). It was nightmare time for CU followers. And Witham.

But one important off-field event took place that fall. Harry Carlson signed on as director of athletics. Like Witham, a quiet, reserved, wise-beyond-his-years easterner, Carlson calmed the waters as he was to do for

with another 5-1 (plus a scoreless tie with DU) campaign. And once again Utah spoiled the season, this time with another avalanche which buried CU in Salt Lake City, 40-0. Witham was reeling now, under constant bombardment by the wolves.

1930

And, once again, it appeared he'd escape the noose as his 1930 team, sparked by rookies Haley and Newton,

Missouri (9-7) and indelibly stained once again by Utah (32-0). This time the wounds were fatal. Finishing wins over CC (17-7) and Arizona (27-7) were mere band-aids on a bloody body. The season was finished, and so was Witham.

In January, he was terminated. He wasn't fired outright. The regents simply failed to renew his contract, thereby creating the same effect. The old "death-by-the-velvet-knife" caper. Witham's record was a glossy 63-26-7

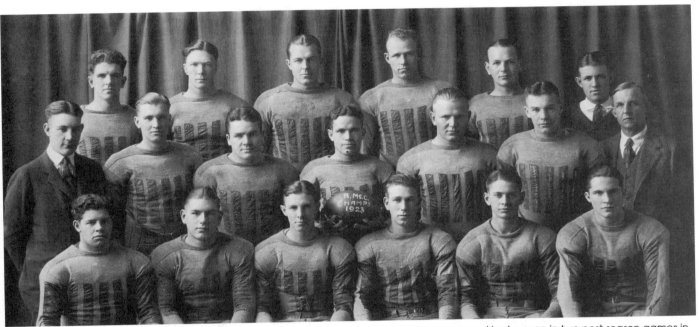

The 1924 squad which was undefeated, untied and unscored-upon during the regular season and broke even in two post-season games in Hawaii. (L-R) *Front row:* Ken Mead, g; Ken Sawyer, g; Fritz Johnson, e; Hatfield Chilson, qb; Dick Handy, e; Bill Bohn, fb. *Middle row:* Walt Franklin, assistant; Bill Pleasted, t; Bill McGlone, g; Capt. Art Quinlan, qb; Fred Hartshorn, hb; Earl Loser, bf; Myron Witham, coach. *Back row:* Bill McNary, c; Jack Healy, e; Don McLean, t; Paul Steward, t; Dave Scoville, g; Ed Montgomery, mgr.

the next five decades. And Witham bounced back with the help of talented performers like backs Buck and Bill Smith, Pete Middlemist, Jim Haley, George Newton and linemen Bernie Buster and Paul Sawyer.

1928

A year later, in 1928, CU reversed the Colorado Aggies and Denver decisions with 13-7 and 7-0 victories, respectively, en route to a comeback 5-1-0 record. But the lone loss was to nemesis Utah, again at homecoming and, again, emphatically (25-6). That was the game fans remembered through the winter.

1929

The comeback continued in 1929

opened with a 9-0 upset at Missouri. After a 0-0 tie at Utah State a week later, CU rolled to four straight victories (over Mines 36-7; Aggies 7-0; CC 14-13, and Colorado Teachers 27-7) to move into the fall's climactic game, in Boulder, against Utah. And once again, the result was a disaster. Utah won the conference championship for the sixth straight year. And they took no prisoners. The final score was 34-0. A closing 27-7 win over Denver brought little solace. The fans wanted Witham's scalp not DU's.

1931

They got the little coach's head on a platter served up by the CU regents a year later after a 5-3-0 1931 season highlighted by a second straight upset of

during his 12 seasons. But winning seasons do not necessarily create longevity. Mostly, they simply raise the standards and Witham was the first of a substantial line of Colorado coaches to learn this sad lesson.

In truth, he had developed a flaw in his off-field approach to the game. Recruiting had by now become a fast-developing facet of the game with coaches becoming actively involved. Witham refused to be drawn into that competition, one which he regarded as unnecessary and unacceptable. His failure to move into this area probably cost him his job. In future years, many coaches would labor furiously, frantically and occasionally, unethically, to recruit prize prep stars from coast to coast, fall short of the mark and get fired, not for failing to recruit but failing

The 1924 CU team aboard the SS Calawaii en route to Honolulu for post-season play.

to recruit successfully. But progress is progress and if Witham's final CU innovation, his refusal to recruit, was fatal to his career, his attitude was "so be it."

He never coached again, returning to New England where he taught mathematics at the University of Vermont until he retired then finished his career with a post-retirement teaching position at St. Michael's college in the same state. His parting comment upon leaving CU was a response to a reporter's question about the reason for his dismissal. His answer was typically short and to the point. A well-phrased "no comment," if you please. "My friends don't need one and my enemies don't deserve one," he replied. With that, he gathered up his 63 victories and his quiet pride and his family and went back "home," taking with him the "Folsom influence" which ended with his departure.

End Harold Graves (27) makes a leaping catch in this 1928 game.

These were the Buffaloes of 1930. *L-R, front row:* Rudy Glehm (physician), Hubert Romans, Earl Schlupp, Neal Stoffle, Bill Berueffy, Otto Staab, Clarence New; *second row:* Earl Rubright, Bill Crosby, Fred Charles, Bob Buirgy, Wayne Ray, A.L. Greene, Virgil Britton, August Zanoni, Oscar Clagett, Dan Beaton; *third row:* Myron Witham (coach), Ken Skaer, George Carlson, Aaron Decker, Warren McKelvey, Bernie Buster (capt.) Sid Pleasant, Jim Haley, Paul Bradley, George Newton, Bill Railey, John Mason (asst.): *back row:* Choice Elliott, Ken Sawyer, Clarence Quinlan, Merle Lefferdink, Bernard Teets, Pete Middlemist, Fletcher Birney, Bus Loucks, Stanford Hartman, Ernest Bolen, Ralph Munns (asst').

Halfback Buck Smith (66) circles left end in 1929 action.

1932

Quite obviously, finding a good recruiter was Carlson's first requirement in hiring a new coach. Witham was gone and so was the recruiting barrier he had established. Personality was the new buzz-word. Get us a coach with charisma, one who can charm high school stars and their parents right out of their living rooms, was the public demand. Carlson quickly found his man a mere 50 miles from the Boulder campus. And in so doing he went right to the opposite end of the personality spectrum.

SAUNDERS

The new coach, named three weeks after Witham's ouster, was William "Navy Bill" Saunders, a familiar figure to the state's football fans. He'd been line coach at Colorado Aggies for six years before becoming head coach at Colorado Teachers in 1928. In three meetings his Greeley teams had never defeated Witham's. But his squads were always well-trained and Saunders had established a reputation as one of the

region's most outgoing and, accordingly, popular coaches in the area.

If Witham was a "New England scholar," Saunders was a "southern gentleman." He had been an outstanding tackle at Auburn before World War I sent him to the navy where he concluded his playing career. He was a popular choice.

Like Witham he used the unbalanced single wing as his basic formation. But his coaching technique was very different. Whereas Witham had been a low-key, quiet, cerebral coach, Saund-

Capt. Bernie Buster poses with a pair of CU coeds in this publicity shot for Christmas Seals in 1930.

The History of Folsom Stadium

Following World War I, as football continued to grow in popularity at CU, it became obvious that Gamble Field was no longer adequate to accommodate the crowds. Built in 1900, it contained permanent bleachers on either sideline, each holding 1,000 spectators. Originally, only the east side bleachers existed. The west side addition was built following the war at a cost of $1,000. It was partially financed by a 25¢ assessment on each student ticket to the Utah and Colorado A&M games. The seating situation was completely unsatisfactory. The majority of the large crowds were standees.

CU's football program reached new heights of fan interest early in Myron Witham's tenure as coach. A new attendance record of 42,480 was set in 1923 when the CU team won nine straight games. That development set the machinery in motion for a new stadium.

The site, a natural ravine just to the east of the new gymnasium location, was recommended by engineering professor Whitney Huntington and endorsed by Fred Folsom, then chairman of the athletic board. President George Norlin turned to Folsom for a financing plan. The ex-coach recommended the formation of a business trust to make the school a legal entity capable of borrowing the construction money. (Let it be noted here that Folsom was just as wise and innovative off the gridiron as he was on it.)

Ground was broken on January 14, 1924. The stadium was completed early that fall, in time for the second home game of the season, a 39-0 defeat of Regis College on October 11. It contained 26,740 permanent seats. The total cost was $69,898 which included some improvements during the next two years. Much of the expense was in excavating approximately 110,000 cubic yards of earth from the ravine to create the natural bowl. The per-seat cost of the original construction in 1924 - $65,000 - was $3.15 per seat, by far the lowest cost for any recently-built stadium in the nation. It was known at first as "Colorado Stadium," then "Norlin Stadium" after the popular, sports-loving president. By official resolution of the regents following Folsom's death November 11, 1944, the stadium was officially renamed "Folsom Field" on November 24, 1944. Subsequent enlargements and additions changed the popular terminology to "Folsom Stadium" in 1956.

CU's entry into the Big Eight conference in 1948 produced another demand for more seating. When CU played Oklahoma in 1952, more than 30,000 fans were squeezed into the horseshoe through the addition of temporary bleachers and sale of standing room admissions. Then began the various improvements and additions which brought the stadium to its present configuration as the first century of football ended in 1989.

In 1954 a new pressbox attached to the east wall of the fieldhouse was built above the west stands at a cost of $19,000. In the beginning, the press workers were seated beneath a canvas cover at the top of the west stands. With the construction of the field house in 1938, the media had watched games through the windows of the fieldhouse with work benches built inside those windows for both press and radio.

In 1956, the first major addition to the stadium, an east side upper deck which dropped down several rows to encircle the south horseshoe, added 15,138 seats at a cost of $1,421,513 to swell the permanent seating capacity to 41,878. An additional 2,000 temporary bleacher seats were available in the north end zone. More temporaries, as the situation required, could also be added at the north corners of the field. The official capacity was 43,878 but at least 1,000 more fans could be squeezed into the corner bleachers when they were jammed into every available opening.

A second major renovation was made in 1967 when the track was removed, the field lowered by approximately 20 feet to make room for 5850 new sideline seats, and a team building added at the north end. Some old seats were lost to make room for the addition and the net gain was 4638 seats, making the total permanent 46,516 and the total capacity 48,516. The cost of this project was $995,000 of which $565,536 was for the new team building. This total also includes the building of a new outdoor track and baseball field on the east campus.

In 1968, a 5-level structure - the top three housing the press facility and the bottom two a new booster organization called "The Flatirons Club" was added at a cost of $562,000, the entire cost of which was paid for by annual contributions of $1,000 from each of the club members. The club section contained 1066 seats; 348 old ones were lost to make room for the structure. The net gain of 718 permanent seats raised the stadium capacity to 49,234 (2,000 of which were bleachers.)

More changes were made in 1972 when 2566 permanent bleacher seats were added at the north end zone, a band stand was erected atop the team building seating 312 musicians, and the visitors' seating section was renumbered for a gain of 362 spaces. Net gain, 1265 seats (the displaced temporary bleachers had held 2,000.)

The final major change was made in 1976 when the dirt sides and end of the original horseshoe were covered with concrete and the old wooden benches replaced by aluminum ones. A small wheelchair section was also added. The entire cost of this project was $985,000 and it was financed totally by an endowment from the estate of John Warkley, an engineering graduate who was a football player in 1909-11-13. The new capacity after this renovation was 52,272, as follows: 48,316 permanent seats, 2566 bleachers, 1066 Flatirons Club, 312 band section, and 12 wheelchairs.

In 1979, the team building was expanded, eliminating 284 bleacher seats but adding six more wheelchair spaces by the team house. And in 1985, the bleachers at the west end of the east upper stands, which held 456 spectators, were removed. Result of these minor changes was a loss of 734 seats.

The total official seating capacity of Folsom Stadium, then, for the 100th season in 1989 was 51,538, as follows: 48,316 permanent seats, 1826 bleachers, 1066 Flatirons Club, 312 band stand, and 18 wheelchairs.

The estimated cost to the university for the stadium, from its creation in 1924 through the 1976 renovation, is $3,013,217.

Some other non-seating improvements should also be noted. In 1976, a new scoreboard costing $250,000, financed totally by the sale of advertising on it, was added. In 1984, an auxiliary scoreboard was built in the southeast corner at field level at a cost of $80,000, also financed by advertising sales.

Modern technology took over on the playing field, too, as artificial turf replaced the natural sod in 1971 at a cost of $550,000. The synthetic covering was replaced in 1977 and again in 1989 at costs of $495,000 and $545,000. In the 1989 project, an additional $100,000 was required to repair the asphalt surface below the artificial turf and at the closed end of the stadium.

ers was an effusive, constantly talking person whose feelings about what was happening were always well known to his players. Witham, though complicated in his approach to football, had kept his instruction simple and basic and sound. Saunders' technique involved precisely working out every move on every play, leaving no detail out in practices. Both were excellent coaches despite their differences in how they coached. Witham was quiet. Saunders was not. Witham was a New Englander. Saunders was a southerner. It was as simple as that.

The big difference in the two men was, of course, their approaches to recruiting. Saunders was aggressive to that end and worked as hard off the field recruiting as he did on the field coaching. Witham, on the other hand, was a teacher once football practice was finished. His organization of fraternity men, in and out of school, were his recruiters. They brought candidates to him. Saunders sought them out, although he continued to use the Greeks as a recruiting aid.

Navy Bill's first campaign was a 2-4-0 loser but coaches get a minimum of one year's grace and he and CU fans looked to the future with optimism. After all, the dour Witham was gone and the sweet-talking charmer, Saunders, was tall in the saddle.

Almost as important as Saunder's coaching debut in 1932 was the arrival of a gritty little freshman from Glenrock, Wyoming named William Lam but known from that point on as "Kayo," a nickname he got after the feisty little character in a popular comic strip of the day. It was a perfect description of Lam, who was not much larger than a strand of leather spaghetti and just as tough. Completely unheralded and unrecruited, and actually lured to the school by an older native of the same tiny Wyoming town, Pete Smythe, who was to become a leading band leader, radio and television personality and piano virtuoso, Lam's greatest problem at CU was getting a uniform as a freshman. The reason? He weighed barely 140 upon his arrival, not exactly impressive credentials for a major college football player. He'd built up to that weight only after three years working as a ranch hand in his native state following high school. If ever an unknown made good at CU, it was Lam.

Bill Saunders replaced Myron Witham as head coach in 1932 and did an excellent job for three years but left unexpectedly, and without explanation, after the 1934 season.

Wearing ill-fitting garb, he toiled obscurely with the other rookies. Carlson, who included the practice fields in his daily walks across the campus, spotted Lam's potential and convinced CU equipment manager Lee Akins to give him better gear plus shoes which fit. Carlson's intervention in behalf of Lam launched a relationship which continued for the next 35 years with the Wyomingite serving as the athletic director's right hand man during those

four decades. But first of all he directed his attention to football. Lam would be prominent on the CU scene for a long time. Saunders would not.

His 1932 team, though a loser which included several veterans who were still unhappy with Witham's abrupt termination, had some excellent players in backs Al Oviatt, George Grosvenor and Jim Counter and end Clayton White, who would become a Rhodes Scholar like a younger brother who came along two years later. After football, White went on to Oxford, then to a brilliant medical career which lifted him to the top plateau of successful CU graduates but got him no higher than a number two ranking in his own family!

Saunders was initiated to the Utah connection with a 14-0 hazing in Boulder. His team had begun with a win at Mines (31-0) as Oviatt broke it open with an 89-yard return of the third quarter kickoff after CU's halftime lead was a nervous 6-0. A week later against Utah State in Saunders' Boulder debut, a 35-yard scoring pass from Counter to White followed by a 45-yard TD gallop by Grosvenor erased a 7-6 halftime deficit to impress the home folks. But a 7-6 loss to Colorado Aggies then the shutout from Utah skidded CU to a finish of four straight losses as the team scored no points in the last three and only one touchdown in the final four. There was hope, however. CU had

Walter Franklin managed CU's athletic business affairs with perceptive brilliance during the decades between the two world wars.

CU was entering a prosperous period in the mid-1930's and these men who played for Navy Bill Saunders in 1933 played an important role. *L-R, front row:* Virgil Britton, Kayo Lam, Robley Nelson, John Slovak, Frank Windolph, Jack Kennedy (mgr); *second row:* John Mason (asst), George Grosvenor, Jim Counter, Frank McGlone, Dick Bailey, Todd Davis, Egon Hansen, Eddie Wagner, Bill Saunders (coach); *third row:* Boyd Bailey, Stanford Hartman, Burt McGhee, Lawrence Moderick, Clyde Gelwick, Ray Stenzel, Ken Anderson, Bill Hubbard, Bernard Teets (asst); *back row:* John Taney, Ken Skaer, Ralph March, Merle Lefferdink, Ken McLean, Vern Drain, Clayton White, Walt Driskill, Del Ritchhart, Doy Neighbors.

BILL
"KAYO"
LAM
QUARTERBACK
UNIVERSITY OF
COLORADO

LOOKOUT!
HERE I
COME

HE GAINED MORE YARDAGE THAN
ANY OTHER COLLEGE BACKFIELD
MAN IN AMERICA LAST YEAR,
CARRYING THE BALL 110 TIMES
FOR A NET TOTAL OF 906
YARDS FROM SCRIMMAGE.
HIS AVERAGE WAS
8.2 YARDS PER
TRY

HE IS ALSO A TRACK
STAR, COMPETING
IN THE 100, 220, AND
440 YARD DASHES
AND THE
BROADJUMP

HOME
ON
THE
RANGE

HE LIVES ON
A RANCH AND IS
A REAL COWBOY AND
BRONCHO BUSTER.

BISHOP-

LET'S
GO!
SIGNALS
20-5-
10!

DIRECTS HIS OWN ORCHESTRA- AND
PLAYS SIX DIFFERENT INSTRUMENTS

HE IS BOXING AND WRESTLING CHAMPION
OF HIS WEIGHT (147 POUNDS)

This nationally-sindicated cartoon extolled the abilities of Kayo Lam in 1935.

1933

With those men in the forefront, CU came out of the starting gate impressively in 1933, winning three straight games by shutouts, including a 6-0 shocker at Oklahoma State. Senior Bob Nelson's 96-yard kickoff return paced a 19-0 opening defeat of Chadron State. Tackle Ken McLean and guard Vern Drain broke through to block an Oklahoma State punt at the four to set up Wagner's winning touchdown two plays later.

A week later a rookie backfield of Lam, Wagner, Anderson and John Slovek exploded a 42-0 bomb on Mines with Lam and Wagner contributing 70 and 30-yard touchdown gallops to the rout.

battled Utah right to the wire, losing only because of two fumbles which gave the Utes possession deep in CU territory to set up their touchdowns.

Saunders would, incidentally, battle Utah savagely during his 3-year tenure. After two tough losses, he finally snapped a 9-game CU losing streak against that arch rival with a momentous victory in 1934. But the most significant development of that first season was the arrival on campus of an outstanding group of freshman which included in addition to Lam, backs Eddie Wagner and Ken Anderson, end Del Ritchhart, tackle Buck Driskill and guard Dave Murphy. The fruits of Saunders' recruiting ability came quickly and these men formed the nucleus of fine Saunders teams during the next two seasons.

Kayo Lam was a brilliant all-around star at CU in the mid-thirties.

But an injury to Grosvenor, the team's leading runner, knocked the team off-stride to a 19-6 loss at Ft. Collins a week later to break the CU bubble. CU then upped its record to 5-1 with easy wins over Wyoming (40-12) and CC (26-0) before running into the Utah roadblock one more time. If the previous five losses to the Redskins had been decisive (by a combined score of 145-6!), the 1933 defeat was an injustice. CU outgained Utah 288-200 and had a 16-9 advantage in first downs. But the Boulder team, soon to be Buffaloes at last, fumbled three straight punts in the first half to fall behind and ultimately bow, 13-6. The pendulum was swinging in CU's direction however, and it would be seven years before Utah would win again.

Grosvenor returned to action a week later to throw a 75-yard scoring pass to Frank McGlone and spark a 24-0 win over Colorado Teachers. McGlone had a field day that afternoon, also spearing a toss from Lam for a 34-yard TD. Wagner also got in on the kill with a 43-yard sprint to the end zone.

McGlone, who was to become a leading physician and medical researcher in Denver, came up with the key maneuver a week later. He lined up unnoticed at the sideline and sped downfield to break away from a surprised Denver secondary and haul down a pass from Counter in a perfectly executed "sleeper play." The pass was

good for a 60-yard touchdown and the winning points in a closing 14-7 win over the Pioneers at Denver before 25,000 fans, the largest crowd to watch a football game in the history of the state at that time.

The finish was good for a 7-2-0 record. But both losses were to league foes and the team finished fourth. It was, however, a great improvement over the eighth place of a year earlier. Saunders had revived CU fortunes and hopes in two seasons. A solid nucleus of fine players would return in 1934. CU would be one of the favorites to win the conference. The future was bright once again in Boulder.

There was more good news. For one thing, the final payment of $2491.75 was made on the stadium. On the other hand, the season ticket price had been raised to $5.50 for the 5-game schedule and pleasure money was hard to come by in those depression years. But the really big news was that the school's athletic teams finally got an official nickname.

1934

A contest sponsored by the Silver & Gold student paper produced more than 1000 responses and from that pool of suggestions, the name Buffaloes was officially bestowed upon the school's teams at the 1934 Homecoming game against Utah. That important landmark

finally out of the way, everyone concentrated on the season. And with one glaring exception, it was just as sound as silver and gold.

The stadium scoreboards didn't indicate it but the Buffaloes got off good that fall, battling favored Big Six foes Kansas and Missouri to scoreless ties. However, the third game, against Saunders' former team in Greeley, produced a stunning surprise. In a bizarre episode of coaching trickery, the sleepy-looking but sly Saunders (he resembled a 1930's version of Jonathan Winters) met his match in Teachers' silver fox, John Hancock. The game would be at night in Greeley. CU had won easily at Boulder a year earlier, 24-0. But Saunders figured he needed an additional advantage this time so he devised a slick plan. Because a white ball would be used for the game, he ordered special white jerseys for the Buffaloes to make the ball harder to find when a CU back had it. In Greeley, Hancock was developing his own strategy. He had brown football-shaped leather patches sewn on both sides of the fronts of Teachers' gold jerseys. Every Greeley back would always have at least two "footballs" showing.

As home coach, Hancock selected the game ball. Quite naturally it was brown. Saunders protested. Hancock whipped out the rule book which upheld his decision. The game was played with a brown ball and CU's

---

EVOLUTION OF SCORING

In case you're wondering about some of the early scores, here is a rundown on how college football scoring has evolved through the years.

From 1869 to 1878 the only way to score was by kicking the ball through your opponent's goal (there were no crossbars.) You could either kick a goal from the field of play or you could have a free kick after your team made a touched down try by crossing your opponent's goal with the ball. Your teammate would then punt the ball in from the point where he crossed the goal and if you made the conversion you scored one point.

Around 1876 some colleges started keeping track of touchdowns and safeties and through 1882 we had scores such as Princeton 2 goals, 2 tries and 6 safeties, Harvard 1 goal, 1 try, 6 safeties. Harvard lists the score simply as Princeton 2, Harvard 1.

When touchdowns (tries) are listed in the score it indicates that the team made the touchdown but was unsuccessful in converting it into a goal.

In 1883 most colleges adopted a scoring system with assigned point values and, in that year only, a touchdown counted 2 points, a conversion after the touchdown 4 points, a field goal 5 points and safety one point.

In 1884 the touchdown was raised to 4 points, the conversion lowered to one.

In 1904 a field goal was lowered to 4 points and then to 3 points in 1909.

In 1912 a touchdown was raised to its present 6 points.

The only scoring change since 1912 came in 1958 when the 2-point conversion was initiated for passing or running the ball into the end zone from the 3-yard line.

SOME KEY DEVELOPMENTS

1896:	Helmets used for first time.
1906:	Forward pass legalized. Game time cut from 70 to 60 minutes. Tripping banned.
1907:	Flying tackles banned. Wedge formation banned.
1912:	Downs increased to 4 (to make 10 yards). Field length cut from 110 to 100 yards.
1939:	Helmets made mandatory.

defense was bewildered. CU's fine corps of linebackers, led by Clyde Gelwick, had to wait till they were sure which "ball" was the real one. By the time they figured it out, the ballcarrier was five yards through the line. Captain Vern Drain called a quick timeout and berated the slow-reacting backers. But the situation was unsolvable. Teachers featured an offense in which the fullback got the direct snap every time and spun, handing the ball to any of the other three backs. Hancock had figured it our perfectly. CU never got untracked. The deception was enhanced by a not-too-bright lighting system. Heavy underdog Teachers got away with a 13-7 upset. CU's only touchdown came when Gelwick blocked a punt. The Buffs and Saunders limped home. Fuming inwardly, Saunders ordered the jerseys destroyed the following Monday.

Like the animal whose name they now bore, the Buffaloes braced themselves, stood their ground and began a stampede which buried BYU (48-6), Colorado A&M (27-9) and Mines (40-6) in the next three weeks. Lam led the BYU blitz, scoring three TDs, the last on a 91-yard run at the final gun to top off a 5-touchdown fourth quarter explosion. The tiny tailback continued to run wild in the next two games, scoring four TDs. CU was getting potent production from the inside-outside combination of Lam and burly fullback Otto Staab. Only the impending arrival of Utah for still another championship clash cast a shadow over the campus.

This time the Buffaloes did not fail although they came close, fumbling away an opportunity to put the game away in the fourth period. A Counter-Wagner pass had produced the only score in the first three quarters as CU carried a 7-0 lead into the final 15 minutes. The defense was stifling and when the Buffs reached the four-yard line early in the period, victory seemed certain. But Wagner fumbled the ball and after an exchange of punts, the Redskins went to a desperation passing attack which found enough holes in the CU

secondary to cover 55 yards in four plays. They missed what would have been the tying extra point but got the ball right back when CU failed to gain and promptly bombed their way to the CU 11. But a point-blank field goal sailed wide and CU's years of frustration ended - and Utah's began, 7-6.

It was downhill the rest of the way for the Buffs as they blasted CC 31-0 then blanked Denver 7-0 to gain a 3-way tie for the championship. Saunders and his Buffaloes were the cocks of the walk. And the good times were rolling. But tranquility has never been a long-time resident at CU and Saunders shocked everyone as he suddenly resigned, without reason, soon after the end of the 6-1-2 season. It was not his first dramatic departure from a coaching job. He had left Colorado Aggies abruptly to enter private business before taking the head job at Greeley. His 6-year stay there was his longest as a head coach. Leaving Boulder, he returned to Mississippi where his family had extensive land holdings and a management position awaiting him. But football was in his blood and he took the head job at Denver within two years.

There was much speculation about his reasons for resigning. Certainly, there was no pressure and the CU outlook was bright with a nucleus of seasoned hands due back in 1935. The most popular guess was that Saunders wanted more support from the CU administration and, upon being told there would be no increase despite the highly successful 1934 campaign, pulled up stakes. No fool, the portly southerner figured it was time to fold up his hand in the Boulder game. So he was quickly and mysteriously gone and CU again searched for a new man to pick up the pieces. The man who was chosen did indeed pick up the pace, leading the Buffaloes to new heights then leaving the program in near-mutiny and disarray. CU's turbulent football history moved on as the new man moved in.

OAKES
1935

With Saunders gone so suddenly, CU officials took the path of least resistance, one which had worked successfully in finding Saunders, and looked to the area coaches for a replacement. They found their man at Montana University in Bernard "Bunny" Oakes, an excellent coach who would take CU to new heights and depths in the next five years. Oakes had been head coach at Montana for four years and, before that, served assistantships for two years at Tennessee and five at Nebraska. His playing background in college was even more impressive: he'd been an outstanding tackle on the powerful Illinois teams which featured the fabulous Red Grange and Bob Zuppke, one of the nation's most innovative coaches.

His credentials were flawless. For the record, no one ever accused Bunny Oakes of not knowing football. His problems would stem from a fanatical approach to coaching. He was totally dedicated, totally committed to driving his teams to their limit. He was intelligent, creative, demanding, suspicious, forceful, energetic with all these characteristics jammed into a one-track mind, a track which led to only one destination: perfect football performance. Not many coaches, or people, come equipped with this nature. Consequently, a lot of people are unable to accept this type of program which, in turn, requires total committment. No matter how successful the results, sooner or later the performers are inclined to feel that the price isn't worth the results. CU's players reached that decision in just three years. As a result, Oakes was in Boulder for just five seasons, four of them winners (one perhaps the greatest in the school's history) and got fired. Not for the way he coached but for the way he treated his teams.

Like his predecessors at CU, and like Dal Ward who would follow him within a decade, Oakes was an ardent advocate of the single wing. He'd mastered its intracies during his two seasons under one of the nation's acknowledged masters, Tennessee's Bob Neyland. Neyland's teams ran from a balanced line. Oakes preferred an unbalanced formation so that he could counter an overshifted defense with a weak side attack. His wingback reverses were devastating to a defense set up to stop the

This was Bunny Oakes' staff when he took over in 1935: (l-r), El Sayre, Frank Potts, Oakes, Frosty Cox, Walt Driskill.

crushing strong side power. He also took full advantage of a single wing staple, trap blocking. As a rookie lineman in the Big Ten, he had been exposed to this inside trickery and he added it to his offensive arsenal. But above all, he was a master of detail. No part of the game was neglected by him. Practice time meant nothing. His practices were long, meticulous and, almost cruel. Lights were installed at the practice field so the sessions could last longer. One thing was certain. His players would be physically prepared. They might be disgruntled and weary of practice but they would know what they were doing and they would know how to do it.

His preparations almost produced a major upset in his first game, at Oklahoma. The vaunted Sooners kicked a first period field goal then were shoved around for the next three periods by a CU team which did everything but score. Led by Lam's whirlwind running the Buffaloes dominated the game and had a great chance to win when a rookie tailback punted dead at the Oklahoma five with time running out. CU got the ball back at midfield then the then-unknown sophomore promptly hit Art Unger with a pass good for 19 yards to the seven. There was plenty of time left to score but CU couldn't do it and that first quarter field goal held up a 3-0 Sooner triumph. Incidentally, that young tailback, who soon after injured a knee and missed most of the rest of the season, would in two years become the most famous player in Colorado history. His name was Byron White.

CU's performance earned the team a favored role against Missouri a week later but the Buffs were flat and bowed 20-6. Oakes' first win was a 58-0 blowout of Mines as Lam scored four TDs and averaged an unbelievable 34 yards per carry in just 12 minutes of action. Then followed relatively easy wins over Aggies (19-6) and CC (23-0) to set up Oakes' first meeting with Utah's wily Ike Armstrong, long a CU tormentor. To make matters worse, the game was at Salt Lake City and the Utes had not lost a conference game there for 10 seasons. But an unbeatable combination of the slippery Lam and a snowstorm which moved in shortly before halftime let the Buffs prevail. The Wyoming will-of-the-wisp streaked 58 yards as the game began in sunshine. He added another just as the storm began with a 40-yard bolt to give CU a 12-0 intermission lead. By the third quarter kickoff, near-

Bunny Oakes with his meal-ticket, Byron (Whizzer) White in 1937.

Byron "Whizzer" White

blizzard conditions prevailed. CU added icing to its victory cake with a late safety when Unger punted out of bounds on the three and center Gene Moore and tackle Walt Driskill blocked the ensuing punt for a safety. The final was 14-0. An Oakes-coached CU team would never lose to Utah. His drill-sergeant practice tactics were already irritating his troops. But he was getting quick results on the field and his detractors were still a minority.

Unfortunately, the Buffs flattened out and lost the next two games as Kansas and Wyoming set its defenses to stop Lam and did so successfully. CU yielded grudgingly, 12-6 to the Jayhawkers and 6-0 to the Cowboys who kept the Buffs pinned down with a fine kicking game. With the ground game sputtering in the face of stacked defenses, Oakes unleashed a surprise weapon in the finale against Denver. It was the strong right arm of Lam, one which had been hardened in the Wyoming wheat fields. Lam hit Ritchhart for 30 yards and Staab for 15 for all the scoring in a 14-0 triumph which gave CU a tie for the league championship.

Lam finished with one of the most sensational seasons in CU history, rushing for a then-national-record 1043 yards in 145 carries, added 364 passing yards, returned punts 530 and kickoffs 288. That all-purpose total of 2225 yards has never been topped during the first century of CU football. There was an obvious reason for Lam's electrifying final campaign. Always tough, gritty and intelligent, he had added one important asset to his 1935 makeup: upping his playing weight to a burly 160. The extra 10 pounds transformed him from merely great to awesome. For his efforts, he became the first CU gridder chosen to play in the Shrine East-West classic in San Francisco.

1936

Oakes' first CU team finished with a 5-4-0 record. Lam was a graduate assistant in 1936 and even such a prospect as White, coming off the knee injury, couldn't fill his shoes. The Buffs labored through a 4-3-0 campaign in Bunny's second season as White had kicking problems early in the opener against Oklahoma, getting a punt blocked for a safety after missing a short field goal try. Oklahoma won 8-0. In a follow-up 33-0 triumph over Mines, White raced 47 yards to propel a 4-

Byron White combined power, speed and brains to lead CU in 1938.

touchdown second quarter outburst. Wingback Joe Antonio's pass interception set up the only touchdown in a 9-7 squeaker over Aggies as White punted out of bounds at the 11 to set up the winning safety. Then CC caught CU looking ahead to Utah and almost upset the Buffs, stopping six deep CU first half penetrations. With the game seemingly headed for a scoreless tie, Unger roared through to block a punt, scooped up the ball and raced 40 yards to give CU a 7-0 win at the wire.

Utah had seen little of White in the previous season as the knee injury and the presence of Lam kept him sidelined much of the time. They got an eyeful this time as he played probably his greatest game, accounting for every point in a 31-7 scalping of the Redskins.

White, who had been nicknamed "Whizzer" as a freshman by Denver Post sportswriter Leonard Cahn, was never more brilliant than on that gray November day in Boulder. He punted out of bounds on the Utah one and promptly returned the following punt 38 yards for the first TD. His next punt hit the sideline at the four and he hauled back the Utah punt 43 yards. The Redskins then threatened to get back into the game but CU stopped them at

the six and White punted the Buffs out of trouble with a 62-yard boomer. In the second quarter he slashed 38 yards off tackle for a third TD. And he didn't cool down at the half, returning the third quarter kickoff 90 yards. For variety he spun a 35-yard scoring pass to Unger. But White sullied, if you can call it that, his sensational afternoon by converting only one extra point. Not exactly a dark stain on his record but a shortcoming which would haunt the Buffs later that season. Almost singlehandedly he had turned an expected close game into a 31-0 rout. From that day on, everyone in the west knew about the latest CU legend and he was beginning to receive national acclaim.

It should be noted that White had an excellent supporting cast. Oakes' offense was beginning to click consistently. Oakes also trained White to catch a punt on the dead run. Once the rockhard 185-pounder mastered this maneuver he was almost impossible to bring down when he broke through or over the first tackler. The Rhodes Scholar, NFL star and Supreme Court justice-to-be was not exactly a gentle person on the playing field. His savage stiff arm and crushing tackles made him just as effective on defense as when the

Byron White is inducted into the football Hall of Fame.

Buffs had the ball. Not blessed with great speed - it has been estimated that he was in the :10.2 range for a hundred yards - he was fast enough, strong enough and tough enough, to handle most tacklers or blockers.

After that easy win over Utah, the Buffs appeared headed for another championship, the school's third and Oakes' second straight. They weren't. In the Beehive state a week later, White missed a PAT and a tough field goal try and the Buffs were edged by Utah State's eventual champions, 14-13. Still the CU-DU finale carried faint championship hopes for both teams, and as an added attraction the Pioneers had a new coach, Navy Bill Saunders, and a fine record, 6-1-1 (CU was now 3-3-0). As another record crowd (27,700) watched, the two teams began with furious first half fireworks, then settled down into a bloody brawl which saw White almost start a riot after a particularly hard tackle at the sideline. DU marched 47 yards to take a 7-0 lead soon after the opening kickoff. Before the Pioneer fans had stopped celebrating, White returned the kickoff 102 yards. But Unger, who had replaced

White as the PAT man, missed the extra point and there was no more scoring, the game ended 7-6. CU reached the five twice in the last half but couldn't get into the end zone as Oakes went for touchdowns both times rather than depend upon his erratic placekickers. The conference finish was a disappointing fourth. Despite the emergence of White as a legitimate national star, 1937 figured to be a difficult challenge for the Buffaloes. As the team put away its gear for the year, not even the wildest-eyed CU fan could have predicted what 1937 would have in store for Bunny, Byron and the Buffaloes.

1937

Before the next season began, one important development took place. A serious competitive gap had developed between the larger and smaller schools of the RMAC. There was great disparity in the quality of play and the home crowds of the two groups. CU, DU, A&M, Wyoming, Utah, Utah State and BYU now formed the Mountain States Conference. The smaller schools - CC, Mines, Teachers, Western State,

Montana State - continued as a 5-team unit.

Oakes' CU team was a well-seasoned one: nine seniors were in the starting lineup. And, significantly, the veteran squad was well conditioned, mentally and physically, by its stern taskmaster with the misleading nickname. Despite CU's promise, the experts remembered their staggering finish a year earlier and proclaimed Utah and Utah State as the co-favorites to be the new league's first champion.

Powerful Missouri, guided by its fine young coach Don Faurot, was the first test for the Buffs. The Tigers started strongly, marching immediately to the CU 15. CU stiffened and White ended the threat with an 83-yard quick kick. The Buffs gained 45 yards on the exchange of kicks and scored from the 40 in three plays, the first two for 35 yards by White and the TD by fullback Erv Cheney. In the second period, White hit end Leon Lavington with a 21-yard scoring pass and the Buffs had all the points they needed in a 14-6 win. Utah State's defending champions visited Boulder next and were promptly dethroned, slaughtered might be a better word, 33-0. White ran wild, gaining 210 yards and scoring two touchdowns. His replacement, Rex Tomlinson, added two more TDs.

Next White used the air lanes to defeat stubborn BYU 14-0, hitting ends Lavington and Monk Saunders for both scores. Those strikes lifted a sputtering offense which netted 333 yards, enough for what should have been a topheavy triumph. White continued his devastating versatility the next week in a 47-0 rout of Colorado A&M, launching the landslide with a 75-yard punt return and carrying 19 times for 138 yards, returning four punts 136 yards, completing five of seven passes for 85 more, punting four times for a 42-yard average and scoring 23 points. In less than three quarters. A routine day for a legend-to-be.

The CU whiz showed another facet of his amazing ability a week later in a 54-0 pasting of Mines: a careless start, he dropped the first snap from center, retrieved it on the bounce and raced 65 yards. Then he scored three more TDs before Oakes sat him down as the second quarter began. The CU coach had his regulars in this game for only 13 minutes. Utah was next. The Buffs would be rested for their trip to Salt Lake.

By now, White's feats had attracted

This is the squad which went undefeated and played in the Cotton Bowl following the 1937 season. L-R, front row: Floyd Trachsel, Erv Cheney, Leon Lavington, Francis Stevens, O.T. Nuttall, Byron White, Gene Moore, Abe Levine, Lou Smith, John Brown, Bill Jump, Joe Davies, Walt Driskill (asst); second row: Bunny Oakes (coach), Jack Rooney, Jim McNeill, Justin Card, Malcolm Anderson, Don Smart, Marty Brill, Alvin McCall, Joe Antonio, Royal Dow, El Sayre (asst), Kayo Lam (asst), Frank Potts (asst); third row: Johnson (mgr), Lex Quarnberg, Morgan Davidson, Harold Saunders, Gene Grove, Lou Liley, Charles Lowen, Bob Hill, Jim Hickey, Rex Tomlinson, Frosty Cox (asst); back row: Paul Reeves, Wilbur Rocchio, Don Smith, Charles Heeb, Henry Brown, Ray Thompson, Joe Kurtz, Reef Fiedelman, Lewis Pugh, Ralph Krieger, Charles Reinhold, Jay Combs, Howard Waite (trainer).

considerable national attention. But distant sportswriters were still understandably skeptical about this apparent superman from the sparsely populated west with its paucity of powerhouses. White was still basically untested, the sports world reasoned. Wins over weaklings BYU, Mines and A&M weren't the stuff to impress. So Henry McLemore, national columnist for the United Press and one of the nation's leading football authorities, decided to come west to see the pivotal game in Utah. That decision was a good one. White was even better than McLemore's Colorado scouts had said. The urbane New Yorker became White's most enthusiastic spokesman after another eye-popping performance by the Whizzer from Wellington. The McLemore endoresement was the second most important factor in White becoming CU's first All-American.

The most important of course, was White, who once again, was almost unbelievable under the spotlight of national attention. Utah, however, didn't die quietly. It was a bare-knuckles brawl which produced no points in the first 30 minutes. But White took over at the start and finish of the second half, turning McLemore's yawns into gasps of amazement. His 25-yard field goal gave CU a quick third quarter lead but Utah came right back to go in front, 7-3. Entering the final period, White who had been named Phi Beta Kappa the night before, had been held in check. The astute Armstrong had devised a defense to halt his off-tackle and end runs. The Utes looked to be in control as time began to be a factor. White then came up with a run which old-timers still describe with awe.

He fielded a Redskin punt at the right sideline on the 14. The kick was high and well-covered. Surrounded by oncoming Utes without much more chance of survival than Custer had at Little Big Horn, he gave ground back to his five before he found a crack in the Utah picket line. Reversing his field, he broke to the far sideline and wove his way to the 20 where he hit daylight and thundered to what was officially, an 86-yard punt return. The run however, required at least 130 yards of frantic footwork. Utah was stunned. White was just warming up. Taking advantage of Redskin shock the next time CU got the ball, he faked inside then wheeled around right end to go 57 yards and put the game away, 17-7. (He was back at his PAT stand in 1937, too.)

This was the very first Folsom Field appearance of Ralphie, then a docile 6-month old calf, October 1, 1966.

THE RALPHIE STORY

Without a doubt, CU has the most spectacular live mascot in college football.

The "Ralphie" tradition began October 1, 1966 when Buddy Hays of Boulder's Hidden Valley Ranch first brought a 6-month old buffalo calf to Folsom Field. The parade around the then-existing cinder track was relatively inconspicuous. Aside from a brief and unsuccessful attempt at taming a buffalo in 1934 and a few quiet appearances by one named "Mr. Chips" in the early 1950's, the buffalo had been inconspicuous by its absence after it had been selected as CU's official mascot in 1934.

The original Ralphie began her career under a curtain of uncertainty. Assumed to be a male (buffalo gynecologists were almost as rare as buffaloes in those days), the youngster turned out to be, upon hurried examination, a girl. CU's sponsoring student body reacted to the news quickly, changing the name from Ralph to Ralphie. The publicity surrounding Ralphie's sex-change made her an immediate campus celebrity. (She was even selected as CU's Homecoming queen in 1971!)

From that time on, the pre-game and second half charges of Ralphie around the perimeter of the playing field (and often through the ranks of startled visiting teams) has been one of the great spectacles of college football.

The tradition has continued through three buffaloes, all trained and groomed by ardent CU fans: originally by Buddy Hays of the Hidden Valley Ranch of Boulder and currently by John Parker, a Hudson rancher and CU alumnus.

Ralphie became an instant CU football fan. Her handlers always found her snorting and ready to get into her trailer each time they arrived to escort her to a game.

It was, they said, almost as though she could sense a football Saturday.

She attended every home game and CU bowl appearance for 13 years until the infirmities of old age forced her reluctant retirement at the close of the 1978 season. She died peacefully at her ranch home two years later.

Her successor was a larger and more ferocious looking buffalo named Moon (short for Moonshine). The original Ralphie was a smallish animal, weighing approximately 900 pounds. Her successors tip the scales at approximately 1200 pounds. (For the record, these are estimates: no buffalo mascot has ever been coaxed to get onto a pair of scales, even for the Guiness Book of Records.)

The CU student body refused to abandon Ralphie as the official name for their mascot and Moon quickly became known as Ralphie II and carried on the tradition gallantly for 10 years before dying suddenly of a heart attack following the 1987 opener against Stanford.

Her replacement was already being trained because Ralphie II was moving into the ranks of senior mascots. The sudden demise forced an early debut for Ralphie III after only five weeks' training but she took to center stage like a veteran and was pounding the AstroTurf fiercely as the Buffaloes moved into their second century of football.

For the record, the Ralphies are 2-1 on opening days. Ralphie debuted during a 10-0 shutout of Kansas State. Ralphie II was greeted with defeats on both her unofficial and official premieres; CU lost to Iowa State, 20-16 when she came to the game with Ralphie November 18, 1978 and to Oregon, 33-19, in her first solo appearance September 8, 1979. Ralphie III launched her career successfully during a 27-10 triumph over Missouri November 7, 1987.

Members of the 1937 Cotton Bowl Team at a 1967 reunion: (L-R) *Back row:* Harry Carlson, Charles Heeb, Walt Franklin, Jim Hickey, Lex Quarnberg, Allen Landers, Alvin McCall, Marty Brill, Byron White, Howard Waite, Louis Liley, Bill Jump, John Brown. *Front row:* Wilbur Rocchio, Elvin Sayre, O.T. Nuttall, Morgan Davidson, Justin Card, Don Smart, Rex Tomlinson, Francis Stevens, and Joe Davies.

When the debris had cleared, White had scored all 17 points, McLemore waxed eloquently about his newly-found high-country hurricane, the Buffs had a cakewalk to the MSC throne room and the Whizzer had all but clinched All-American honors. Not a bad game, season and career - all in one afternoon - for this quiet, handsome, unassuming small town boy from modest circumstances. It was the stuff soap operas were made of and the world would know about him as soon as McLemore got back to Broadway.

A week later however, CU got an early jolt from a weak CC team which was now a non-conference opponent. Oakes elected to start his second team because of the inequity between the two squads. Mines wasn't buying that and fought to a scoreless first quarter. Oakes confidently sent his regulars in to end the suspense. They weren't awake yet, either. When Mines intercepted a White pass and returned it 66 yards, the Golden team had a shocking 6-0 halftime lead. Oakes flew into his team with

a rage unmatched in CU history during intermission. The Buffs and White got the message. The Whiz scored three TDs in the first 10 minutes of the third quarter and Mines was buried 35-6.

Another fine Saunders-coached Denver team was the final regular season foe and the Pioneers out-first downed the Buffs, 14-4, but couldn't stop White's long distance hauls. Closing out his career in typical fashion, he scored three touchdowns on scrimmage runs of 51 and 19 yards and a 46-yard pass interception, threw two touchdown passes to Lavington and kicked four extra points. That farewell flourish accounted for all of CU's points in a 34-7 victory.

The brilliant White performance in the Utah game projected CU into the national limelight. The far-away Buffaloes were suddenly destiny's darlings, thanks to the word spread by McLemore. White made every All-American team that December. To cap the campaign, the Buffaloes were invited to play Rice in the Cotton Bowl on New Year's

Day. The school had its first All-American and first bowl team. Pandemonium reigned in Boulder. And where was White? Preparing for his Rhodes Scholarship tests much of the time. He was in fact, in San Francisco taking his examination when the team departed for Dallas, joining the team two days later, simultaneously with the announcement that he had earned one of the two regional scholarships and would do graduate study at Oxford. A Hollywood script writer couldn't have made the CU star's path more exciting. (And by the way, he also married the daughter of CU's president.)

But once in Texas for game preparations, Oakes' fanaticism darkened the CU picture. Bad weather forced the team to work out much of the time indoors in Boulder, setting the coach on edge as he feared his team had lost valuable practice time. The weather was worse in Ft. Worth. It rained constantly and the TCU practice field quickly became a mudhole. Oakes kept his team outside most of the time despite the miserable practice conditions. The practices were long. The players were wet, weary and disillusioned. The bowl experience which had seemed so exciting now became drudgery. There were two workouts a day. Their uniforms and equipment never had time to dry.

But Oakes kept cracking the whip. He knew Rice was the better team: bigger, deeper and with two backs of White's calibre in Ernie Lain and Ollie Cordill, two great sophomores. Oakes figured he'd out-prepare Rice. His plan backfired. The Buffs were an unhappy team. There were murmurs of mutiny. They would not be ready to play.

Word of the team's poor mental attitude and resentment toward Oakes did not get back to Boulder where 7000 fans headed for the Dallas classic.

Largely because of White plus the two Rice standouts, the game had drawn considerable national attention. There were even predictions of a CU victory. But the dean of American sportswriters, Grantland Rice, had the game figured. CU had one great back, Rice two he reasoned, predicting that White would play well but that Rice's superior manpower would prevail during the last stages of a wide open game.

He couldn't have called it any better. White was just as sensational as advertised, scoring the first 14 points in a 28-14 Rice victory. After Joe Antonio recovered a Rice fumble at the outset, White sparked a 59-yard scoring drive, carrying the ball on six of the first seven plays and gaining 34 yards before he hit Antonio with a 7-yard TD pass. Then he intercepted Lain's first pass and returned it 47 yards to the end zone. His two extra points gave CU fans a lightning-like 14-0 lead. But CU's impossible dream would end at the quarter. Rice's power took command and the Owls scored twice in both the second and third periods and its defense completely bottled up White the rest of the day.

The Buff All-American worked hard but Rice defenders never gave him much opportunity to run. He netted only 20 yards in his next 16 carries after that sensational beginning for a total of 23-for-54 yards. His TD pass was his only completion in five tries and two were intercepted. He caught one punt with no return and punted eight times for a 42-yard average.

The statistics showed Rice's total domination. The Owls rolled up these margins: 20-6 in first downs, 257-87

rushing, 158-7 passing and 415-95 in total offense. It was a dismal finish for the Buffaloes. Yet they had faced one of the nation's top teams and come away with honor, if not victory. White's first quarter one-man show drew most of the post-game praise from the media. The consensus in the press box was that CU was no match for Rice but that White was the best man on the field and that Gene Moore could play center for any team in the country.

The train ride back to Colorado was fraught with tension. There was even talk of rebellion among the underclassmen on the squad. Many vowed they would not play for Oakes again. Oakes had never courted the favor of his players or fans. Consequently, he was an unpopular man even though he was a successful coach. The public, unaware of the pre-bowl practice problems, still respected his ability. But the feelings of his players ran deep. They would never heal.

1938

As soon as he got back to Boulder, he began preparing for the 1938 season. One thing could be said about Oakes. He worked his teams hard. But he drove himself even harder. It's doubtful he even realized that others were not as driven as he. And his stern personality prevented anyone from telling him. The 1937 champions had been basically a senior team so 1938 would be a rebuilding year. Realizing this, Oakes had recruited a fine freshman squad. But they wouldn't help for a year and when the Buffs dropped their first three games of the season: to Missouri (14-7), Utah State (20-0) and George Washington (13-0), fears of a disastrous season blanketed Boulder. But Bunny's teams didn't fold, whatever their feelings about him were. They had to be tough to play for him and that toughness carried through to Saturday afternoons.

Besides, the losses hadn't been that lopsided. The Buffaloes weren't exactly patsies and they proved it, going undefeated in the next four games. They came back to rip the Aggies 31-6, and Wyoming 20-6, tied champion-to-be Utah 0-0, and nipped BYU 8-0, to enter the final game against Denver with a chance to tie for the title. But Denver won 19-12 and CU finished 3-4-1 and tied for second place in league play.

1939

The strong 1938 finish seemed to soothe the troubled waters and the outlook seemed bright for 1939 as the talented group of sophomores joined the varsity. But the calm ended as quickly as fall began, as seniors Marty Brill and O.T. Nuttall quit and 2-year letterman Lou Liley soon followed. All had been stalwarts on the Cotton Bowl team, Brill and Nuttall starters as guard and blocking back. Liley was the top returning end. They minced no words: they would not play for Oakes. The struggle was out in the open. Oakes would be gone before the spring quarter began.

Predictably, the vaunted sophomores weren't early dazzlers and when Missouri, a team CU had battled evenly in four of the last five seasons, butchered the Buffs in the 1939 opener, 30-0, the wolves began to scent Oakes' blood. When Utah State bounced the Buffs 16-6 and Kansas State made it three losses in a row with a 20-0 shutout, the grumbling turned to howls of displeasure. The CU athletic committee, also weary of Oakes tyrannical demeanor, then got into the act, recommending that Oakes be dismissed immediately. But the board of regents vetoed that recommendation, giving the beleaguered coach an unenthusiastic vote of confidence. The turmoil turned the spotlight off the struggling sophomores and they promptly came to Oakes' rescue, amazing everyone with a furious finish which produced five straight victories and seemingly saving their coach's job.

With rookie backs Paul McClung, Leo Stasica and Ray Jenkins leading the charge, CU snapped back to whip A&M 13-0, then Wyoming 27-7. Undefeated Utah's defending champions were next and Oakes still had their number. After spotting the Redskins a 14-0 lead in the opening quarter, ends Lex Quarnstrom, Vern Miller and John Pudlik caught a barrage of Stasica aerials to lead the comeback and when the CU tailback hit still another end, Oscar Jacobsen, for a 35-yard TD, the Buffs had the upset, 21-14. The amazing Buffs led by their resilient coach were on the way to a championship.

It took a miracle to win at BYU but the Buffs performed one to pull out the 12-6 victory. Trailing in the closing minutes 6-0, they unfolded one of the wildest plays in CU's first century, an 81-yard punt return, in which six men handled the ball, to set up the tying touchdown. Stasica fielded the ball at the CU four and raced to midfield where he lateraled to Ray Thompson who flipped it to Pudlik who tossed it back to Jenkins who gave it to Lloyd Oliver who finally ran out of open teammates and was hauled down at the 15. CU punched it in from there and won when Stasica hit Monk Saunders with a 55-yard bomb. Shades of Byron White!

CU and DU met for the championship with the Pioneers taking an early 10-0 lead, their touchdown coming on an intercepted fullback pass from big Jenkins. But CU's "Pole-to-Pole" combination of Stasica and Pudlik, the latter one of Oakes' severest critics, connected for 51 yards on two passes to pull the Buffs to within three points at the half. It was CU all the way in the final 30 minutes and the 27-17 triumph gave Oakes his third conference crown in five seasons. This one was by far the most amazing title of all, coming despite the horrible beginning, the constant clamor for Oakes' scalp and a tough closing schedule. No one could shoot down the Bald Eagle after that finish. After all, the 1939 crew was a young one with an even brighter future.

Oakes still had three years remaining on the 5-year contract he had been given following the Cotton Bowl season. He gratefully gave a dinner for his saviors in December and even Pudlik was in good spirits, collecting money from his teammates for a gift to show their appreciation for their coach. Life seemed serene in the shadows of the Flatirons. But there was danger lurking for Bunny in those shadows.

The storm broke on February 20, 1940 as a Denver Post 8-column headline blared, "CU PLAYERS PETITION FOR OAKES' REMOVAL!" Similar headlines burst forth from the Rocky Mountain News and Boulder Camera. Actually, the newspapers were late with the news. The petition had been presented to the regents at their monthly meeting four days earlier.

After the euphoria of the championship campaign had worn away and the "morning after" syndrome took over, the Buffaloes began plotting their coach's removal. The petition calling for his dismissal was signed by 35 of the 40-man squad, including every player who had started the Denver finale. Pudlik, guard Justin Card and fullback Jim Hickey had presented the 13-page complaint. The threat was explicit: the team would quit en masse if Oakes returned in 1940. Obviously, the championship season had only healed the wounds superficially. The team's resentment had to be bitter to trigger the threat of mutiny.

The petition was never made fully public. But the 9-count indictment was soon public knowledge. The charges were: (1) use of physical discipline in coaching; (2) violation of the conference rule limiting practices to two hours; (3) antagonizing the press; (4) failing to meet the public well; (5) criticism of opposing coaches; (6) fomenting hate and discontent among squadmembers; (7) promising jobs to men who would play for him; (8) encouraging players to cut classes before practices; and (9) criticism of faculty members who failed to pass athletes.

President Robert Stearns and the regents summoned Oakes for his rebuttal on February 23. The embattled CU coach, as belligerent as he was bald, promptly went on the offensive, downplaying the credibility of the charges, defending his coaching ability, and demanding the dismissal of athletic director Carlson, graduate manager Franklin and Franklin's assistant, Mark Schreiber. Each of them was derelict in his duty, he snorted, and even worse, disloyal to him through their lack of cooperation. With that bombshell he rested his case.

Stearns formed a faculty committee to consider the case. It was not an easy decision. Oakes had a fine record, 25-15-1. His teams had won three championships and never lost to Utah. Never had his teams failed to respond to his leadership and chances were, the current players could very well settle down and forgive him before the next season. After all, many of their charges were in areas in which they had no real expertise and probably were not totally accurate. But the man was an untamed tiger in all his dealings with players, public, faculty and administration. Nervously, because they knew the public judged a coach on his record and not on his personality, the committee recommended dismissal. By this time, everyone - administrators and regents - felt the same way. Oakes had given his ultimatum: get rid of the administrators.

The following Monday morning, Stearns and Oakes met for two hours. The waiting press assumed that, because of the meeting's length, Oakes had

Early Support

With the establishment of football as the major sport on campus, a supporting cast was quickly formed.

An informal CU band was assembled in 1891, the forerunner of the permanent group which followed quickly.

There was already in place, the school song, "Glory, Glory, Colorado," adapted from the song "Battle Hymn of the Republic" which was traditionally played at academic processions in early commencements.

There were official school colors, "Silver and Gold," adopted by the Class of 1888, a tribute to the mineral wealth which led to the early population of the state.

There was still no nickname, "Buffaloes" was not to be selected until 1934, but there was great spirit and there were cheerleaders and there was the school's first popular yell which went like this:

From Boulder's rocks,
We come in flocks,
And yell for the U of C.
We grow men tall,
And play football,
And yell for the U of C.

The pageantry, such as it was, was in bloom, if not full bloom, and would develop in unison with the football program, then as now, the top spectator attraction on the CU campus.

dodged the bullet. Actually, he was fired almost as soon as he sat down. Most of the time was spent in negotiating the dismissal terms. The settlement was never revealed. But his salary was $5,000 and he had three years remaining on his contract. The consensus was that he probably received $10,000.

Bunny left Boulder almost as soon as the ink on his final check was dry. His successful but stormy CU career was finished. And so was the best part of his coaching career. He returned to Illinois and completed work on his master's degree then was named head coach at Wyoming in 1941. His first squad went 2-7-1 but showed definite signs of improvement in 1942 when the record was 3-5-0. World War II interrupted his coaching tenure as he served in the navy for the next three years (he had been a decorated U.S. Marine in World War I after enlisting at the age of 18.) When his 1946 team tumbled to 1-8-1, Bunny resigned under fire.

He moved to tiny Grinnell College in Iowa for the 1947 and 1948 seasons but, again, was unsuccessful as his teams could do no better than 3-5-0 and 1-7-0. Once again, he resigned, never to coach again. Oakes finished his life as a salesman for a sports equipment manufacturer which specialized in producing baseballs for minor league teams, working out of his home in Traverse City, Michigan where he could pursue his hobbies of hunting and fishing. He died of a heart attack October 22, 1970 while vacationing with his wife in Virginia. He was 72.

Twenty-two years later when CU scaled almost the same heights with another Rhodes Scholar All-American and a coach whose nickname rhymed with "Bunny", history would repeat.

Succeeding years indicated that Oakes' almost psychotic distrust of both friends and enemies might have been his own worst enemy. The ensuing careers of the men he demanded be fired proved him wrong. Carlson continued as an able, respected athletic director for another quarter-century. Franklin wearied of the constant turmoil in athletics and became a business school professor, a position he held until his retirement in 1965. Schreiber left the university later to become a prominent Denver advertising executive. That artful gridiron dodger, Kayo Lam, became athletic business manager, a new title for what had been most of Franklin's job. CU named its men's

gymnasium after Carlson and a playing field adjacent to the stadium after Franklin when he called it a career. Oakes most certainly would have had a longer and more enjoyable career at CU had he had better relationships with his fellow workers. Not to mention his players.

POTTS
1940

The search for Oakes' successor never left the campus, primarily because his financial settlement had depleted the following year's salary budget. A staff member was the logical, not to mention necessary, decision and Carlson turned to Frank Potts, who had been head track coach and assistant in football since his arrival in 1927. Potts was a popular choice: familiar with the players and the strategies, quiet and totally non-controversial and a man who had great relationships with his athletes. The quiet Oklahoma native also had one other strong recommendation: he would require no additional salary. For Carlson, who managed his money as the laws of decency and poverty permitted, this was perhaps the most important consideration of all although he and Potts were, and remained to his death, the closest of friends. Additionally, Potts was an excellent football man. He had been an outstanding back on fine Oklahoma teams in the mid-1920's. He would be a good coach although he took the job only on the basis that he would do it on an interim basis. He was happy to be a track coach and grid assistant and he wanted no part of the pressures which came with the head football job.

Peace, if not immediate prosperity, returned in 1940 under Potts, a man frequently referred to as "fatherly" during his 41-year tenure at CU. A solid nucleus of players, plus the return of Brill and Nuttall, 10-returning-starters-strong greeted Potts enthusiastically. The Buffaloes were favored to repeat their championship season. But an almost-forgotten problem, Utah, would shatter that dream.

Potts couldn't have picked a tougher opponent against whom to open his head football career. His Buffs faced mighty Texas in the opening game of 1940 at Austin. The brilliant Stasica twisted 53 yards to give CU an early 7-6 lead and the Buffs trailed only 12-7 after three quarters. But the Buffs wore

out and the Longhorns stampeded in the fourth quarter for four touchdowns and a 39-7 victory in a game that was closer than the final score. CU's home opener was a 7-6 comeback against Kansas State as Vern Miller's sparkling catch of a Stasica pass produced the 55-yard touchdown and set up Pudlik's vital conversion. It should have been a more decisive victory but a penalty nullified a Paul McClung lateral which broke Ray Jenkins free for an apparent 40-yard touchdown. CU picked up the pace as conference play began, belting three brother schools: Utah State 26-0, as Harvey Click returned two interceptions for touchdowns; Colorado Aggies 33-14, with Stasica scoring three touchdowns, one on a 97-yard kickoff return, and set up a fourth with a 57-yard punt return; and Wyoming 62-0, when everyone got into the act.

That set the stage for the by-now traditional game against Utah for the MSC championship. The Redskins unleashed their version of Kayo Lam, a will-of-the-wisp named Izzy Spector who dazzled the Boulder crowd and led Utah to a 21-13 win. Now in his first year as business manager, Lam was still a prominent figure with post-game heroics as he shinnied up the goal post and balanced on the crossbar trying to keep the Utah partisans from ripping them down. His gallant effort was in vain and the posts toppled. He had the last laugh though. Before the season, he had replaced the expensive and non-repairable metal posts with wooden 2×4's. So the Utahans left Boulder with cheap souvenirs, CU's scalp and a lock on the title.

The Buffs ran into another offensive buzz saw a week later as Missouri's All-American quarterback, Paul Christman, passed for two touchdowns and ran for a third to lead the Tigers to a 21-6 win. The Buffs snapped their 2-game losing streak with a harder-than-expected 25-2 decision over BYU to give them a 5-3 record going into the traditional Thanksgiving tilt at DU. Nothing was on the line this time except intra-city pride and there was plenty of that always.

Those partisan emotions spilled over into the usual post-game melee between the student bodies as the game finished in a 3-3 deadlock in which there was more controversy than scoring. The game was basically a bruising infantry battle until the final period when Jenkins booted a 42-yard field goal from a difficult angle for a 3-0 lead

Jim Yeager in his first pose as CU coach in 1941.

too gentle for the post-war period when the game was taken over by aggressive young coaches determined to reach the top regardless of how they made the trip. But he was perfect for Boulder and CU in 1941, more outgoing than Oakes and more personable than Potts. He was a man who could charm and entertain professors or the public equally well.

Yeager had impeccable credentials, too. he had lifted Iowa State to its greatest heights in 1938 as his till-then undefeated team bowed to Oklahoma 10-0 in the game which decided the Big Six championship. Iowa State fans were very unhappy when CU lured him away. But Yeager liked Boulder and the mountain country and felt that CU offered more possibilities for success than Iowa State so he came west. And never left, remaining in the women's apparel business after leaving coaching. His Cyclone teams were always tough for other Big Six teams to handle despite the fact Iowa State was one of the conference's "have-not" schools.

Yeager had been a fine pulling guard at Kansas State in his native state. He moved to Iowa State as line coach then to the head job after an assistant's post at Ft. Hays State.

After a shaky start — few first year coaches explode triumphantly on the scene - he led CU back to the top. Unfortunately, the clouds of World War II were hovering on the horizon when he took over. No sooner had he built his team to a championship level than the war erupted and he and most of his players went into service. When the war was over and Yeager and his men -now older and fatter and slower -returned, the magic was missing. Nothing was ever quite the same for the smiling Kansan whose trademark was a nervous shrug of the shoulders, a constant characteristic.

His immediate job was difficult. Gone were six 1940 regulars, including such standouts as Brill and brothers Harold and Max Punches. Top returnees were center Lloyd Oliver and workhorses McClung and Jenkins but the star tailback went down for the season with a knee injury after throwing a touchdown pass to Dick Woodward for CU's only points in another getaway gouging from Texas, 34-6. A promising rookie, Tex Reilly, replaced McClung and fellow sophomores such as end Stan Hendrickson, guard Gus Shannon, center Bud Schwayder and tackles Jim Smith and Jack Griffith performed creditably if erratically because of

only to see DU come back with a 28-yarder. The officials drew most of the crowd's attention. A penalty had erased a 46-yard Pioneer touchdown in the first quarter. A countering decision negated McClung's apparent touchdown plunge in the third period, the linesman moving the ball back two inches from the goal line on the fourth down effort. So it was a completely acceptable season in which the Buffs lost only to the conference champion and to powerful Texas and Missouri. Most importantly, Potts' presence had calmed the situation. For his good work, Potts was offered the permanent

position. Predictably, he declined and Carlson looked to the midwest for a replacement.

YEAGER
1941

That coach was at Iowa State and his name was Jim Yeager and he was a man much more like Potts than Oakes: strong, personable, friendly and with an excellent sense of humor and timing in contrast to the serious, taciturn track coach. His nickname was "Gentleman Jim" and it described him perfectly. He was a generous, gracious man, perhaps

Yeager's first staff: (l-r), front, Paul Bradley, Yeager, Frank Potts; back, Frank Prentup, Roland Balch (trainer).

inexperience.

After losing to another fine Missouri team, 21-6, CU duplicated its performance of a year earlier. The Buffs won three straight over Utah State (13-7), Colorado A&M (26-13) and Wyoming, coached now by Oakes, (27-0.) Bunny had tightened the Cowboy defense considerably but his Wyoming team was still no match for the Buffaloes even though the loss was by 34 points less than the year before.

The 3-game streak again set up a critical game at Salt Lake City. CU was never in it. Utah scored on the first play of the game and went on to a 46-6 decision. The Buffs then staggered to a 13-13 tie with BYU before taking a final walloping from DU, 27-0. Yeager's first season ended 3-4-1. But those sophomores had earned their battle ribbons and would be a factor for the next two years, WW2 permitting.

1942

Yeager added a trio of fine backs to his already-loaded arsenal in 1942, John Zeigler, Walt "Kaiser" Clay and Carl "Steamroller" Stearns. Unfortunately, none would be available for more than a year but they added firepower to Yeager's short punt and modified Notre Dame box formations. After an opening 54-0 waltz over Mines, the Buffaloes lost at Missouri, 26-13, with Hendrickson's 76-yard return with an intercepted lateral providing the major highlight. A week later, Stearns sped 64

yards with a lateral from Reilly in a 34-14 win over Utah State. Next it was a 12-0 decision over New Mexico as Stearns again carried a lateral, this one from Clay, for a 20-yard TD and Woodward blocked a punt for the other. Stearns continued to run wild

A pair of CU players who made good in later years (l-r) Walt Koelbel (1944-5-6-7) and Don Brotzman (1940-1-2) are honored at midfield ceremonies in 1965.

against Colorado A&M, scoring two more touchdowns. So did Zeigler. And Clay added another in a 34-7 field day. The Buffs made it four straight as Clay scored twice and Zeigler went 76 yards with a pass from Reilly to conquer Wyoming and Oakes, again, 28-7. It was the last game Oakes was involved with against CU. He was still at Wyoming a year later but, because of travel restrictions, the two teams never met.

The 4-game winning string sent CU against Utah as the favorite on Homecoming day. The game was tough and tense and, from CU's standpoint, unproductive. The Utes punched out two touchdowns and completely stymied the CU attack. The Buffs' only deep threat came when Clay broke through then lateraled to Stearns who flew 40 yards to the 22. But the CU drive ended at the 12 and the Buffs were frustrated again. But all was not lost. The Redskins weren't perfect either and the two teams finished in a tie for the championship as the Buffs finished furiously with 48-0 and 31-6 clubbings of BYU and Denver.

1943

The CU outlook was bright but the world picture was not. The war was now in full swing. Athletes began disappearing into the armed services. The college talent pools consisted primarily of players still underage for the draft and rejectees. But CU got a break when the Navy chose Boulder and Colorado Springs (CC) as sites for its V-12 training program. The good news was that the Buffaloes would get constant transfusions of new navy personnel. The bad news was that they would leave when their expedited classes graduated, often in mid-season. Yeager himself would enter the navy following the 1943 campaign, a good one in which the Buffs defeated three service teams and broke even in four contests with area colleges for a 5-2-0 record. In a 38-0 breeze over Ft. Warren, sailor Bob Dal Porto, whose son Steve would play for Eddie Crowder, opened the scoring after burly Paul Briggs, who would become a postwar CU standout, blocked a punt. Bluejacket Bob Maddalena, formerly of San Francisco U., sparked the 19-6 win over Lowry Field and still another bell-bottomed Buffalo, Roland Rautenstraus, who would become CU's 12th president in 1974, blocked a punt to set up a touchdown in a 14-0 win over Salt Lake City AFB. In a war-caused unique schedule arrangement, CU played Utah home-and-home and got a double-dose of revenge for the three straight defeats at the hands of the Utes. Rookie QB Jim Hammond, and tailback Dick Morrow, a fine sailor athlete by way of Oregon, paced the Buffs to a 35-0 laugher in Boulder. And, in the shadows of the tabernacle, Dal Porto returned a kickoff 83 yards in a 22-19 thriller.

The Buffs lost only twice that season, to Colorado College, 16-6 and 6-0, and ironically, both whippings were triggered by the play of Zeigler, one of Yeager's rookie flashes the previous year and now in the V-12 program at the Colorado Springs school. The luck of the draw had sent him to Colorado Springs instead of Boulder and CU paid the price as his running and kicking were key factors in both contests. His 35-yard sprint was the only touchdown in the final game of the abbreviated season. Once it was over Yeager traded his silver and gold coaching outfit for a navy blue uniform and, again, old reliable Potts took over for the 2-year interim.

This trio of CU linemen (l-r) Aubrey Allen, Bill Simons and Paul Briggs checked out uniforms in 1946.

POTTS II
1944 - 45

Those two seasons were relatively undistinguished ones as the combination of navy trainees and fuzzy-cheeked freshmen managed 6-2-0 and 5-3-0 campaigns in 1944 and 1945 over basically undermanned opponents. Three of those five defeats were administered by service teams who were by now, as the armed forces began to funnel good talent to its various bases, not undermanned. A typical naval maneuver bottomed out the 1945 campaign. CU went into November with a 4-1 record, defeating all four college foes and bowing only to Ft. Warren. The team defeated Utah for the fourth straight time. But the navy graduated the class which included six regulars and three top reserves and the riddled Buffs lost two of their last three games, including a 14-8 decision to Denver in Potts' last appearance as a head football coach.

1946

With the war's end, normalcy returned to the country. CU fans assumed Yeager and his men would pick up where they left off in 1943. They were wrong. Those bright-eyed eager young athletes were now older

with different outlooks and, in many cases, wives and families. Back to earn their degrees, they had a different set of values. Football was still fun but it was not a life-or-death matter any more. Life-or-death was what they had been going through in the far corners of the world for the previous three years. As his personality might have indicated, Yeager was never a harsh disciplinarian like Oakes. It was obvious that his paunchy veterans required considerable motivation: with a stick not a carrot. Yeager's approach leaned more toward the carrot. Consequently, his final two years in coaching were not pleasant ones.

All seemed in order in the 1946 opener against his former team as Reilly returned to lead the Buffs to a 13-7 win over Iowa State. But then came a nightmare at Texas, a 76-0 slaughter at the hands of possibly the finest team in the nation. The Buffaloes never recovered from that drubbing and they were an inconsistent team for the next two years. Nevertheless they bounced back to shut out Utah State (6-0) and Wyoming (20-0) as fullback Roland Gregory and tailback Don Evans assisted Reilly with the attack. But just when they seemed to be gaining momentum, old Mr. Inconsistency

jumped up, and CU lost its first game in history to BYU, 10-7. After edging New Mexico, 7-0, they were blanked by Utah (7-0) and Missouri (21-0). Big Jim Smith, who carried the nickname "Ox", barely missed a 40-yard field goal try as the clock wound down and CU had to settle for a 13-13 tie with DU in a game they should have won.

But the Buffs put everything together in the finale against A&M, ambushing the Aggies in the second half, 18-0. One of Yeager's favorite weapons in short punt formation was the screen pass and Dick Schrepferman, son of a great CU athlete, Chet Schrepferman (1918-19-20), grabbed one from Evans for a 34-yard scoring play to launch the attack.

That strong showing in the finale gave CU a creditable, if not satisfactory, 5-4-1 record. CU fans were still confident about the future. It stood to reason, they reasoned, that the returnees needed a season to get readjusted to campus and gridiron life. And there were still some more due to return. 1947 would be more like what was expected, they believed. But it was a belief strongly tinged with nervousness. The 1946 team had been a group of listless plodders.

1947

But 1947 was almost an exact duplication of the preceding year. Almost eerily, the first two games followed the same pattern. First came a 7-0 close call at Iowa State as Yeager finished 2-0 against his former team. And then there was another crushing encore, this time a brutal 47-0 beating at Army. In fairness to Yeager's offense, Reilly had injured a leg in pre-season drills and never recaptured his 1941 form. A talented and tough rookie, Harry Narcisian, teamed with veteran Schrepferman to give Yeager good strength at tailback. But Narcisian suffered a knee injury at West Point and was of little help the rest of the fall.

Once again the Buffs were demoralized. But this time they had to face a strong Missouri eleven and the Tigers toyed with CU in the Boulder opener, 21-0. A week later in Folsom Field, the Buffs struggled almost as badly, needing a dramatic John Zisch field goal with five seconds remaining to rally past a weak BYU team, 9-7. They made it two straight with another wobbling win over an equally inept A&M team at Ft. Collins, 14-7, and it required a late Art Tanner interception at the goal line to prevent a possible tying touchdown. Utah was again the Homecoming foe and the Buffaloes gathered themselves and played the favored Redskins tough but a blocked punt then an interception

Athletic Harry Carlson's steady leadership from 1928-65 guided CU into the "big time."

Jim Yeager (l) and publicist Dan Partner (r) check signals with star quarterback Maurice (Tex) Reilly in 1947.

let Utah off the hook, 13-7. Evans, prominent primarily as still another great CU punter, kept the Buffs in this one with a pinpoint passing performance. He took CU to the Utah 27 in the final minute.

With Utah's secondary expecting another tailback pass, Yeager sent in a perfect trick play with Reilly, a forward pass off an end around. Lanky Jack Pixler took the handoff from Reilly and circled deep as the Utah defense closed in on him. Reilly slipped out into the flat and was wide open for what would have been an easy touchdown. The strategy was perfect except for one thing: Pixler was not accustomed to passing and he overthrew Reilly. The game ended and so, for all practical purposes, did Yeager's coaching tenure. The expected letdown followed and a great athlete, Jay Van Noy, led Utah State to an easy 35-12 win at Logan. Only Wyoming and DU remained and there was little to salvage from wins over these teams even though the annual bloodletting with the Pioneers would heat up both schools. As expected, CU dumped woeful, unwonderful Wyoming, 21-6. But Denver got a brilliant performance from an Hawaiian named Howard "Pineapples" Benham and the Pioneers made Yeager's last game a disappointment although it was a thrilling

26-20 loss, if losses can be thrilling. Reilly played the greatest game of his post-war career but it came too late for his coach. It was obvious that Yeager had lost his zest for coaching. He had been considering a business opportunity and less than two weeks after the final game became a partner in a Boulder department store and managed that business successfully, becoming one of Boulder's leading businessmen until his death from a heart attack in 1971. Boulder mourned the death of this personable midwesterner who might have become a gentleman Kansas farmer had it not been for the athletic ability which earned him a chance to play and get a college education at Kansas State.

His departure in 1947 marked the end of an era. Football had been taken over by a pack of young coaches who eagerly accepted the recruiting challenge which was so contrary to pre-war traditionalists like Yeager who felt a football coach was hired to lead young men not hit the road to lure them to enroll.

1948

College football would quickly grow into one which would transcend regional lines and rivalries into a more demanding and expensive sport. Emphasis moved quickly to over-emphasis. Pressures on coaches mounted. Fundraising emerged as a necessary means to help finance the programs. World War II had separated the kindly old-style coaches from the sharply-dressed, nononsense newcomers. Bunny Oakes would have loved it. Jim Yeager didn't. He was glad he was out of the coaching business. Selling women's clothing wasn't as exciting. But it was much easier on his stomach. His 24 years after coaching were peaceful and prosperous, and he remained a gentleman to the end. Jim Yeager wasn't treated kindly at the end of his career. But he never regretted coming to Boulder. He didn't get his fair share of years. Jim Yeager was only 62 when he died.

CU now needed a man to perform a difficult two-part assignment. First of all, he had to upgrade the football program and additionally, it had to be a better overhaul than any before because the Buffaloes would enter the rugged Missouri Valley Intercollegiate conference that fall. Nebraska and Oklahoma, then, as at the end of CU's first century, were national powers. Missouri and Kansas consistently fielded high quality teams. If there is such a thing as culture shock, athletically speaking, the Buffaloes faced it. There would not, for long, be the Utah States and Wyomings and BYUs to kick around. The challenge would be great. Many football observers in the Rocky Mountain region felt that CU was taking on more than it could successfully digest. Despite the elation which accompanied the school's step up the collegiate ladder there were a considerable number of doubters in the CU ranks.

Strangely enough, there was not high excitement surrounding this search. The apparent lack of interest was undoubtedly due to the drop in CU performances the previous two falls. 1946 and 1947 had produced nine losses. No back-to-back campaigns had lost that many since Witham's 1926 and 1927 teams dropped five each fall.

The early frontrunners were a pair of current head coaches, Dudley De-Groot of West Virginia, and Bill Glassford, of New Hampshire. DeGroot was a scholarly mentor with fine credentials, but at little-known West Virginia. Glassford was a fiery individual who had raised the New England school's football fortunes. He would soon get the Nebraska job. New Mexico was a later stopover for DeGroot.

These CU dignitaries posed before plane trip to Army in 1947. *L-R*, Amy Stearns, Jim Yeager, President Bob Stearns, Governor Lee Knous, Denver Post sports editor Jack Carberry and Walt Franklin.

WARD
1949

A relative unknown assistant at Minnesota was the surprise winner. He was Dallas Ward, a grim-visaged, stern tactician who had apprenticed during the golden years of Bernie Bierman's Minnesota juggernauts. Ward had been a do-everything coach with the Golden Gophers. He'd served as freshman coach then varsity assistant joining Bierman after nine highly successful years at Minneapolis high schools. He was heavily involved in the Minnesota recruiting. Competition for the top athletes was brisk in the Big Ten, a conference far in front of the rest of the nation in those pre-war days. And for the most part during the 1930's and early 1940's, Minnesota was in front of the Big Ten. At first glance, Ward appeared more in Oakes' mold than Yeager's. He was never a gifted orator. Phrasemaking was definitely not a leading feature of his public appearances. He appeared to be a gruff taskmaster to the public. What he was was an excellent coach, more than ready to head his own program. He owned one of the finest offensive minds in the country. His unbalanced single wing attack, featuring the savage old-fashioned power plays interspersed with inside and outside wingback reverses and a deceptive buck lateral series bewildered Big Eight foes for a decade.

Ward was also an excellent organizer insofar as recruiting was concerned. Predictably, he concentrated on the territory most familiar to him from his Minnesota experience — the midwest. He also mined some diamonds in the rough from sparsely populated and lightly recruited states like South Dakota, Montana and Wyoming. But in particular he looked to the midwest and the highly concentrated Chicago area for his first recruits. When his teams made the school's first serious move toward the Big Eight top in 1951, there were 14 players from Illinois on the roster. The banquet circuit suffered considerably when Yeager yielded the podiums to Ward. But speech-making, to the new coach, was a necessary evil. He was adequate but not much more. Certainly not a gifted phrasemaker like Eddie Crowder or a powerful spellbinder like Bill McCartney in later seasons. If Ward were compared in that category to future CU coaches, he'd be in the same row as Bill Mallory.

But he could recruit and he could coach. And, above all, he had a talent associated with the old line of football

coaches: generating intense loyalty from his players. Even though he could be grim and tough at times, not unlike Oakes, but only when goaded by poor performance by a team or individual and not as a general rule, the men who performed for him developed a lasting affection for this product of western Oregon's farm country by way of Oregon State. He had been a great end there and his ends were always the class of the Big Eight.

There was no magic on opening day as Ward dealt the hand which had been left him by Yeager. There were few face cards in it. The line was shallow but with decent ability. The backs were quick but small. Burly tackle Paul Briggs was the best man. Harry Narcisian, Malcolm Miller and Don Hagin were fiery little runners. Narcisian was the best CU jump passer since Hatfield Chilson. He had to be. He was only an inch taller than the tiny star of the 1920's. Co-incidentally, Narcisian's number was 20 and his nickname was "Roaring Twenty."

Ward's debut was a wretched 9-7 loss to tiny New Mexico, a team the Buffs were favored over by at least three touchdowns. But career-opening losses were nothing new for CU coaches. You had to go all the way back to 1934 and Saunders to find a CU coach victorious

Dal Ward in a familiar sideline pose as Frank Prentup and Frank Clarke stand by.

in his first game. And no coach since Saunders had won his first game. Of all the CU coaches who lasted more than two seasons, only Folsom, Witham and Saunders won their openers. So, putting it in perspective, Ward simply was following a long CU tradition in losing to the Lobos.

The next seven games following the opening loss were offensive orgies. Even though the Buffs won only two of them, the word was soon out in the conference: watch Ward's team! The Buffaloes were pushovers no longer. So what if the defense still didn't measure up! That would follow. In the meantime the Buffs would have to rely on the offense.

Two touchdowns by Hodel and a 46-yard interception return by Brookshier sparked a 28-point second half and a 34-6 win over Kansas State. (Ward's teams would reach that exact figure four times in wins over that school.) But the defense did buckle a week later at Lawrence. CU couldn't hold a 21-0 lead and Kansas got four TDs in the last 20 minutes to win, 27-21. Ironically, the Jayhawkers, who hadn't completed a pass all afternoon, hit three straight en route to the winning score with 1:30 left.

Next, CU threw a 28-19 roadblock into a cinderella Nebraska team and its sensational sophomore, Bobby Rey-

These men led CU into the Big Eight Conference. L-R, Bus Gentry, Frank Prentup, head coach Dal Ward, Ray Jenkins and Marshall Wells.

nolds. CU's young trio of Hodel, Jordan and Shelton were more than a match for the Cornhusker All-American. This time the Buffs did not blow a 14-0 halftime lead. Brawny Punches, one of the best-named players in CU history, pounced on a Husker fumble in the end zone to wrap up the win. The Buffs let down after that big win but managed to survive against Arizona, 28-25, in a game which began as a waltz for CU. The Buffs scored with their first two possessions. But it took a full afternoon of work and Hodel's 73-yard burst up the middle late in the game to put it away. The big guy could bull for short yardage and outrun a secondary. His speed was authentic. Hodel was the Big Eight indoor low hurdles champion. He used his football strength and a pair of slashing elbows to intimidate rival hurdlers on the tightly-turned indoor ovals. At Utah, the Buffs again sputtered on defense but a 45-yard interception return by Branby boosted the Buffs into a 20-20 tie and a win seemed certain as the usually reliable Venzke eyed a 22-yard field goal with 37 seconds left to play. But it was wide and the deadlock remained. It was

the beginning of the end of Venzke's placekicking career. He missed three straight PATs a week later and yielded to fellow quarterback Roger Williams for the rest of his career.

Then came the biggest game in CU's young Big Eight existence. Mighty Oklahoma, riding a 27-game winning streak, was due next in Folsom Stadium. The Sooners were heavy favorites. Increasing the CU problem was the absence of the injured little sparkplug, Shelton. But Jordan, whose booming punts and ground-gobbling quick kicks would plague Oklahoma for three seasons, put the Sooners in an early hole as he punted dead at the two. Following the return punt, CU drove right in with Hodel getting the TD. Venzke missed the PAT. The 6-0 lead was the only one the Buffs would enjoy as they matched the Sooners' first three touchdowns but came up short on all the PAT tries. The final was, 27-18.

A week later, Missouri, which would make a career of deflating Ward's teams after its close calls against Oklahoma, somehow topped the Buffs, 21-19, despite a huge CU statistical advantage. The Buffs rolled up 17 first

downs in the first half against the Tigers' two and continued to dominate the second half, but led only 19-14 late in the game. The Tigers then got a big break when Brookshier was flagged for pass interference at the CU 12 in the closing minutes to put Mizzou in position for the winning touchdown.

Undaunted, the Buffs chopped down Oregon, 21-7, as Jordan punted for a 55-yard average en route to a national season's average record of 48.2 yards. CU called it a season by ending the 2-year frustrations dealt by Colorado A&M with a 5-touchdown, 31-6 barrage highlighted by Dalthorp's 30-yard TD with an intercepted fumble.

CU's Big Eight debut was terrifying, too, as Kansas administered a 40-7 flogging. Ward's first victim was, of all teams, Nebraska. But then Dallas enjoyed playing the Cornhuskers. In 11 meetings, Ward's teams built a 7-3-1 margin and outscored the Huskers, 223-163. Those 1948 Nebraskans were heavy favorites over a CU squad which had been unimpressive, to say the least. But Ward's intricate single wing required a lot of adjustments by his players who were coming out of a com-

CU's "Roaring 20" Harry Narcisian runs wild against Utah State in 1948.

pletely different offensive scheme. Trap block timing and double-team co-ordination took a lot of time to master. His single wing always looked simple from the stands and to the press box. Actually its combination of power and deception made it one of the most diffi-

Kayo Lam was just as dashing a figure as athletic business manager as when he starred on the field for the Buffaloes.

cult to defend against. Lining up against it was a lot more complicated than watching it.

After three weeks of pre-season practice and two games, the Buffaloes were beginning to get the feel of it. Nebraska was the first team to pay the price. The first half was even until Nar-

cisian hit Ed Pudlik for a TD and a 13-6 halftime lead. In the second half the defense took over and blanked the Cornhuskers and Narcisian found Miller for a 21-yard score which iced the game. CU's tiny trio had a field day against the bigger and slower Nebras-kans. Narcisian ran and passed for an awesome 195 yards. Hagin added 116 and Miller 42 on the ground. It was a huge victory, one which would go on CU's all-time list of major accomplishments.

But that was the high point of Ward's first season. CU won only two more games and finished 3-6-0. After Nebraska the Buffs traveled to Iowa State and made the best beginning in history when Pudlik recovered Iowa State's fumble of the opening kickoff in the end zone for a 7-0 lead with only 15 seconds played. But that was it for the day and CU fell, 18-7 The team roared back behind "Roaring Twenty" next week with a 51-7 Homecoming win over a Kansas State team rated even with the Buffaloes. Narcisian was up to Byron White standards in that one, scoring touchdowns the first three times he touched the ball on scrimmage runs of 15 and five yards sandwiched around a 67-yard punt return. For good mea-sure he set up a fourth with a pass to John Strobel which gained 40 yards to the five from where he scored. Ward sat out the Wheat Ridge whirling dervish in the second half but Narcisian's under-study, Dane Graves, continued the assault with three TDs of his own. K-

State, for what would be the first of many times, left Boulder in disarray.

But a week later, Pudlik's two missed conversion attempts let Utah escape at Salt Lake, 14-12. In the next game, against BYU, Narcisian caught fire in the fourth quarter which began with the Buffs trailing, 14-7. He bolted 35 then 16 yards for the tying touch-down, then, following a 29-yard gallop, sent CU in front with a 13-yard strike to Pudlik. He iced it with still another TD. CU won, 28-14, and fans were again excited. But that was the last hur-rah for 1948. The Buffs couldn't hold a 7-0 halftime lead and lost to Missouri 27-13, then were victimized by a tall, skinny Colorado A&M quarterback named Bob Hainlen, who kicked three field goals in a 29-25 Aggie upset.

As anticipated CU had neither the talent nor the depth to face the rugged Big Eight schedule. They did, however, escape the basement. K-State was last. The record was bad, 3-6-0, but aside from the Kansas game, the Buffs were in every battle. Omitting the KU disaster, the other five losses were by a total of only 34 points, less than a TD and PAT per game. Ward was on his way. Still, 1949 would be even worse as the seniors graduated and his recruits began to move in despite their inexperience.

1949

The road back under Ward in 1949 continued to be laborious. After an opening 13-12 win over KU in which

Dal Ward always had outstanding ends, beginning with this quartet in his first year, 1948. L-R, John Zisch, Harry Robertson, Jack Pixler and Ed Pudlik.

This quartet of Dal Ward-era stalwarts suited up for an alumni game in 1963. Shown with line coach Marsh Wells they were (l-r) Vic Thomas, Tom Cain, Fred Johnson and Sam Catanzaro.

Buffs reached double figures in each of the last nine games, nearly doubling their 1949 point total, 227-129. Ward's single wing power was beginning to grind out the yards. Now he had the horses to pull the team. They were talented sophomores named Tom Brookshier, Ralph Curtis, Woody Shelton, Roger Williams, Larry Horine, Lee Venzke plus Zack Jordan, a transfer from California with three years' eligibility remaining, in the backfield and solid linemen in Don Branby, Bill Allen, Jack Swigert, Dick Dietrich, Jim Dalthorp, Tom Evans and Roy Shepherd. This imposing roster of rookies, blending with such solid veterans as Vic Thomas, Dick Punches, Joe Nix, Pete Thompson, Don Gorman, Dick Stevens, Tom Hancock, Ray Jump, Jack Jorgenson, Cliff Vandeventer, Bill Allen and Chuck Mosher and backs Arlie Beery, Dane Graves, Don Hagan, Hugh Davidson and Hodel, gave Ward the tools to make his move.

Miller scored twice and the CU line blocked both Kansas PAT attempts, CU dropped three straight: to Kansas, 27-13; Iowa State, 13-6; and Oregon, 42-14. The defeat at Eugene was particularly painful as the Ducks jumped to a 28-0 halftime lead. Even the fates seemed to be frowning on the Buffs by now. On the trip home Sunday morning, CU's chartered airliner blew an engine and had to make an emergency landing.

But the Utah schools, so often jinxes in past seasons, uncharacteristically came to the rescue. CU ended its skid with a 20-7 win over Utah State at Logan as Miller scored twice. The slender New Mexican had developed into a Buff workhorse. Against Utah the next Saturday in Boulder, a sudden snowstorm swept into the stadium just before the half. But Ward had the answer in a human snowplow, sophomore fullback Merv Hodel, who would become one of the finest offensive fullbacks in CU history. The big guy from Illinois dug out 100 yards and two touchdowns despite the soggy sod. CU won, 14-7.

That was the last time the victory chimes rang in Old Main that fall. Once again, lowly New Mexico administered the death blow, winning at Albuquerque, 17-15. Nebraska battered the Buffs physically — Hodel, Dane Graves

and star tackle Pete Thompson went out early with injuries — to win at Lincoln, 25-14, and Colorado A&M made the final chapter of 1949 a sad one, 14-7. The record was 3-7-0, a game worse than 1948. But Ward was beginning to assemble the makings of a fine squad. He was ready to fine tune the offense. It would become one of the most feared in the Big Eight within two seasons.

1950

The warning to opposing defenses was sounded loudly in 1950. After an opening 14-7 loss at Iowa State, the

1951

There was guarded optimism as 1951 approached. Ward had proven his teams could move the ball. But the CU defense was still suspect. So the accent was on the offense as eight starters, including the entire backfield, returned. Branby, Jorgenson, Shepherd and Brookshier were proven standouts. But there were holes. Ward, however, felt good about his team. CU was the only team in the league using the single wing. That gave his already effective offense an added advantage. Opposing teams were never fully prepared to stop the Buffs after only a week's practice. They worked against the T-formation in

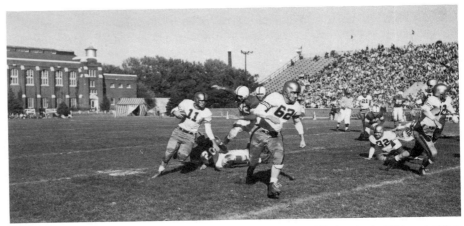

Jack Swigert (62) leads Zack Jordan (11) for good yardage at Nebraska in 1951 rout of the Cornhuskers.

Merv Hodel was a great fullback in 1949-50-51.

CU's first road victory in the Big Eight and ended a string of eight straight losses away from Boulder. Blocking back Roger Williams dove in for two touchdowns, one set up by Shepherd's alert interception of a fumbled pass.

Now the Buffs were in the title hunt. They headed for Norman to meet the Oklahoma team they had scared badly the year before. The Sooners would take them to the woodshed and administer a 55-14 walloping. It was a nightmare in which all of CU's plans went awry. Defensive ace Brookshier was injured and out. Not to worry. Sooner quarterback Eddie Crowder, a magician at disguising the ball on his handoffs to a fleet of good running backs, wasn't noted for his passing ability. Besides, Wilkinson preferred that his teams stay on the ground where the going was safer. Two things happened, both bad. First, Vandeventer, another secondary stalwart, was injured early. Second, the Sooner press-box observers spotted a tendency of CU's deep backs to come up quickly to support against the run when the Oklahoma option developed to the outside.

Crowder got the word. His arm was only average. But it was quick and it was accurate and his fakes to the outside brought up the CU secondary and left wide open spaces for the OU ends to occupy. The result was an Oklahoma dream and a CU nightmare. Crowder completed five straight passes in the first quarter, three for touchdowns covering 27, 67 and 38 yards. Another, good for 23 yards, set up a fourth. The Sooner blitzkreig produced a first quarter lead of 27-0. CU never got out of intensive care. Only 136 yards from Hodel, including a 66-yard TD gallop, brought consolation to the Buffaloes.

If upcoming foes thought the Buffs would be demoralized by the knockout at Norman, they were in for a surprise. CU rebounded savagely, averaging six touchdowns per game in hammering Iowa State (47-20), Utah (54-0), and Nebraska (36-14.) The Cyclones were subdued quickly as the Buffs drove 74 yards with their first possession, detonated a Jordan-Shelton bomb for 48 yards the next time, then put the Cyclones away as Shepherd intercepted a pass at the 10, returned it to midfield then lateraled to George Figner who bunny-hopped the rest of the way. Before the rout was over, four more Buffs had joined in the scoring: Ron Johnson for 36 yards, Carroll Hardy for 38, Hugh Davidson for 17 and Larry

every other week. One fact dampened CU optimism. Two of the Big Ten's top teams, Northwestern and Michigan State, were on the schedule, making the 1951 slate the toughest ever faced by a Colorado team.

The beginning was a routine victory over Colorado A&M as the Buffs pulled away in the fourth quarter to win, 28-13. The fears about the defense were not unfounded. Northwestern riddled the secondary, hitting two bombs in the first four minutes and went on to a 35-14 victory. The defense continued to yield points in the next three games but the offense prevailed. Kansas fell, 35-27. Missouri followed, 34-13. The Buffs made it three straight at Kansas State, 20-7.

Shelton and Brookshier teamed up for one of the most spectacular plays of the season against Kansas. The tiny wingback fielded a KU punt at the CU 35, slipped it to Brookshier, who raced 65 yards to the end zone as most of the Kansas team chased the faking Shelton.

In the Missouri rout, Curtis gouged out 121 yards and Shelton reversed for 93 more and guard Tom Cain's fumble recovery enabled the Buffs to pull away after an early Tiger lead. A transfer from Notre Dame, Cain was one of CU's first widebodied middle guards. He surrounded the Tiger fumble at the 17 and Shelton scampered all the way on the next play. The relatively routine win at Manhattan was a highlight of Ward's career for one reason: it was

Horine for 25 with an interception.

The Utah jinx never applied to Ward. His CU teams went 9-0-1 against the Utes after that opening loss in 1948. The Buffs showed no mercy this time. The attack was awesome, producing 627 yards and the worst defeat in the 49-year history of the series, 54-0. Ward's three fine tailbacks feasted that day. Johnson got 90 yards, Jordan 81, and Hardy 80. Shelton slid back to the weak side for 79. Fullbacks Hodel and Davidson took it easy, netting a mere 39 and 36. Second place was at stake against Nebraska and CU was a slight underdog on a bitter cold November day in Lincoln. The game was on national television, CU's first appearance. 7,000 Nebraska fans stayed home because of TV and the weather. The Cornhuskers took a quick lead, an interference call at the goal line setting up its touchdown. Then a CU avalanche of five touchdowns and a safety buried them. Hardy had 107 yards, Hodel 103 and Jordan hit six of eight passes for 110 yards. The versatile CU tailback put on an eye-popping punting exhibition to set up nine third-quarter points. First he punted out of bounds at the four to pave the way for the safety. On his next kick he knifed it out at the one and the Buffs got an easy TD.

Now the Buffs had to travel to Michigan State for the final game. It was a tough assignment. The Spartans had been ranked number one in the nation for most of the season but had just been

Jack Swigert, the fine guard in 1950-1-2 who became an astronaut, receives a university citation from president Fred Thieme in 1970.

1952 All-American end Don Branby poses at picture day with Denver radio-TV personality Starr Yelland.

displaced by Tennessee which had finished the season undefeated. State's only chance to overhaul the Volunteers was to whip CU decisively. They did, 45-7, but it was not enough. The Spartans still finished second. So did CU in the Big Eight, an almost unbelievable accomplishment for the Buffaloes who had literally come from nowhere in four seasons to join the league's elite. Hardy's 67-yard third quarter TD capped a brilliant year for the fleet frosh.

1952

The outlook was rosy for 1952. No longer were the Buffs question marks. They had established themselves as a solid football team with the 7-3-0 record in 1951. 39 lettermen were back. There were good replacements for the departed seniors. Only the reliable workhorse Hodel left a void in the backfield. But Ralph "Cactus" Curtis was a slasher who could run to daylight.

This was the senior class of 1952 which propelled CU into the top ranks of the Big Eight. *L-R,* Don Branby, E; Jerry Raveling, E; Larry Horine, S; Jim Dalthorp, LB; Roger Williams, QB; Bill Allen, T; Tom Brookshier, DHB; Roy Shepherd, C; Coach Dal Ward, Woody Shelton, WB; Lee Venzke, QB; Jack Swigert, G; Zack Jordan, TB; Tom Evans, E; Ralph Curtis, FB; and Bob Klamann, T.

CU had Oklahoma at Boulder early. Maybe they'd catch the Sooners off stride. It would be Oklahoma's opener. CU would have what should be a breather, San Jose State, the week before. The Buffs would profit from the tune-up.

The beginning was good. Almost perfect. The season was one of frustration, 6-2-2. CU came ever so close to reaching the top. Eleven more points in the right places could have meant a championship. So instead of a title, the Buffs wound up talking to themselves about what might have been.

San Jose State was not a soft touch. CU's 20-14 win required a 63-yard third quarter punt return TD by Frank Bernardi, a transfer who stopped for a visit in Boulder en route from Indiana to Arizona and remained to become a Buffalo. Bernardi had taken over at wingback when Shelton was shelved by a dislocated elbow. Bernardi went down three weeks later with a knee injury.

The Oklahoma game was an epic. Folsom Stadium bulged with the largest crowd in history, 30,732. Maybe the Sooners, who were riding a 26-game winning streak, were overconfident. They had basically the same cast back, too, and they had to remember the 1951 laugher.

Whatever, the Buffaloes took the fight to them from the beginning. Jordan's kicking was magnificent, a major factor in the game. He punted and quick

kicked seven times for a 56-yard average, including a 77-yarder from the CU one-yard line. The Buffs rallied from a 14-7 halftime deficit to take a 21-14 lead on a 60-yard drive midway through the final quarter. They stopped the Sooners and came right back and appeared headed for a clinching score when Figner recovered a fumble at the OU 29. The Buffs tried to fool the Sooners with a quick pass on first down. It was intercepted at the 22. Nevertheless, the Sooners were in deep trouble as three plays netted only eight yards. This time they gambled. And won. Crowder, who had been held well in check by a vicious CU defense sparked by ends Don Branby and Tom Evans, slid down the line on the option, pitched to Billy Vessels and the Heisman Trophy winner roared 18 yards to midfield. That play ignited the Sooners. They scored to tie the game with 1:51 left. Colorado reached for a miracle and almost got it. The Buffs roared 62 yards, from their 17 to the Oklahoma 21. With a first down there but no time outs left, they were stopped by the final gun.

Jordan had a tremendous game, scoring all three touchdowns and passing for 66 key yards in addition to his superb punting. Crowder, the star the previous years, finished badly battered and leaking blood from a savage pounding from Branby. OU coach Bud Wilkinson protested bitterly about the

Colorado terminal's rough play and asked the conference to suspend him the following week. Ward, who had been a Minneapolis prep coach and good friend of Wilkinson's when Bud was a star quarterback and guard for the Gophers, snorted that aggressive shadowing of the quarterback was the only chance a defense had to stop the option. Crowder never complained. After all, he had guided the Sooners to the come-from-behind triumph. Branby had the last laugh. He was named All-American two months later, primarily with the momentum of that early-season performance against the top team in the nation.

But CU promptly faltered the next week at Lawrence, losing to Kansas 21-12 when they failed to punch the ball into the end zone after twice reaching the KU one. This was the time Hodel's absence was devastating. He had been faulted often for his lackadaisical play in the middle of the field. But there was no Buffalo who was ever better inside the 10.

His replacement, Curtis, did come through a week later against Arizona, ripping out 122 yards and catching two passes for 43 more in a 34-19 win over the Wildcats. And for a change, the defense dominated a game as the Buffs throttled Iowa State at Ames, 21-12. Then came Nebraska and its superstar Reynolds. But the Cornhusker smoothie had another rough day against the

CU defense. It was a wildly fluctuating game. CU went ahead quickly as Curtis raced 49 yards on the fourth play of the game. Nebraska tied it, then took a 9-7 halftime lead when they blocked a Jordan quick kick out of the end zone, the only kick the CU star ever had blocked in a brilliant 3-year career which made him the leading college punter in history, 139 punts for a 43.3 average. The finish was furious. CU led 10-9 on Roger Williams' third quarter field goal. Nebraska drove the length of the field to go in front, 16-10, with 2:11 left. Hardy promptly raced 84 yards with the following kickoff. But Williams, a reliable placekicker, missed the extra point which would have won the game. Reynolds, who never played on a team which beat CU in three years, then got his final frustration as he missed a 33-yard field goal attempt with no time remaining on the clock.

Zack Jordan, Bill Horton, Carroll Hardy and Ron Johnson (l-r) formed a fleet foursome of tailbacks in 1952.

The Big & Little of 1952 were wingback Woody Shelton and tackle Jack Jorgenson.

pass aimed at an end. Missouri was always tough against the run. So Ward figured he'd come out throwing against the Tigers. When it came out raining, his plan was foiled. Missouri won in the mud, 27-7.

The Buffs took out their frustration on hapless Kansas State and Colorado A&M in the final two games. It was too late to salvage anything but pride. But they did that as they hammered the Wildcats, 34-14, after spotting the cellar dwellers a 14-0 lead. The Buff seniors, who had played such a vital role in building CU's Big Eight fortunes, exited with a flourish, slaughtering Colorado A&M on a gray late November day, 61-0, as eight men scored touchdowns: Jordan, Curtis, Hardy, Shelton, Ron Johnson, Shepherd, Don Shelley and Gary Knafelc (2). Williams booted nine straight extra

Williams atoned for his bad boot with his finest day, catching four Jordan passes and scoring twice, as CU escaped a Utah ambush, 20-14. Hardy was the leading rusher with 103 yards. A driving rainstorm which began moments before the opening kickoff to end a 3-month drought in Missouri, ruined CU's strategy for that game. Ward was never a disciple of the passing game. His aerial attack consisted primarily of short throws from the tailback to the blocking back in the flat with an infrequent

Trainer Jack Rockwell (r) and Dick Freund (52) help Frank Bernardi off the field at Columbia after he got his face bashed while blocking an extra point against Missouri in 1954.

Fullback Emerson Wilson plows for yardage against Utah in 1953 as guard Dick Knowlton *(left)* and tackle Jim Stander *(on ground)* block and end Gary Knafelc heads downfield.

points. The 6-2-2 record wasn't all that bad, though good for only a fourth-place tie. But it was a disappointment, coming after CU had almost defeated the nation's number one team. Now Ward faced his second rebuilding job. Sixteen senior stalwarts played their last game against A&M. CU's locker room would be full of empty shoes in 1953.

1953

Sixteen starters were missing as practice began. If there was any consolation it was that a rules change had ended two-platoon football and fewer players would be necessary. A team possibly could get by with 22-25 performers. Still the holes to fill were large. No linebackers or blocking back returned. The experience was thin at the other positions. Ward, who had learned gloominess from Bierman, the nation's master of the gloomy outlook, presented a properly long face to the public. Inwardly, he confided that the Buffaloes would not be that bad.

One major experiment held the key to CU's chances. To plug the blocking

Equipment manager Lee Akins checks out gear to sophomores Bill Kucera *(l)* and Sam Salerno *(c)* in 1953.

Carroll Hardy (27) breaks open in a record-setting 238-yard afternoon against Kansas State in 1954. Convoying him are Les Lotz (80), Don Karnoscak (56), Dick Stapp (74), John Bayuk (30) and Wally Merz (88).

back hole, Ward shifted Roger Hunt, a fine offensive guard the past two seasons, to that position. A good athlete, Hunt was an obvious candidate. Ward's blocking backs were little more than third guards wearing an eligible number. All Hunt had to learn was how to catch the safety valve passes in the short flats. If he could do that, CU would have a presentable starting unit. One thing was certain. Ward's offense would be in good hands - and feet - with excellent backs in Hardy, Johnson, Bernardi, Bill Horton and Shelley. The line was thin but there were two outstanding veterans: guard Dick Knowlton and end Gary Knafelc, already one of the finest receivers in CU history.

Two-touchdown favored Washington was the opener in Seattle. CU spotted the Huskies an early touchdown when a big tackle intercepted a fumble and lumbered 77 yards. Hardy and Knafelc were as good as expected but

the fleet tailback went down with a rib injury early in the second period. A much-ballyhooed sophomore, Homer Jenkins, replaced him and performed at the same level. So did another rookie, fullback Emerson Wilson. Jenkins passed to Knafelc for 16 and 50-yard TDs. Hunt kicked all three extra points. CU won, 21-20, and Hardy supplied a key punt return, re-entering despite his pain to field a kick deep in CU territory and run it out of danger 54 yards. In the depleted secondary, the swarthy, stocky Bernardi was scintillating, bumping receivers off-stride and ankle-tackling like the departed Brookshier.

On a day dominated by President Dwight Eisenhower's heart attack in Denver, Bernardi tormented Arizona, the school to which he had almost transferred. Sound again after a knee operation, his wingback reverses and southpaw passes would be a vital part of CU's attack. The Buffs held on to win,

20-14, despite yielding another freak opening TD on a Wildcat tackle's fumble interception return, the second in two weeks. Bernardi's 33-yard TD pass to Knafelc provided the winning points. Then misfortune struck the backfield again. Horton went down with a dislocated elbow, Shelley with a knee. The Buffs went down too, losing to Missouri, 27-16, despite continued excellence from newcomers Jenkins and Wilson. A week later against Kansas, still another ace went down, when Johnson collapsed with an asthma attack, triggered by Band Day dust stirred up on the cinder track surrounding the field, after returning a kickoff the length of the field. Later in the game Jenkins' leg was broken. Forced into action too soon, Hardy re-injured his ribs. The Buffs fought courageously after falling behind 14-0 in the first quarter. They crept even at 14 and 21 but finally lost, 27-21, to the Jayhawkers.

A CU lineup in 1953 included (l-r) linemen Alabama Glass, Bob Morton, Dick Knowlton, Jim Stander, Don Karnoscak, Ken Huffer and Gary Knafelc, and backs Don Neary, Roger Hunt, Bill Horton and Carroll Hardy.

Now reeling from the epidemic of injuries, the Buffs were jolted 28-14 at Kansas State. Up next was Oklahoma, as usual scenting another national championship and rolling along in their undefeated streak. CU was a heavy underdog at Norman. But Bernardi slithered 13 yards on the first play following the Sooners' fumble of the opening kickoff and Ward's single wing continued to baffle Oklahoma. CU appeared to have fashioned an amazing upset when the still-ailing Hardy came in long enough to break a 35-yard lightening bolt to give CU a 13-6 halftime lead. Oklahoma edged back ahead 20-13 in the second half but a brilliantly improvised play by Hunt capped an 80-yard CU comeback to tie the score. On a fourth down buck-lateral play, Hunt, realizing his trailing back Johnson was covered, pulled in the ball and wheeled back to the weak side and rambled 26 yards to the end zone. The tie didn't last long. The Sooners, getting a break when linebacker Ken Huffer was called for holding on an incomplete pass, broke Merrill Green for 51 yards on a counter play to win, 27-20. CU's coaches lamented long and loudly after reviewing the movies that Oklahoma's right guard had jumped offside on the play. But it was too late. Wilkinson, the acknowledged master of college football semantics, simple smiled that the guard had moved with the snap while the rest of the line was behind by a count. Astute answers aside, Ward was furious. But the score never changed and

undoubtedly Wilkinson considered it repayment for league officials' failure to follow his "ban-Branby" edict of the preceding year.

Iowa State figured to catch CU flat the following week. The Cyclones had a good team, paced by a sensational sophomore in Gary Lutz. The game was one of the wildest ever played in Folsom Stadium. The visitors struck savagely at the outset, taking a 21-7 lead in an opening avalanche in which the Buffaloes had only one scrimmage play. The opening point parade went like this: Iowa State drove 80 yards with the opening kickoff. Ron Johnson returned the next kickoff 97 yards. Iowa State took the next kickoff and marched to the end zone again. On CU's first scrimmage play of the game, a Bernardi pass was intercepted and returned for a third Cyclone TD. But the Buffs regrouped to cut the deficit to 28-20 at the half and won it, 41-34, on Hardy's dazzling 17-yard burst with 1:22 remaining. Now labeled CU's "twin torpedoes," Bernardi (104 yards in 12 car-

John Bayuk (30) bursts through the line against Kansas State in 1954.

The CU starting lineup in 1955 consisted of (l-r) linemen Wally Merz, Sam Salerno, Dave Jones, Dick Stapp, Don Karnoscak, Dick Golder and Lamar Meyer, and backs Emerson Wilson, Sam Maphis, John Bayuk and Homer Jenkins.

number 30" be pointed out. Bayuk graciously visited briefly with her, never realizing that he would forever after be known as "The Beast." As for Bernardi, he was more than alert after missing his Lawrence exit. He made two sensational diving catches to set up CU's first two touchdowns after a scoreless first half, leading KU's renowned publicist, Don Pierce, to remark after the game, "I wish that train had gone on to Wheeling, West Virginia instead of Kansas City!"

In a night game at Tucson, Arizona provided little resistance after Wilson was ejected from the game early for riding Wildcat star Art Luppino to the ground more enthusiastically than the rule book permitted. Bayuk came on in relief and lived up to his new nickname, thundering to four touchdowns in a 40-18 exercise.

ries) and Hardy (17-103) were unstoppable.

The Buffaloes finished the season with routine wins over Utah (21-0), Nebraska (14-10) and Colorado A&M (13-7). CU's wingbacks, because they carried the ball infrequently on reverses, never piled up the yardage like the workhorse tailbacks. Bernardi, in particular, took a publicity backseat to CU's bevy of tailbacks like Hardy, Johnson, Jenkins and Horton. But he was a standout both ways and never did he demonstrate his value more than in the Nebraska win. His pass defense was flawless all afternoon. With CU trailing, 10-7, late in the game he hit Knafelc for 48 yards then followed with a short pass for the winning TD. He still wasn't finished. Nebraska marched right back to the CU goal line and powered into the line on fourth down from the three behind a good hole. But Bernardi filled it quickly, ran through a blocker and made the tackle to save the game. The finishing 4-game winning streak gave the Buffs a 6-4-0 record. It would undoubtedly have been better had it not been for the early injuries. Ward's offense was always better than his luck. His bad luck continued in 1954.

1954

Once again established as a legitimate Big Eight contender, the Buffs opened 1954 with impressive routs, blanking out-manned Drake (61-0) and Colorado A&M (46-0) then continuing at Kansas (27-0). That game was noteworthy for two reasons. First Bernardi, failed to get off the train at Lawrence and had to be driven in from Kansas

Dal Ward always had good punters. Two of his best were Homer Jenkins and Carroll Hardy (l-r).

City. Then one of CU's most famous nicknames, second only to White's "Whizzer," was pinned on fullback John Bayuk after the brawny sophomore had punished a tired KU team with a 71-yard fourth period and the final touchdown. As the Buffs awaited their night train back to Denver, a tiny old lady wearing KU's blue and red entered the Hotel Eldridge lobby and asked that the "beast who wears

But the cruelest blow in Ward's career cut him down personally as his undefeated Buffs hosted an underdog Nebraska eleven. An old back ailment flattened him and he was under sedation all week and unable to prepare the Buffs. The old-fashioned mentor's practices were literally a one-man show, particularly the offensive preparations. He tried to attend practice on a golf cart but the pain prevented him from doing any-

Frank Bernardi, a wingback throughout his brilliant CU career, practices taking a T-handoff from backfield coach Frank Prentup as he prepares for the Shrine East-West game in 1954.

kept his balance when hit by using his free arm for leverage for 113 yards. Wilson contributed mightily, too, with 124 yards including a 95-yard dash up the middle which gave CU a 19-0 half-time lead.

When the Kansas State slaughter was over, CU had established a national single-game rushing record of 493 yards. The single wing was impressive despite the beginning mutterings that Ward's alignment was old-fashioned and that he would do well to move to the T-formation. That complaint would haunt him until his coaching demise four years later despite the fact his next-to-last team, in 1957, would lead the nation in rushing and finish second in total offense. But those two tortured weeks in late October when Ward and the Buffaloes lived in pain had wrecked

thing and the sedatives dulled his mind. An air of gloom hung over the team. The game would decide the Big Eight's Orange Bowl representative. A new agreement prevented a conference team from playing there two straight years and Oklahoma had been there already. CU was the favorite to finish second and earn the trip. Nebraska and Kansas State were also in the picture. The Cornhuskers were fired up and upset CU, 20-6, running down Bayuk in the open early then bottling up the CU offense the rest of the way. It was a crushing setback for Ward who had to watch the game from a straight-backed chair on the sideline, unable to be a factor for his team.

Oklahoma followed a week later and by now CU's gallant efforts against the Sooners were a source of constant pre-game talk. Oklahoma had another streak going, winning 17 and tying one game following Notre Dame's victory over them in 1952. Snapping back surprisingly after the Nebraska disappointment, the Buffaloes carried a 6-0 lead into the final period, on a Sam Maphis-Frank Bernardi 19-yard connection in the second quarter. It was the first time a Wilkinson team had ever been blanked that long. The Buffaloes appeared to be driving to a clinching

touchdown late in the third period but stalled at the 12. Superior Sooner manpower prevailed in the final 15 minutes as the Oklahomans drove 88 yards then hit a long pass to win, 13-6.

CU didn't lose another game although it took a heroic PAT block by Bernardi to save a 13-13 tie at Missouri seven days later. The gutty little wingback deflected the ball with his face, a very un-Italian maneuver which broke and dislocated his nose and closed both eyes. Despite those wounds, he reported for practice early the following Monday to get used to the birdcage he would wear to protect his face, growling to a questioning sports writer, "Why shouldn't I practice, I don't run with my nose."

The Buffs clubbed Utah, 30-7, at Salt Lake City then eliminated Kansas State from the Orange Bowl with a 38-14 runaway. The Hardy-Bernardi connection made a memorable exit that day. Carroll, dubbed "Preacher" by his teammates because of his ministerial-like dedication to clean living, set a national record with 238 rushing yards in only 10 carries. The mark survived until the heavy duty I-backs took over nearly two decades later. Not to be outdone, Bernardi bounced along in his unique "3-legged" gait, as he constantly

Regents Recognized Folsom

The massive contributions of Fred Folsom to CU's athletic program was recognized by this regents' resolution two weeks following his death on November 11, 1944.

"RESOLVED: We record here the services of Frederick Gorham Folsom to the University for a period of 41 years; and in keeping with his own character, we do so in direct, simple, straightforward terms. First, on our athletic fields as a coach he elevated football contests from mere brutal, physical encounters to engagements of skill and strategy requiring self-control, moral discipline and high sportsmanship. He, himself, and a host of athletes trained by him later employed those qualities in life and in defense of our country in its armed forces. Then, for 37 years, in our Law School he taught that law suits were to be prosecuted vigorously and faithfully in the interest of one's client but always honestly and in keeping with the higher interests of society and the state. He taught that the law and the courts afforded not only a mechanism for the solution of commercial disputes between private litigants but that they should conserve and protect civil liberties and the public welfare.

"He has left high standards for us to attain.

"To his wife and children we express our sorrow and our sympathy."

CU's chances for 1954's Big Eight Orange Bowl bid. They finished third behind Nebraska. The overall record was 7-2-1. And Ward had the winter in which to heal and launch another bid for New Year's Day in Miami.

1955

Going into 1955, the Buffaloes would be without their touchdown twins, Hardy and Bernardi. But there was a good nucleus of 25 lettermen, 18 of them linemen, returning. Jenkins had recovered from a leg operation and looked to be an excellent replacement for Hardy. The big experiment of 1955 was the switch of Wilson from fullback to wingback to make room in the starting backfield for Bayuk. Unlike Hunt's move to blocking back in 1953 this one would not go smoothly. Wilson, a 2-year starter and excellent blocker as well as runner, had trouble making the adjustment. He'd been hampered by an early elbow injury the year before. Now as he entered his senior season it was at a strange position, one in which he would carry the ball infrequently. After his standout sophomore campaign it was a huge letdown. Bayuk didn't have as good a year either. His yardage

CU alum and prominent Denver radio-TV personality Pete Smythe was the first sideline announcer at CU. Here he broadcasts the coin toss against Kansas in 1955 as game captains Bill Lamont and Emerson Wilson watch.

dropped from 824 to 460 as his carries went down from 145 to 95. Part of the reason was a greater emphasis on passing because of the arrival of a talented junior college end, Frank Clarke. The Buffs threw the ball nearly 50 times more than the year before. Clarke caught 13, as many as CU's top three receivers totaled in 1954. But still the forward pass was not a vital part of

This was the lineup at Dad's Day in 1955. Shown with their parents are *(l-r)*, Les Lotz (80), Bob Boyer (25), Jerry Leahy (84), Bill Lamont (41), Chuck Joslin (61), Greg Lefferdink (62), Ken Schlagel (82), Bill Mondt (79), Dick Golder (71), Arlin Hubka (70), Les Welker (23), Gene Worden (22), John Bayuk (30), Stapp (66) and Bob Stapp (63), Lamar Meyer (86) and Rodger Lindwall (51).

Ward's offense. Despite the increase, the Buffs averaged less than 12 passes per game.

Defense took the Buffs to a pair of opening victories over Arizona (14-0) and Kansas (12-0) and eight Oregon fumbles, CU covering every one of them with center Don Karnoscak personally getting four, helped the Buffs to a struggling 13-6 win in rain-soaked Eugene. When Kansas State turned the ball over three times the next week, CU had its fourth straight win to enter the annual Oklahoma showdown with a perfect record. For 20 minutes it looked as though another stemwinder was in store. The Buffaloes stunned the Sooner crowd with touchdowns by Wilson and Bayuk to lead 14-0 after 20 minutes. Then misfortune struck. A third-down Oklahoma pass sailed high over the receiver's arms but an official called CU's defender for interference and the Sooners took advantage of the break and went on in to score.

The questionable interference call unnerved the Buffaloes. A CU man made a critical error when Oklahoma punted next, getting too close to the ball as he threw an unnecessary block - CU's safety was letting the ball roll dead. The ball took a crazy last bounce and grazed his leg. Oklahoma pounced on it and had a first down at midfield. Were it not for the mistake, CU would

CU's "touchdown twins", Carroll Hardy (27) and Frank Bernardi (18), watch the coin toss before running wild in their final game, a 38-14 rout of Kansas State in 1954. Hardy ran for 238 yards and Bernardi 113 that day.

have had excellent field position with a 14-7 lead. Oklahoma then surprised the Buffs with a no-huddle offense. The faster OU ran their plays, the more the crowd roared and the more confused the Buffs became. Ward's bewildered warriors, who had seemed so much in command a few minutes earlier, trailed 21-14 at the break. The Sooners didn't ease up in the second half, upping their lead to 35-14 before reserve quarterback Dick Hyson hit Clarke for a 54-

yard bomb. The final score was 56-21 in a game that had begun so promisingly for the Buffs.

Now Missouri, as usual, awaited CU in the post-Oklahoma week and the Tigers took a 20-0 lead and held on for a 20-12 win as CU rallied late with TD passes from Bob Stransky to Clarke (27 yards) and Jenkins to Jerry Leahy (23 yards). But CU missed both extra points and never really had a chance to pull it out.

Taking a cue from Oklahoma, the Buffaloes detonated a 21-point explosion of their own to bury Utah, 37-7. The salvoes included an 81-yard punt return by sophomore Stransky, on his way to becoming one of the top backs in the Big Eight, a 63-yard bomb from Stransky to Clarke, and a 39-yard fumble return by guard Joe Connors. Nebraska used the same shock treatment to upset the Buffs, 37-20, a week later at Lincoln. The Cornhuskers sandwiched two quick touchdowns around a 95-yard pass interception by CU nemesis Willie Greenlaw to take a 21-0 lead in the first 10 minutes. CU tried hard but couldn't catch up, going down, 37-20.

Then the Buffaloes turned in a near-perfect performance to blast Iowa State, 40-0. But if 1955 was one thing it was inconsistent. The Buffs dipped from perfect to pathetic in seven days, falling futilely at Colorado A&M, 10-0. It was the first time in eight years a Ward team was shut out. The Buffs contributed to the loss almost as much as the Aggies. Wilson was injured early. Bayuk got tossed out in the first half for unneces-

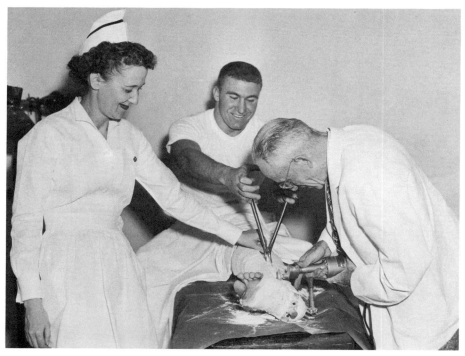

Star tailback Homer Jenkins, injury-plagued throughout a fine CU career, watches as team doctor G.O. Giffin removes a cast while nurse Naomi Wright assists.

Newly-enlarged Folsom Stadium was packed to the hilt for the 1956 game with Oklahoma.

sary roughness. CU lost four fumbles and had a pass intercepted. The 6-4-0 record and third-place tie gave the critics more reason to complain. Like the preceding year, CU had been undefeated in the first month to whet its followers appetites. Then came the closing collapse: four losses in the last six games including the disaster at Ft. Collins.

1956

Ward now faced an uncertain future. The pressure was on him for the first time. He'd already lasted eight years, longest tenure for a CU coach since Witham. But the prospects for 1956 weren't rosy. Only three regulars were back. But Ward had a flock of sophomores to come to the rescue.

The Buffaloes were picked to finish no better than fourth in 1956. But the rookies came through. Ward's greatest hour was just ahead. It would also lead to disappointments in the two succeeding seasons which would end his coaching career.

There was a whole new look to CU football as the 1956 season began. That flock of promising sophomores, the second best crew Ward ever recruited (he brought in an even better one in 1958), was on hand. So was an enlarged Folsom Stadium. A million-dollar addition had added 15,138 seats above the east stands and curling around the south horseshoe. Its metal benches were in sharp contrast to the old wooden planks which still sat above the bare ground in the original bowl. And pulling the

Frank Clarke catches one of his two touchdown passes against Missouri in 1956 to lead CU to an Orange Bowl bid.

Eddie Dove's teammates inspect the broken nose he received in the 1956 Oklahoma game. *L-R, front,* Bob Stransky, Dove, Jim Uhlir; *back,* Howard Vest, Wally Merz, Jerry Leahy.

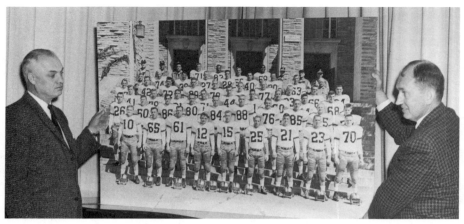

Dal Ward and KOA sports director John Henry (r) with an enlarged photo of the 1956 squad which was made for Ward's TV show hosted by Henry.

weeds which had grown up beneath the boards since spring was still an important late-summer job for summer school athletes. But the CU stadium now had the look of a big-time operation. And the stadium architecture blended in nicely with the other campus buildings. It was a needed improvement. And a well done one.

Now the Buffs were ready to make their 1956 debut in their new setting. An expectant crowd of 40,500 - understandably the largest for an athletic event in the state - gathered for the unveiling. CU wasn't expected to be great. But the opening opponent was

lightly-regarded Oregon. The Buffs were 2-touchdown favorites. The crowd anticipated a feast. They got a famine, wrapped around a nightmare. The rookies weren't ready and the veterans didn't lead. Oregon steamrollered the Buffs, 35-0. The game wasn't that close. The Ducks out-first downed CU, 24-7 while rolling to 444 yards. In disgust, Ward played the last half mostly with the sophomores. If this was going to be a reconstruction effort, he figured he might as well get started early. The veterans were shocked, then angered, at his treatment. But it worked.

A week later, the Buffs traveled to Kansas State and rebounded, 34-0. The sophomores led the way. Tailback

The CU backfield poses for photographers at Orange Bowl press day in 1956. L-R, Eddie Dove, John Bayuk, Boyd Dowler, Bob Stransky and center Jim Uhlir.

Tri-captains Wally Merz (88), Dick Stapp (74) and Jerry Leahy (84) listen to pre-kickoff instructions from referee Cliff Ogden at the 1957 Orange Bowl.

Howard Cook scored two touchdowns and intercepted two passes. Eddie Dove made CU followers forget Woody Shelton and Frank Bernardi as he twisted for 73 yards in five carries, one of them a 27-yard TD. The veterans got the message. Against Kansas, end Jerry Leahy got the Buffs rolling as he plucked the ball out of the KU quarterback's hands at the seven and stepped into the end zone as the game began. But the Jayhawkers fought back and Stransky had to break loose for 80 yards to rally the Buffs to a 26-25 win. Even then, they needed a break. Moments earlier, an overeager Kansas lineman had jumped offside on a successful PAT kick which would have meant a tie.

But the team had blended and the combination of new and old hands caught fire. The Buffs came just this close to going undefeated the rest of the way. Only the annual Oklahoma heartbreak prevented that. But that was still a month away. The CU firestorm cindered Colorado A&M (47-7) and Iowa State (52-0). Nebraska was next and Ward showed unexpected mercy on his tormenters of the preceding two sea-

74

Gene Worden (22) and Sherm Pruit (67) lead Howard Cook against Clemson in the Orange Bowl.

John Bayuk (30) follows Bill Mondt (66) and Dick Stapp (74) into the end zone for the winning touchdown against Clemson in the 1957 Orange Bowl.

sons, buttoning up the offense three times inside the 20 in the last 20 minutes after building a 16-0 lead, the final score. Big Bayuk, who had been a primary target of Ward's early exasperation, finally got untracked, scoring both touchdowns from 23 and 12 yards out.

Now it was time once again for the Oklahoma invasion and a packed house of 47,000 squeezed into Folsom. They saw one of the best Big Eight games of the decade. CU surged to a 19-6 half-time lead over the confident Sooners who had a week earlier demolished Notre Dame, 40-0, for their 58th game without a loss. Only ties with CU in 1952 and Pittsburgh in 1953 soiled that streak. But on this gray Boulder afternoon, the Buffs were in complete charge during the first 30 minutes. Leahy had started it by blocking a quick kick which Bayuk ran down in the end zone. Stransky and Dove contributed touchdowns. At the intermission, a CU victory seemed probable. At the least, very possible. But the Buffs needed to maintain their momentum in the third quarter.

Oklahoma prevented that with a daring gamble on their fourth play after receiving the kickoff. The situation was fourth-and-two at the 28. They went for it and made three yards. That payoff awakened the sleeping giant. They outscored CU 21-0 the rest of the way for a 27-19 triumph. The Buffaloes, like the year before at Norman, were victims of a disputed call in the third quarter when the Buffs were still in front. A clip was called on a CU blocker to nullify a Stransky run into Sooner turf.

The Buffs were crushed by their latest heartbreak at the hands of the Sooners. And, one more time, Missouri's Tigers licked their lips in anticipation of catching a letdown CU. The Orange Bowl bid was at stake. Oklahoma would be staying at home this year, its every-other-season price for dominating the conference. The game was at Columbia, a death trap for Buffaloes. But CU had one advantage. Even a tie would probably send them to Miami. Missouri had to face Oklahoma at Norman the following Saturday. And the Tigers always played as poorly against the Sooners as they did well against CU. A CU win would send the Buffs to Miami without question. A tie would undoubtedly mean that the team which played Oklahoma the closest

Leroy Clark (31), Larry Call (68) and Bill Mondt (66) carry Dal Ward off the field after the 1957 Orange Bowl win over Clemson. Ellwin Indorf watches.

would go.

CU's chances were fading away in the last half as Mizzou controlled the game, taking a seemingly safe 14-0 lead into the third quarter. The Tiger defense was too strong for the Buffs. But big Bayuk recovered a fumble at the Missouri 27 and quarterback Boyd Dowler hit Clarke with a 17-yard TD pass and suddenly the Buffs were back in business. But Ward's new multiple offense - he had finally mixed in the T-formation with his beloved single wing - still couldn't get untracked. It took a crazy sequence to rescue them. Bayuk was buried on a third down attempt in the final period. A Missouri guard poked a forearm inside the Beast's face-bar. Bayuk did what any frustrated beast would do. He bit it. The Missouri player pulled it out and bounced a fist off Bayuk's headgear. The referee, busily untangling the pile, missed the bite but saw the blow. The 15-yard penalty gave the Buffs their badly-needed first down. They went on in, with Dowler and Clarke again connecting for 18 yards and the tying TD. Cool Ellwin Indorf, primarily a place-kicking specialist in those pre-platoon days, converted both PATs and the 14-14 tie meant Miami for the Buffs. Utah and Arizona were easy. The Redskins yielded, 21-7, at Salt Lake and the Buffaloes celebrated with a riotous Saturday night party and a Sunday excursion to exotic Nogales, Mexico, sandwiching those escapades around a 38-7 romp in Tucson. And suddenly everything was coming up roses for Ward. Or rather, oranges. The state was on fire with pride in the Buffaloes. Ward was being hailed as the offensive master he was. Not for his bread-and-butter single wing but because of his addition of a few winged-T plays to calm his critics. Whatever, the Buffaloes were tasting the heady wine of post-season bowl play for only the second time in history. This time the experience would be better.

Unlike the Ft. Worth-Dallas experience in 1937, this New Year's treat was everything it promised. Good weather, good entertainment, good quarters and good practices sent CU against Clemson ready to play. The Buffaloes wasted no time taking command. Both schools had been criticized as unworthy of their Orange Bowl invitations because of their imperfect records. They answered their detractors with one of the most exciting games in Orange Bowl history.

The game began as a rout. CU

Dal Ward with Orange Bowl trophy upon arrival back home in Boulder.

turned loose its tailback terrors, Stransky and Cook, against unsuspecting Clemson. The Buffs rolled to a quick 20-0 lead and would have made it a touchdown more had not third-string quarterback Bud Morley failed to sneak his way into the end zone after his pass to Clarke had moved the Buffaloes 40 yards to a first down at the three in the final two minutes of the half. But not to worry. The Buffs were in total command as they pranced into the dressing room at the half.

But a funny thing happened on the way to the trophy. Clemson awakened. With a roar. The Tigers came out furiously and before CU could get re-organized, went in front, 21-20 midway through the fourth quarter. Then the

Tigers got too greedy. After their third touchdown, they tried an onside kick. Not bad strategy. If they recovered - and the maneuver would be a surprise to CU - they'd be in great shape to move in for the clincher. But the kickoff went straight to CU sophomore guard John Wooten who covered it deftly. Now it was the Buffs who had field position. With the slender Dove driving for early yardage and Bayuk taking over inside the 15, the Buffs scored to win it, 27-21. Clemson came back for one last try to win but Stransky's interception - the CU All-American was as nifty on defense as on offense - secured the CU victory.

Now Ward was again the toast of the town. The state legislature hailed his efforts with an official proclamation. Fans sang his praises. The amazing 1956 campaign had seemingly pumped new life into his career. And 1957 looked even better. Where 1956 had begun with great concern, the talented sophomores from that squad would now be solid regulars for the next two years. The diversification of the offense would continue to improve the CU attack as the players got even better acquainted with the combination of single wing and winged T. In particular, the presence of the lanky Dowler, who was an adequate blocker and fine pass receiver in the single wing, and a good ballhandler, passer and runner from the T, and a great punter, guaranteed superb quarterbacking. His backup, Ralph Herbst, was much better than average, good enough to have been a fine starter but for Dowler's presence.

1957

1957 would be another offensive sideshow for the Buffs who would lead the nation in rushing with 3224 yards and rank second in total offense. The slippery senior, Stransky, would become the first CU back since White to top 1000 yards rushing, ranking second nationally with 1097 to become CU's third All-American (after White and Branby.) And yet there would be familiar frustrations for Ward. Only six points kept his team from a perfect record. His honeymoon would begin to deteriorate. He was only two years from his finish. Unfortunately for him, and for CU, the 1956 truce was only temporary. The slightest slips of his team would become major catastrophes in the eyes of his detractors.

An underdog in the 1957 opener at Washington, CU should have won but didn't. The Buffs reached the five-yard line twice in the fourth period but couldn't push it in and settled for a 6-6 tie. The Buffs then had to rally for a touchdown with 41 seconds left to nip Utah, 30-24, despite Stransky's runaway afternoon of 162 yards. Then a horrible break late in the game let Kansas nick the Buffs, 35-34. CU had battled back to lead 34-28 with five minutes remaining after falling behind 0-14 and 14-28 at the beginning of each half. Fullback George Adams moved into perfect position to intercept a desperation Jayhawker pass but deflected the ball to the KU receiver who ran 58 yards to the six. Kansas required three running plays to score and in so doing chewed up valuable time. In the final 30 seconds CU crossed midfield but was stopped by the gun. The excruciating defeat nullified three fourth quarter touchdowns: runs of 37 by Stransky and 90 by Dove plus a Dowler-Gary Nady 11-yard completion.

Two familiar punching bags were next and the Buffaloes wore them out, trampling Arizona 34-14 with Stransky scoring three times in the first half before sitting down, and obliterating Kansas State, 42-14. The Buffs nearly wore out the Manhattan scoreboard, rolling for 647 yards and 35 first

Howard Cook takes a pitchout from Boyd Dowler and follows Gene Worden in the start of a reverse which scored against Missouri in 1957.

Cook prepares to hand off as Sherm Pruit (67) blocks out two men.

Eddie Dove (11) takes the handoff as John Wooten (69) whirls to lead the interference.

Dove heads downfield.

The CU wingback is all alone as he nears the goal line.

Bob Stransky (20) follows the blocking of Bill Mondt (66) and Eddie Dove (11) for yardage which helped him win All-American honors in 1957.

career died in February. The beginning, however, gave no signs of the impending disaster as the Buffs breezed past K-State, 13-3; Kansas, 31-0; and Arizona, 65-12. Tailback Howard Cook tied a school record with 25 points in the annihilation of Arizona. The Buffs ripped out a school record 551 rushing

A pair of All-Americans, tailback Bob Stransky (1957) and guard John Wooten (1958) check an assignment before practice.

downs, both school records. The freakiest play of the season saw Stransky run down a speeding Wildcat runner and strip the ball from him into Gene Worden's possession. CU wound up with a first down after a 73-yard K-State gain. That third quarter play completely collapsed the Wildcats who were already trailing at the time, 21-0.

Now 3-1-1 and only three more points short of being perfect, the Buffs moved on to Oklahoma's Owen Stadium, dubbed the "Snake Pit" by Big Eight teams. But it was "Heartbreak Hole" for CU teams and the Sooner jinx held forth again. Stransky ran for a 40-yard score then hit Dowler with a great off-balance 6-yard TD throw to give the Buffs a 13-7 lead then had the Sooners on the ropes with a third-and-two at the OU seven later in the period. But the Sooners got help from their band, playing loudly in that end of the stadium. The Buffs couldn't hear Herbst's snap count and jumped offside. The threat died, and so did CU, as a 24-yard field goal by center Charlie Brown was blocked. OU then drove for a fourth-quarter score to win, 14-13.

Missouri again followed up by upsetting a flat CU team in the rain at Boulder, 9-6. The Tigers used a pair of familiar, and oft-criticized, Ward weapons - the quick kick and third down punt - to keep the Buffs in the hole all afternoon. A motion penalty cost CU a long pass completion to the Tiger 10 on the opening series and the Buffs failed to take advantage of an offense which outgained Missouri, 346-126. That sharp Tiger kicking game forced the Buffs to start from far upfield on every possession and completely frustrated

Ward's team.

Showing fine resiliency, the Buffaloes rallied to finish with a rush, stomping Colorado A&M, 20-0; Nebraska, 27-0; and Iowa State, 38-21. But the record was a disappointing 6-3-1, good only for a third-place Big Eight tie. Ward was in trouble again.

1958

1958 was a nightmare. The vaunted seniors, who had been brilliant for the preceding two seasons, almost to a man had disappointing finishes. The season was devastating and Ward's coaching

yards in that game. Then the defense stepped forward to hold Iowa State to 43 rushing yards in a 20-0 shutout. The stubby power runner Cook continued torrid against Nebraska, running 71 yards to set up a touchdown and passing 20 yards to Dowler for another as the Buffs overcame a 16-13 deficit to overhaul the Cornhuskers, 27-16.

Then it was Oklahoma weekend again and CU entered as an even choice

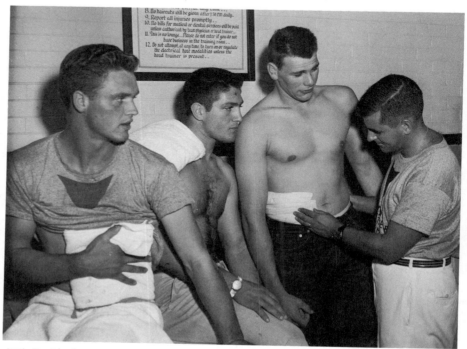

Jack Rockwell was a popular trainer for the Buffaloes in 1953-59. Here he checks (l-r) Bill Mondt, Bob Salerno and Jack Himelwright in 1958.

against a Sooner team which was still sound but not as strong as in previous years. The Buffs got off impressively as Dove returned a first period punt 40 yards to the 30 to set up a 7-0 lead. But the Sooners caught the Buffs slanting the wrong way and broke fullback Prentice Gautt 48 yards then took advantage of the newly-adopted 2-point conversion to take an 8-7 lead. Oklahoma then

ing a 420-160 margin in total offense. But the Buffs fumbled 12 times, losing seven to neutralize their statistical superiority. The Falcons won it on a Mike Rawlins interception and TD run with an intended CU screen pass from Dowler to Leroy Clark. Still, CU almost pulled it out in the final seconds, reaching the Air Force three. But reserve tailback Dave Garvin twisted

Sonny Grandelius at his first press conference following his appointment as CU coach in 1958.

out of bounds to stop the clock after what he thought was a first down on a fourth down carry. It wasn't. The Buffs were down in flames. So was Ward although it would be more than two months before he was dismissed.

Ironically, the 11-year veteran had assembled his finest freshman team headed by such future stars as Joe Romig, Gale Weidner and Jerry Hillebrand. Those rookies would lead CU to its first Big Eight title in three years. Unfortunately, Ward wouldn't be around to coach them. He was fired in late January. The decision was made by

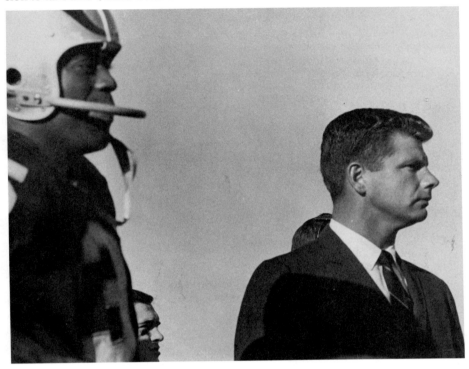

Sonny on the sideline with Teddy Woods.

used a time-consuming option game featuring a converted defensive end, Gene Calame, at quarterback to stifle CU's chances, 23-7. The script continued to be a carbon copy of previous seasons as Missouri erupted in the final 20 minutes for 33 points to erase a 9-0 CU lead and win, 33-9.

The Buffaloes collapsed after that one, winning only one of the final three games, a 7-0 mudfest at Utah. Colorado A&M lined Ward up against the wall with a come-from-behind 15-14 triumph in Boulder as vicious CU fans actually cheered for the Aggies in the final period. CU's play did nothing to aid their besieged leader. Air Force's yound Falcons, completing their first season of major college competition, supplied the firing squad for Ward as they hung on despite being pushed around most of the afternoon to win, 20-14. CU had an unbelievable statistical advantage in this game, out-first downing the Falcons, 26-5, and build-

Sonny's first CU coaching staff in 1958. *L-R, front,* Chuck Boerio, John Polonchek, Sonny, Frank Johnston, Bob Beattie; *back,* Ralph Herbst, John Mack, Buck Nystrom, Bob Popp, Bob Ghilotti.

79

the regents who, realizing his record didn't justify the act, explained only that the decision "was in the best interests of the university." The vote was 5-1. Athletic director Carlson was not consulted. Ward had no opportunity to plead his case. The act was totally unexpected because of its timing. The normal month for firing football coaches is early December. Ward's record was a highly respectable 62-41-6. More than that, he was a respected figure in the Big Eight. His teams had earned him that reputation.

Throw out his first two rebuilding years and he was 56-28-6. But no matter. He was gone. Ward remained as a professor of physical education, an almost menial postion for the man who had led CU into the Big Eight. Later he became an assistant to Bud Davis in 1962. When Eddie Crowder took over he continued to use the expertise of Ward and elevated him to assistant athletic director before his retirement in 1975. Ward remained in Boulder, finishing his life in great pain from a circulatory problem which necessitated amputation of several toes and ultimately of his lower leg. Worn down by his long battle with the circulation problem, he developed cancer and died soon after that diagnosis on February 15, 1983.

1959

Furiously — there was not much time before the start of spring drills — the search for a new coach began. And the names began to fly as the guessing game began. Terry Brennan, recently ousted at Notre Dame, and ex-Irish master, Frank Leahy, were early speculations. Former DU coach Bob Blackman, who was doing a fine job at Dartmouth, had support. But the CU search committee, limited to two men - Carlson and business professor Bill Stanton - because of the need for haste not committee entanglements was interested in a bright young face. The "now" generation was fast approaching. Delaware's Dave Nelson and a pair of young Michigan State assistants, Bill Yeoman and Sonny Grandelius, quickly surfaced as leading candidates. The name of Eddie Crowder, another bright young prospect on Wilkinson's Oklahoma staff, also received brief consideration. But he withdrew almost immediately, feeling correctly he would benefit by more experience under Wilkinson, who was acknowledged as the finest coach-

administrator in the nation. Crowder knew there would be ample opportunity for a good head job down the line.

The press bloodhounds soon exposed the committee's intentions. It would be Nelson, Yeoman or Grandelius. The first two were the top candidates. Grandelius was a long shot. But the personality, good looks and impressive playing and coaching background of the 29-year-old Grandelius ended the race almost before it began. He was exactly what CU was looking for: an excellently prepared young man who would be a great recruiter and, most all, a glamorous public figure.

GRANDELIUS

Grandelius' blitzkreig won him the job on February 9, 1959, just 17 days after Ward's firing. CU fans were elated. Grandelius was exactly the type coach they had wanted. Ward's quick kicks, third down punts, horse-and-buggy single wing would bug them no more. Now there'd be a total T-formation attack, lots of passing and gambling game plans. Not only that, Grandelius captivated everyone when he boldly announced in his opening press conference that his CU teams would beat Oklahoma, not come close. No other coach in CU history, especially the ultra-cautious Ward, had ever made such public proclamations. Still, there were many who wondered whether the good-looking, baby-faced Grandelius would deliver his promises. There may have been doubts in some quarters. But never in the mind of one

man. That man was Everett Grandelius, of Muskegon, Michigan and Michigan State. But everybody called him Sonny. That described Colorado's outlook, too. The cloud that covered the CU football picture lifted almost instantly despite a gloomy winter followed by almost torrential spring rains.

Sonny and his greatest star, Joe Romig.

The rains forced CU indoors for workouts in much of April. But Grandelius had a mission and there was no time to waste. When the stadium field was too soggy for the first Saturday scrimmage, he ordered the fieldhouse clay to be plowed and worked his team on the pavement-like surface. His practices were much more punishing than Ward's and the veterans couldn't believe the difference. But if this was the way the Big Ten did it, then it was the

Sonny Grandelius gets a ride off the field after his team's sensational win over Missouri in 1959.

Offensive line coach Buck Nystrom huddles with three top candidates in 1959. *L-R*, Bob McCullough, Jim Howell and Bill Eurich.

right way for CU.

Grandelius inherited basically an inexperienced team. Ward's 1958 crew had been almost exclusively a senior group. But his promising freshmen were there for Grandelius to use. Still, the prospects for 1959 were not bright. It would be a season of adjustment for both the sophomore players and the rookie coaches. And it would not be a vintage season. The Buffs slipped to 5-5-0 and a third place tie in the Big Eight. Still they were in the race for the Orange Bowl (which went to the runnerup that season), losing the bid in a tough 2-point loss at Nebraska in late November.

Grandelius immediately created an uproar among CU loyalists when he ordered black jerseys and silver headgear and pants for his team. Only a thin gold stripe, which barely could be seen from the stands, represented that traditional school color. The headgear included a modernistic buffalo horn which reminded many complainers of a racing stripe on one of the monster models coming out of Detroit's automobile plants. We're Buffaloes not Plymouths, lamented the old grads. No matter. But the Buffs wore black and, except for brief and unhappy switches to yellow then blue, have worn it from then on. Black, silver and gold would designate CU teams of the future. If nothing else, the new color combination would offer a greater contrast than the old silver and gold uniforms which had first been criticized so roundly by the Silver & Gold editorial in 1921. For the

record, no CU team, including Ward's, had been sartorially splendid up to that point. The addition of black was an improvement whether or not the traditionalists approved.

Grandelius didn't draw any soft touches in his first month at the helm. First came Washington, a team which would wind up a surprise participant in the Rose Bowl. CU unveiled a bright new backfield star that afternoon as sophomore quarterback Gale Weidner's passes and 95-yard interception touchdown were the chief bright spots

in a 21-12 loss. Weidner, recruited as a tailback by Ward, hit 11 of 19 passes. Despite playing 6-man football in high school at Troy, Montana, Weidner had impressed Grandelius quickly in the spring and would be Sonny's main man for three seasons.

A fine Baylor team had an even more impressive sophomore the following week. Ronnie Bull scored twice as the still punch-less Buffaloes bowed to the Bears, 15-7. Then came Grandelius' first confrontation with Wilkinson. Ward's longtime friend from Minneapolis days Wilkinson, happy not to be facing the annual CU single wing challenge, showed some mercy on Sonny. But not much. He called off his troops after they had built a 40-0 lead in three quarters. The final was 40-12, as Joe Dowler and Kirk Campbell got CU touchdowns against the Sooner reserves.

The Buffaloes were reeling. Captain Bob Salerno, Chuck Weiss, Jerry Steffen, Reed Johnson and Chuck McBride, all regulars, had gone down in September with injuries. Still Grandelius maintained an air of icy calm in his public appearances. His staff was near panic. One assistant even went so far as to suggest a "disaster plan" in which the Buffs would concentrate more on holding the score down than winning. Grandelius dismissed the suggestion with a snarl. He had another idea.

The Buffs finally got their first win, 20-17, at Kansas State. Once again,

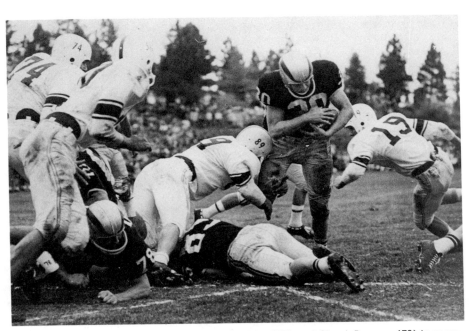

Chuck Weiss (30) drives over the blocks of Bill Elkins (85) and Chuck Pearson (78) to score the only touchdown in CU's first Big Eight victory over Oklahoma in 1959, 7-0.

Everybody called him "Snappy" and Floyd Walters shot more photos and movies of CU players and teams than any other photographer during a career which spanned almost half a century.

Weidner took charge, scoring two TDs, passing for the third plus a 2-point conversion. That benchmark passed, Sonny began devising a new offensive plan, a spread formation with Weidner at tailback. The Buffs had been unable to develop a running attack. Therefore, reasoned Sonny, he'd switch to a pure passing offense with only an occasional draw play interrupting Weidner's aerial barrage to a fleet of fine ends which included Jerry Hillebrand, Ken Blair, Gary Henson, Bill Elkins and McBride. After all, that's basically the way the pros played the game. Why not CU?

The new formation was still developing and the Buffs continued to operate out of the Winged-T. Iowa State delivered a 27-0 thrashing in Boulder, probably the most humiliating defeat in

Grandelius' meteoric but brief coaching career. The Cyclones did it with the single wing, pouring through the CU defense much as Ward's teams had done to opponents in the preceding years. Aware that he was supposed to improve upon Ward's offense, Grandelius was furious. His practices the following Monday and Tuesday made Bunny Oakes sessions look like a boy scout outing. Six CU players were dragged off the field with injuries. But the Buffs got the message: shape up or ship out. The Buffaloes shaped up and won four of the last five, narrowly missing the Orange Bowl bid and actually getting serious consideration for a new post-season game, the Gotham Bowl. Grandelius would have gone but CU officials said no.

NICKNAMES

Nicknames, once an important part of sports, are not as prominent, or colorful, as they once were. But CU football has had its share, some arriving in Boulder with their bearers, others being applied by teammates or publicists or the media and still others by seemingly innocent comments.

Probably the three most famous nicknames of CU gridders were Whizzer (White), Kayo (Lam) and The Beast (John Bayuk). A special word about each one's origination is appropriate. White got his from Denver Post sports writer Leonard Cahn, who spotted his obvious talents during a freshman game and reported to his editor that the young Buff was "really a whiz of a player."

Lam brought his with him. It came from the pugnacious little character in the Moon Mullins comic strip and described the feisty Wyomingite perfectly. Bayuk's was applied innocently by a little old lady who was an ardent Kansas fan. During a hot 1954 afternoon in Lawrence, the beefy Bayuk had pulverized a worn out KU team in the fourth quarter of a tight game. As the Buffs were awaiting their train to Boulder that evening, the woman came into the team's hotel lobby and asked CU publicist Fred Casotti "Could I see that beast who wears No. 30?" No publicist, not even CU's green rookie, could have passed that one up.

Those describing a players's lifestyle or background have been popular. There has been a Kamikaze (Tom Brookshier), Cactus (Ralph Curtis),

Sun Devil (John Wooten), Crazy Horse (Leroy Clark), Rocky (Martin), Iron Man (Bernie McCall) and Pearl Street Paul (Arendt).

Nicknames which describe a player's running style have been predominant. CU's gallery includes a Stop-and-Go (Bob Stransky) who was also a Traffic Light Tailback, Hot Rod (Homer Jenkins), Crazy Legs (Frank Cesarek), Earthquake (Ray Jenkins), Bullets (Horace Perkins), Steamroller (Otto Staab), Bunny (George Figner), Bronco (Don Hagin), Slick (Jim Haley), Roaring Twenty (Harry Narcisian) and Scooter (Eric Bieniemy).

Teammates can often be humorously cruel in applying nicknames. Some of these types include Bonzo (Ron Gray), Toad (Joe Romig), Baby Huey (Jerry Hillebrand), Fang (John Farler), Dippy (Don Evans), Hawk (Bill Horton), Flamingo (Bill Scribner), Pappy (Chuck Joslin), Cookie (Dick Knowlton), Rickets (Bill Lamont), Cyclops (Jim Perkins), Howdy Doody (Jim Raisis), Bones (Lamar Meyer), Treetops (Jerry McClurg), Tree (Jim Stander), Fireplug (Larry Plantz), Pinky (Dick Stapp) and Trash Compactor (Kyle Rappold).

One of the first, and most unusual, nicknames was hooked onto a player at the turn of the century, O.S. Fowler, who was known simply as "Spit."

For some reason, probably because CU teams have never been pass crazy, passers have been spared. Gale Weidner was "The Whip" and the fine combination of Polish players, Leo Stasica to John Pudlik, was

known as "Pole-toPole."

For the religious minded, there has been a Preacher (Carroll Hardy) and a Monk (Harold Saunders.) One to appeal to devotees of the quick lunch is Soupy (Jeff Campbell.) Royalty hasn't been in great prominence at CU. There was a Duke (Don Karnoscak) and a King (David Williams), a Kaiser (Walt Clay), and a Count (the chronicling Casotti.)

The best father-son combination? Easy. It's Steamer (Carl Stearns) and Bad Dude (John Stearns). And the most unusual way to acquire a nickname? No contest. Dick Robert, a freshman punting candidate in 1967, got a headgear without a facemask when he checked out his equipment. A manager slapped a piece of adhesive tape on the front of it with the words "HOOKS" on it to indicate that attachments for a facemask were still to be added. Frosh coach Dan Stavely assumed it was the newcomer's name (all freshmen are identified that way at early practices) and listed him on the roster as Hooks (first name unknown.) Robert was forever known as "Hooks" from that day on.

But nicknames haven't been the only unusual labels for CU footballers. Bull Stirrett, a fine quarterback in 1908, may have appeared to have had one. But a check of the records reveals that his proper name was William Bull Stirrett. And in the late 1950's there was a Robin Cherp. Then a Tom Catt.

So what's in a name? Or a nickname? Nearly anything you want it to be. Or, most of the time, what your teammates want it to be.

After the Iowa State debacle and the following week of terror, the Buffaloes went to Arizona to face one of their favorite "get-well" foes. Ward never lost to the Wildcats. Neither did Grandelius. CU breezed, 18-0. Now it was time to spring the surprise. Three key Big Eight games were next and the Orange Bowl bid was up for grabs. At 1-2, CU was still in the hunt. Three straight wins would win the prize.

Still Sonny sat on his new formation through the first three quarters against Missouri. The proud CU leader hated to give up on the Winged-T he had begun at Boulder. He had little choice when the time came. CU was dying, 20-6, entering the fourth quarter. Sonny gave his offense the word. His men responded. With Weidner deep, the Buffs began to move: 54 quick yards, three of them completed passes, the third to Hillebrand for a touchdown. When Weidner hit Nick Counter for a 2-point conversion, the Buffs sensed a victory. Weidner was up to the challenge, passing for 64 of the 69 yards which ended with his one-yard dive into the end zone. Then the new CU ace calmly held the ball for Counter's winning PAT. The 21-20 win got Sonny his first ride off the field on his players' shoulders and CU fans tore down the goal posts. Grandelius had made good, despite the fact that the victory brought CU's record to only 3-4-0. He'd shown the world he could adjust to adversity and come up with new strategies when the old ones failed. That was what everyone had needed to know. Sonny was good!

A solid Kansas team was next and the Jayhawkers suddenly had to prepare to stop two formations. Sonny's strategy kept them off balance as CU won, 27-14. When KU expected the Winged-T they got the spread and vice versa. Weidner wasn't as sharp as the previous week but Henson, Elkins and McBride were spectacular on the receiving end of his passes, each making sensational end zone catches. And when Weidner was shaken up in the fourth period, the clinching TD drive was engineered by reserve quarterback Frank Montera, who would be a reliable backup and sometime starter for the next three years.

But the critical Nebraska game on a bitter 19-degree day in Lincoln a week later was a 14-12 disappointment. The Buffaloes yielded two long first quarter touchdowns and could never recover despite dominating the last three periods. The Cornhuskers went to Miami and CU closed out the fall with a 15-7 win over Air Force as Weidner threw scoring passes to Weiss and Steffen and linebackers Joe Romig and Walt Klinker personally derailed a late Falcon threat which reached a first down at the CU eight before the two native Coloradoans stopped the march.

Though not impressive as a won-lost accomplishment, the 5-5-0 record was a noteworthy achivement for the youthful Grandelius. A much tougher taskmaster than Ward, he had imposed his disciplines successfully on his young team. The Buffaloes were on the road to the top. They had the right coach, the right young men and the right attitudes. Prosperity was about to return to CU. So were a lot of other things, not all good.

1960

But 1960 produced a temporary setback for Sonny. A mid-season outburst of injuries sent the Buffaloes, who had won five straight after an opening loss to Baylor, skidding to three losses in the last four games. It was almost an exact reversal of 1959's path. The beginning wasn't impressive. The Buffs got past midfield only once in bowing to Baylor at Waco, 26-0. Once again Grandelius went to the whip. His charges responded with four straight wins: pounding Kansas State, 27-7, and Arizona, 35-16 (there were those two favorite doormats again!); Iowa State, 21-6; and Nebraska, 19-6. The Buffs finally uncovered a breakaway threat who would be the main ground gun for the next two years in Teddy Woods, who broke up the Cornhusker game with a third quarter 96-yard kickoff return. CU had its WOW Boys (Weidner or Woods) to lead the way to an ultimate Orange Bowl. But not in 1960.

These four men were inducted into the Alumni C Club in 1959. *L-R,* Father Charles Forsythe, Gary Imig (accepting for his father Warner Imig), Father Pat Patterson and Floyd Walters.

First there was serious business in Boulder with Oklahoma. Grandelius made good on his promise to CU fans. With Romig prowling in awesome fashion behind a rock-ribbed defensive line, the Buffaloes blanked the Sooners, 7-0. Fullback Weiss was the big gun in this bruising defensive struggle, digging out 75 yards in 22 carries, including the game's only touchdown. The blond Minnesotan also came up with the game's biggest defensive play when he hauled down an in-the-open Sooner

---

CU's Conference Affiliations

CU has been a member of an intercollegiate athletic conference since 1893. During this time, the school has belonged to five different groups.

In 1893 the Colorado Inter-Collegiate Athletic Association was organized and the members were CU, Denver, Colorado College, Colorado Mines and Colorado A&M.

In 1909 four of the schools (Denver was not included) formed the Colorado Faculty Athletic Conference. A year later in 1910 the name was changed to Rocky Mountain Faculty Athletic Conference and Denver and Utah joined to make it a 6-team league. The conference was expanded steadily as follows: Utah State, 1914; Montana State, 1917; Brigham Young, 1918; Wyoming, 1921; Western State and Colorado Teachers, 1924.

In 1937 the larger schools (CU, DU, A&M, Wyoming, Utah, Utah State and BYU) formed the Mountain States Conference.

CU left this alliance in 1948 to join the Missouri Valley Intercollegiate Athletic Association (then the Big Six.) CU made it the Big Seven and Oklahoma State joined in 1960 to make it the Big Eight and that is now the official name of the conference.

halfback after a 69-yard chase deep into CU territory. His effort gave Romig and his mates a chance to brace. They did, stopping the Sooners at the four to preserve the victory.

CU fans had always felt that the reason for a loss to Missouri following an Oklahoma game was because of the letdown caused by a Sooner defeat. But this year's team proved it could do it after a victory as Missouri prevailed in Columbia, 16-6, handing the Buffaloes a solid trouncing. It didn't begin that way. CU scored right away on a 38-yard Weidner-Henson pass then came right back as Eddie Coleman intercepted a pass. But the Buffs stalled at the four and could never get going again as a rugged Missouri defense took control. The Tigers scored in each of the last three quarters to win going away. The Buffs lost guards Romig and Tom Wilscam and halfbacks Jerry Steffen and Dave Rife within a 2-week span beginning with that game. Their absence and a fleet of Kansas racehorses, one of them determined later to be ineligible, made life miserable for the Buffs at Lawrence, 34-6. The game was declared a forfeit in December but that was little consolation to Grandelius and his men who had absorbed their worst beating of the year.

The finish was disappointing. CU recoverd six fumbles against conference newcomer Oklahoma State but had to sweat out a 13-6 win then played dismally against Air Force to close 1960 with a 16-6 defeat.

Despite 1960's foldup at the finish, the 1961 outlook was excellent. The team had proven it could hold its own against all comers. The Buffs would field an all-veteran team. Eight starters would be 2-year lettermen. Of 38 lettermen the year before, 25 were due back, including three regulars, 10 from the second unit (remember, this was still 2-way football) and seven from the third team. There was experience and there was talent returning. The Buffaloes would be a solid contender for the Big Eight championship which had eluded CU in its first 13 years of competition in that conference. In contrast to previous seasons when Sonny publicly exuded confidence, he was tightlipped about this campaign. His former backfield mentor at Michigan State, Forrest Evashevski, now a highly successful head coach at Iowa, had given him this sound advice: talk up a weak team, play down a good one. And this was a very good team. Sonny was quiet

CU featured a fine foursome of fullbacks in 1961 in *(l-r)* Bill Harris, Loren Schweninger, Jim Raisis and Noble Milton.

Backfield coach John Polonchek huddles with his three quarterbacks in 1959: Frank Montera (11), Gale Weidner (10) and Joe Dowler (14).

The starting backfield for CU's 1961 Big Eight champions included *(l-r)* Ed Coleman, Loren Schweninger, Ted Woods and Gale Weidner.

in early September. His team would do his talking once the season began!

1961

The beginning of the 1961 campaign couldn't have been more sensational. In the season's opener against Oklahoma State in Boulder, the Buffaloes exploded for long touchdowns the first three times they touched the ball en route to a 24-0 triumph. First, Weidner hit Hillebrand for a 40-yard score. Woods ran back the next punt 82 yards, helped by a finishing block by Coleman. After OSU failed to gain, sophomore Leon Mavity twisted its punt back 60 yards, escaping four traps on the way. Just for kicks, in the second period Hillebrand drilled a 54-yard field goal, longest in Big Eight history and best in the nation that fall.

Could the Buffs top that opening day? They did the next Saturday. Subdued solidly for three quarters by an outstanding Kansas team and trailing 19-0 with 13:38 left, Weidner launched an aerial bombardment to produce a 20-19 comeback win in perhaps the most exciting CU triumph in Folsom Stadium history. Weidner rallied his troops with a 58-yard toss to Blair then followed up with another bulls-eye which Blair alertly snared after a deflection to go 48 yards and tighten the score to 19-14. The crowd was on fire now and so were the Buffs. Kansas tried to run off time but when Klinker nailed John Hadl for no gain on third-and-two at the KU 45 the Buffs got the ball back. Starting at its 21, CU began a steady drive, mixing up flat passes, draws and screen passes. Spotting a drawn-in secondary trying to stop CU's short game, Weidner threw deep to Hillebrand 17 yards away in the end zone. The big end missed the PAT but the TD was all they needed. CU had come off the deck with three touchdowns and an extra point in barely more than 11 minutes to score the winning points with 2:56 remaining. It was the highest of drama in the high country. The victories continued but the fireworks subsided. CU had to battle to win the next four games.

Hillebrand's fumble recovery late in the game followed two minutes later by his 37-yard field goal brought CU from behind over Miami, 9-7, as the big end from Iowa went quickly from goat to hero. His earlier missed PAT had the Buffs headed to defeat until his late heroics. A last-minute addition to the

Ed Coleman (46) runs to daylight in 1961 game against Air Force as Nick Graham (17) and Joe Romig (67) help.

All-American end Jerry Hillebrand hauls down a pass against Iowa State in 1961.

Fullback Loren Schweninger breaks open behind Ted Woods' block for big yardage in CU's dramatic 20-19 win over Kansas in 1961.

85

CU's 1961 Big Eight champions (L-R) Front row: Gale Weidner, Reed Johnson, Frank Montera, Ted Woods, Chuck McBride, Bob McCullough, Jerry Hillebrand, Jim Perkins, Joe Romig, John Denvir, Walt Klinker, Ken Vardell, Loren Schweninger. Second row, Jon Mars, Ken Blair, Roger Wissmiller, Chuck Morris, Bill Frank, Mike Bolan, Dale Christensen, Ralph Heck, Bill Bearss, Dan Grimm, Dick Harper, Ed Coleman. Third row, Pat Young, Jerry Watkins, Leon Mavity, Ted Somerville, John Lockwood, Kirk Osborn, Marty Harshbarger, Ronnie Jones, Pat White, Jim Raisis, Dave Young, Dave Vivian, Cliff Houk. Fourth row, Tony Stricker, Dean Lahr, Alan Cleavenger, Donne Pitman, Claude Crabb, Bob Bell, Frank Cesarek, Leroy Loudermilk, John Willman, John Meadows, Jerry McClurg, Mark Cohn, Pete Wahtera, Noble Milton. Fifth row, Lloyd Williams, Lee Akins, Jim Hold, Dick Mankowski, Tim Monczka, Mike Bennis, Albert Hollingsworth, Bill Harris, Boris Tabakoff, Gordon Swanson (Mgr), Art Ritchart (Mgr). Back row, Frank Johnston, Rollie Dotsch, John Polonchek, Buck Nystrom, Sonny Grandelius, Chuck Boerio, Bob Ghilotti, John Mack.

traveling squad, sophomore Bill Harris, scored both touchdowns in a 13-0 struggle at Kansas. The big hitter from Hackensack, New Jersey, who hadn't even traveled to Miami, became one of CU's top running threats the rest of the season. Mavity, and Jim Hold and fullback Loren Schweninger were the leaders of the Buffs second straight win over Oklahoma, 22-14, at Norman. Mavity scored CU's first touchdown on a twisting 39-yard run, Hold made a key recovery of a fourth quarter kickoff and Schweninger surged for two final period TDs.

Now it was time for a Big Eight showdown. But neither Kansas, the preseason favorite along with CU, or perennial champion Oklahoma was involved. Instead Missouri's Tigers, who had moved up sharply under the direction of Dan Devine and with every offensive play starting with a snap from a senior center named Bill McCartney, were the surprise mid-season challengers. The Boulder meeting would decide the championship.

This would be a clash of two physically-strong ball control teams. Devine's teams always featured a bruising defense. Grandelius by now had shelved the spread formation which had served CU so well, figuring his Buffs were strong enough to ram their Wing-T power through an enemy then field a defense strong enough to shut down any opponent. Privately, a CU coach felt so confident about the CU defense that he confided that one touchdown would win the game for the Buffs. CU got one early, Weidner hitting Harris for a 21-yard TD in the second quarter. If the assistant's prediction was accurate, the Buffs were on their way to Miami. But a second half combination of CU conservatism and a ferocious Tiger counter-attack made it a stemwinder. Mizzou scored with 6:14 left and went for two. But diminutive Reed Johnson batted the pass down and CU still led, 7-6. Missouri got the ball back and promptly came right back, reaching the CU 27. The clock stopped the drive as the Tigers were forced to try a long field goal as the game ended. It was long enough but off to the right.

Doubling the taste of victory was the fact that a national TV audience watched the game, the first national telecast ever from Boulder. Famed sportscaster Mel Allen called the play by play. CU wasn't exactly the New York Yankees but Allen did utter his trademark phrase, "How about that!" as he described the hectic finish. Now only games with weak Nebraska and Iowa State stood between CU and the championship. The title and bowl bid were practically a sure thing. Unfortunately, a so-so Utah team with a .500 record was preparing to upset the Buffaloes who spent most of the week reflecting on the Missouri win.

CU drove 80 yards after taking the opening kickoff, scored, had the TD nullified by a penalty and promptly scored again on the next play to take a speedy 6-0 lead. Hillebrand missed the kick but that didn't seem important at the time. Then for some reason, Grandelius, overconfident too soon, put in the second unit. Utah came back against the reserves and regained its poise. But CU's regulars couldn't recapture their opening effectiveness. The result was a resounding 21-12 upset. And it wasn't even that close. The Buffs trailed 21-6 before getting a consolation TD just before the end.

Its confidence shaken by that reversal, the Buffs met Nebraska in the sleet on a muddy Lincoln field. There would not be much scoring on this wretched afternoon. CU forged a smashing statistical triumph, outgaining Nebraska, 343-31 while rolling up 20 first downs.

Meanwhile, CU's defense held the Huskers without a first down. But the Buffaloes lost four fumbles to stop themselves each time they moved in for the kill. Schweninger gained exactly three times as much as the entire Nebraska team, 93 yards. In the end a modest 11-yard third quarter drive, begun by a fumble recovery by tackle Jim Perkins and ended by a one-yard Weidner sneak decided the game, 7-0. The Buffs then breezed past Iowa State, 34-0, as Harris scored three times, then finished the season with a 29-12 struggle past Air Force. Woods got the Buffs off and running in that one, speeding 42 yards on the first scrimmage play then returning the third quarter kickoff 55 yards to set up a pair of TDs.

The Buffaloes were in the Big Eight throne room and its partisans were delirious with joy once again. Before the team even began preparations for the Orange Bowl game, supporters gave Sonny a sleek white Cadillac, a fitting tribute for a handsome knight in shining armor. Step to one side, Galahad! Romig was well on his way to a Rhodes Scholarship after his second straight consensus All-American season. Hillebrand too, was an All-American. Klinker and Weidner were All-Big Eight selections. Aside from Utah's Redskins turning Folsom Stadium into another Little Big Horn, it had been a fabulous fall.

But the clouds of scandal had begun gathering over the Flatirons in late November. They were brushed aside as CU readied for its Miami meeting with Louisiana State. But they persisted. Area newspapers began hinting of an NCAA investigation and impending sanctions against the school. The smoke was too dense for there not to be a fire somewhere. Understandably, the ugly rumors distracted the Buffaloes not to mention Sonny.

Suddenly CU's outlook wasn't sunny. Still the Buffaloes went into battle against LSU as an even choice. Unlike 1956 however, CU's Orange Bowl excursion was filled with foreboding. Talk of an NCAA penalty would not die. Miami's weather didn't help either. The pre-game week was rainy and cold. Practices didn't go well. Wives and fellow-travelers, cooped up in their expensive Miami Beach hotel rooms fretted. Through it all, Sonny kept cool. After all, his team had proven it could perform under adverse conditions. An Orange Bowl victory would save the day.

These standouts played important roles in CU's 1961 championship season. *L-R*, Dan Grimm, Claude Crabb, Ralph Heck *(kneeling)*, John Denvir and Bill Frank.

This trio of fine CU backs huddles at the 1963 alumni game. *L-R*, Bill Symons, Ted Woods and Ben Howe.

Dal Ward returned to the coaching ranks in 1963 to lead CU's alumni team. He posed with three of the best players he recruited for CU. *L-R*, John Bayuk, Joe Romig and Jerry Hillebrand.

All-American guard Joe Romig is dwarfed by his CU tackle teammates (l-r) Dan Grimm, Bill Frank, Jim Perkins and John Denvir.

All-Big Eight center Walt Klinker was a CU stalwart in 1959-60-61.

Unfortunately, the game was an extension of the preceding month. For the first time in the history of the Orange Bowl, it rained. CU's fans were soaked and the Buffaloes were drenched 25-7 by Louisiana State as the CU attack was strangled by LSU's Chinese Bandits defense. The Buffs were outgained, 343-143, out-first downed, 19-7 and suffered a pair of blocked kicks for good measure. Only Schweninger's second period 59-yard interception TD averted a shutout. That burst gave CU a brief 7-5 lead which changed to an 11-7 deficit by the half and to 25-7 by the end of the third quarter. LSU reserves played much of the fourth. Weidner's vaunted passing arm showed only its durability that day. The CU star set an Orange Bowl record with 36 attempts. Unfortunately, he completed only 11 for a skimpy 98 yards.

CU's disintegration was as total as it was unexpected. Now the post-game discussions quickly got back to the NCAA problems. Suddenly, Sonny was suspect. Was he a white knight or just another get-rich-quick opportunist who had short-cut his way to the top. There was little talk about the 9-2-0 season and CU's first Big Eight title and the host of returnees who would again make the Buffaloes a force in 1962.

Instead, all speculation centered on the NCAA decision which would be forthcoming the following spring: the wheels of NCAA justice grind slowly and, most of the time, mercilessly. The continuing rumors no longer mentioned the possibility of a penalty. Instead, they concentrated on how tough the sanctions would be.

1962

Before that happened, however, CU's regents came up with a decision of their own. They ordered CU's administration to launch its own investigation. CU's president, Quigg Newton, who had been a productive but controversial young Denver mayor with an Ivy League background, turned the request over to private investigators. There were easily-proven cases of illegal payments to players to cover personal expenses, travel to and from homes during holidays and other incidental expenses. Perhaps insignificant monetarily, but nevertheless wrong. CU coaches and a Boulder druggist had established a collection site near the campus. The results of the official investigation were never made public. The sins of Sonny and his staff probably were not as serious as the rumors indicated. But there were

Sophomore John Meadows goes high to spear a pass against Louisiana State in the 1962 Orange Bowl.

goat. It wasn't a pleasant time for the CU president. He would call it quits to move to an eastern-based educational foundation in little more than a year.

But for now, Grandelius was gone and the line quickly formed for his job. The good news for the new coach would be a fine returning nucleus of talented players. The bad news was that spring practice was only two weeks away. The sinister news was that almost certainly there would be NCAA disqualifications of players involved in the violations and there would undoubtedly be underclassmen in this group.

As for Sonny, he joined the Philadelphia Eagles staff then switched to the Detroit Lions where he came close to getting the head job then left football to begin a career in the Detroit business world in addition to becoming a color analyst for Detroit radio and television stations. He re-surfaced briefly on the CU scene in 1967 when he did the color for a national radio network

enough violations to produce a stiff NCAA penalty. The CU regents decided to jump the gun on the NCAA and possibly ease the penalty by their advance actions.

On March 17, 1962, Grandelius was fired by a 5-1 vote. Ironically, it was the same margin as the one which had confirmed him. And it was exactly the same regential tally which had ousted Ward three years earlier.

It was an historic decision. College coaches are fired for losing. Grandelius had won a championship. The Cadillac proved how everyone felt. Many CU fans stood by him. He'd proven he was a good coach. Nobody else had reached the heights he had. But he was gone, just as quickly as he had come. Sonny rode off to the east in his white Cadillac, not to return to Boulder until a special reunion for his team which was one of the highlights of the centennial season celebration. Unfortunately, most football fans demand only results and do not seriously question the means of obtaining them. Unfairly, Newton was criticized for his role in the Grandelius affair. It was a no-win situation for the CU president. His detractors came at him from several directions: (1) he had permitted the cheating to develop through poor controls or (2) he had permitted a university investigation to supersede the NCAA findings or (3) he was a party to making Sonny the scape-

Gale Weidner was noted primarily as a passer but he could run, too. Here he scores against Kansas State in 1960.

Ted Woods was CU's power back in 1960-61. He heads to the end zone against Air Force in 1961.

which broadcast the 1967 Bluebonnet Bowl game between CU and Miami.

DAVIS

The time factor meant that a new coach would have to be in place by April 1. There was no time for a search. Besides, any possible nominees might be reluctant to sign on with a school which had fired a coach after a championship season. A logical move would be to hire someone currently on the campus. Or just off it. Grandelius' end coach, Bob Ghilotti, was an immediate nominee. He was a popular member of the staff, quiet with a low profile but a producer of fine ends. And he was interested. Line coaches Chuck Boerio and Buck Nystrom, extremely competent coaches, were aligned with Ghilotti. But the regents ruled that there was enough guilt to cover the entire Grandelius staff and none would be considered for the job. The void continued. Suddenly in a desperate move, William "Bud" Davis, CU's alumni relations director and a former outstanding high school coach, was appointed with the unstated qualification that he would be a temporary coach to guide the Buffs through the 1962 season while the CU authorities selected a permanent coach. Or, if he performed a miracle, he would continue on the job.

There was strong resistance from all quarters. Even though he had won state prep championships in South Dakota and Colorado before returning to his alma mater, Davis wasn't considered qualified because he had been only a marginal collegiate gridder and had never coached at the college level. Captain-elect Blair told CU's authorities, "You've got a coach, now get yourself a team." But the threat of mutiny never developed. Davis then compounded his problems by hiring a staff of mostly coaches with high school backgrounds. Exceptions were Dal Ward, Davis' old coach who returned to the ranks as a defensive assistant, and Ed Farhat and Don Stimack, two Grandelius appointments made after the 1961 season and before the firing. But these men had come out of the high school ranks, too.

The NCAA decision was handed down in March. Graduation had taken a big enough toll on the Buffaloes. Thirteen 3-year veterans were gone via this route. The NCAA edict came out in April: CU would be on probation for two years with no television or bowl

A pair of brilliant sophomores played key roles in CU's 1961 Big Eight championship season. Bill Harris (33) runs through a big hole as Ted Somerville (41) blocks. Ralph Heck (51) cleared the other side.

End Ken Blair races toward the end zone with the first of his two fourth-quarter touchdown receptions against Kansas in 1961.

This group of outstanding CU exes got together at the 1963 alumni game. *L-R*, Ken Blair, Boyd Dowler, Joe Romig, Jim Perkins, Gale Weidner, Don Branby, Bob McCullough and Mel Semenko.

HOW THE BUFFALOES GOT THEIR NAME

Until 1934, CU teams were given a legion of labels, none of them sticking. The nicknames came in all sizes, colors and species. Most were favorable, some were not and some were almost silly. Here are a few which failed to pass the test of time:

Tea Sippers (in the early days, apparently there were those who considered CU a highbrow school for the sophisticated drinker); Silver & Gold (for the colors but too unwieldy); Silver Helmets (too closely identified with football); Eagles, Elks, Moose (all state natives but too closely linked with fraternal orders); Yellowjackets, Greyhounds, Silvertips (for uniform colors); Hornets (for Yellow-jackets); Arapahoes (for the regional Indian tribe), Sour Doughs, Fifty-Niners (for the state's mining tradition); Big Horns, Grizzlies (for more native animals); and Fron-tiersmen (the eastern press liked to use this one, undoubtedly because they considered Colorado to still be unmapped territory.)

A contest by the Silver & Gold student newspaper in 1926 came up with "Wolves" but that didn't stick, either, and it was quietly abandoned without objection. Finally, in 1934, an energetic campus sports editor, Bill Bartleson, launched what would be a successful effort. Undoubtedly, the optimism which enveloped the CU football team as the season approached supplied the stimulus because the response was impressive. More than 1000 people responded with suggestions. Duplications and eliminations reduced the list of names to 400. Included were such varied titles as Puddle Jumpers (for the train which connected Boulder and Denver), Submarines and Tanks (even though the nation was between world wars), Boulders (obvious to anyone who ever tried to plant a lawn in Boulder), Spartans (settling Colorado did require a lot of toughness), Eaglets (this one was quickly eliminated), Zephyrs (for mountain breezes), Chinooks (for mountain-spawned tempests) and Flatirons (obvious).

Bartleson and fellow scribe, Ken Bundy, athletic director Carlson and graduate manager of athletics Walter Franklin burrowed through the nominations. Despite some objections to the use of an animal to represent athletic teams from a small but vocal faction of animal lovers who probably didn't love football, the selection committee chose "Buffaloes." The winning bid was submitted by Andrew Dickson, a printer at the Boulder Daily Camera newspaper whose name was plucked out of a hat which also contained those of Claude Bates of New Madrid, Missori and James Proffit of Cincinnati, Ohio, who had also suggested "Buffaloes."

The committee's reasoning was that the Buffaloe was a Colorado native, courageous, powerful and intelligent - everything a football player ought to be. Football, obviously, then as later, occupied center stage for CU fans. Certainly, basketball players, tracksters, baseballers and the other sports participants required none of the physical attributes of a buffalo. Be that as it may, the nickname was unveiled at Homecoming and from that day on (November 10, 1934) would forever be CU's official athletic designation. And that selection meant there would be formidable mascots to come.

It also meant there would be several variations of the theme: Stampeding Herd and Golden Avalanche early on, then Golden Buffaloes and Thundering Herd in later times. Whatever, the mighty symbol of the high plains reigns supreme on CU's athletic scene. And what would CU name its massive mascots in future seasons? A name to strike even more fear into foes? Not on your life. More than 30 years later, in 1966, the official school animal got an unofficial but permanent name. CU's rumbling representatives would be known as "Ralphie."

Bud Davis in his first pose as CU's head coach in 1962.

Bud Davis and his 1962 captain, end Ken Blair.

appearances during that time. More importantly, the NCAA named 21 players, 12 of them seniors, as recipients of illegal financial aid. Because the NCAA did not take away eligibility, decreeing that the two years' probation was a sufficient penalty and easing up the punishment because CU had fired the coaching staff and aided in uncovering additional violations.

So the nine underclassmen named participated in spring practice. The squad Davis inherited wasn't all that bad. But within a month following the end of spring drills, the Big Eight ruled all nine men ineligible for 1962 competition and furthermore counted that year against their eligibility. Since eight of the nine were juniors that meant the end of their collegiate careers. Davis' staff, unfamiliar with eligibility rules, failed to enroll five other athletes in summer school to make up deficiencies. When the carnage was complete, only six of 35 men who had lettered in 1961 - Leon Mavity, Bill Harris, Ted Somerville, Dan Grimm, Dale Christensen and Nick Graham were eligible in 1962.

The less said about 1962 the better. The Buffaloes tried hard early in the year but were too thin to maintain a 60-minute effort. Second-half collapses were the order of the day in the first part of the season and 60-minute ones followed. The defense was horrible. CU's opponents scored 346 points and

gained 3862 yards, both negative records for a CU team. The Buffaloes kept their hopes alive for two weeks, extending Utah in a 37-21 loss then blanking equally-hapless Kansas State, a school with a long history of hopelessness, 6-0 behind a record 35 carries (for 156 yards) by Harris. Even then, the Buffaloes had to repel three fourth-quarter deep penetrations by the Wildcats to preserve the victory. Then the dam broke.

CU's next seven foes were Big Eight teams and their coaches showed no mercy, possibly because CU may have established a dangerous precedent: firing winning coaches for sinning. Regardless, the Buffaloes were overwhelmed by Kansas (35-8), Oklahoma State (36-16), Iowa State (57-19), Nebraska (31-6), Oklahoma (62-0) and Missouri (57-0). By now CU was negotiating terms for Davis' resignation at the end of the season. And Davis, who had entered the campaign so optimistically, was ready to step aside. He became Dean of men in a wise step which opened the door to a new career in education as he became president of Idaho State, then New Mexico, then head of the Oregon system of higher education, and then Louisiana State Chancellor.

But there was still non-conference business left in the season and the Buffa-

loes made a last-gasp effort. Previously winless Texas Tech had used a length-of-the-field interception to edge the Buffaloes on a snowy afternoon in Lubbock, 21-12. Davis revealed his resignation to his squad on the eve of the Air Force finale. The Buffaloes rallied to give their coach an honorable exit, hammering Air Force, 34-10, driving 80 yards with the opening kickoff then setting up another quick touchdown by recovering a Falcon fumble to take a 14-0 lead. When the Falcons threatened

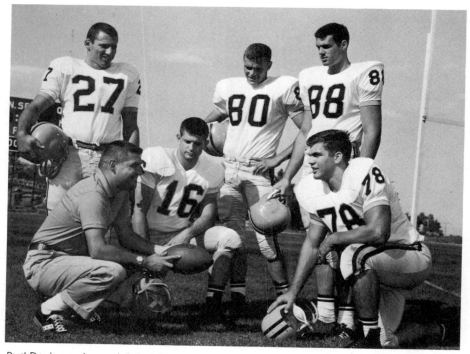

Bud Davis greets a quintet of Illinois athletes during picture day in 1962. *L-R,* Leon Mavity (27), Frank Cesarek (16), Roger Wissmiller (80), John McGuire (88) and Dale Christensen (78).

to come back, Bill Symons promptly lugged a third quarter kickoff 79 yards and Mavity returned an interception seven yards to the end zone. Celebrating CU players hauled Davis off the field and into his new career.

Once again, CU searched for a new coach. This time there would only be complete chaos to greet the new man. The program was in shambles. There was a Dal Ward faction still disgruntled over his firing. And a similar group who resented the Grandelius axing. Plus even a small contingent of understanding alums who felt that Davis should have been given at least another year. But the three men were gone and CU was picking up the tab. Ward and Davis were still on payroll in non-athletic capacities and Grandelius was still collecting his year's salary settlement. Colorado didn't have a coach. But the school had three ex-coaches on payroll.

CROWDER
1963
This time there was no contest. Eddie Crowder, who had withdrawn from the race in 1959, was a unanimous choice as athletic director Carlson finally was permitted to make a unilateral decision. Carlson was a great admirer of Bud Wilkinson through his athletic director associations with the Oklahoma AD-coach. Crowder's brilliant playing career plus experience under Wilkinson and Army's legendary Red Blaik were more than enough credentials for the job. Whether he could heal the wounds was another matter. He was named on January 2, 1963. Crowder faced a tremendously difficult challenge: bringing the factions together, rebuilding morale and, most

Assistant Coach Phil Cantwell checks in with three of CU's top receivers in 1962 (l-r) John Meadows, Stan Irvine and John McGuire.

importantly, finding some football players - legally! The prematurely balding 32-year old with the hyper-active mind was up to the assignment.

Crowder promised no miracles and delivered none. It would have taken one to win his debut. The Buffaloes were matched against Southern California's defending national champions in Boulder. It was like a dive by a novice swimmer from a 10-meter platform. But Eddie had run a rough spring camp. His Buffaloes were lean and mean if not overly talented. He got a break when a rainy week prevented CU grounds-

keepers from mowing the grass short. Or maybe his chief assistant, Rudy Feldman, who was in charge of overseeing details like that, wanted it that way. Certainly USC's fleet of great backs, led by eventual Heisman Trophy winner Mike Garrett, wouldn't be helped by an off track. At any rate, the Buffaloes hung on for their lives and escaped with honor bowing, 14-0. USC's volatile coach John McKay was properly infuriated at the result and, in particular, the height of the grass. No matter. Crowder had gotten through the opener relatively unscathed. After that came a 41-6 flog-

One of the few bright spots during the 1962 season was the performance of the CU pompom girls.

The 1962 cheerleaders form a pretty frame around Bill Harris (33) and Leon Mavity (27) at picture day.

ging from Oregon State before Crowder took advantage of an old CU ally to win his first game at Kansas State, 21-7. The Buffs made it two straight with a 25-0 shutout of Oklahoma State before the home crowd. But then came six straight losses, four of them shellackings: 19-7 to Iowa State, 41-6 to Nebraska, 35-0 to Oklahoma in Crowder's first meeting with his former mentor, 28-7 to Missouri, and 43-14 to Kansas.

The finale was delayed a week because of the assassination of President Kennedy and CU dropped a bitter 17-14 decision to the Falcons when quarterback Frank Cesarek fumbled the snap over the center's head and straight into the arms of a surprised Air Force middle linebacker to destroy a closing CU drive which had reached the Falcon 34. The 1963 record, 2-8-0, wasn't any better than Davis'. But Crowder was on

his coaching honeymoon and honeymoons are nearly always pleasant affairs.

1964

The 1964 record was the same: 2-8-0. But the Buffaloes were starting to benefit from a Crowder trademark, excellent recruiting, and his team was now highly competitive. Six of the eight losses were by a touchdown or less. CU lost the opener to USC in Los Angeles, 21-0, as quarterback Dan Kelly broke his arm making a tackle. Hale Irwin had previously been moved to safety so Kelly's injury opened the door for still another rookie, Bernie McCall. McCall was one of the most durable QBs in CU history, taking repeated poundings from superior opponents as he ran Crowder's option offense. McCall had

Leon Mavity scoots into the end zone as the 1962 Buffaloes upset Air Force 34-10 in Bud Davis' final game.

A well-groomed Eddie Crowder worked the sideline in 1964.

The press grills Eddie at picture day in 1965. *L-R,* Frank Haraway (Denver Post), Chet Nelson (Rocky Mountain News), Howard Baxter (Boulder Camera), Crowder, Dennis Hutchinson and Lu Monroe (Boulder Camera).

Eddie Crowder inherited three fine running backs in 1963 *(l-r)* Leon Mavity, Bill Harris and Bill Symons.

Eddie greets his 1965 squad at picture day.

prepped at tiny Yuma in northeastern Colorado but he became a solid performer for the next three seasons. After a 41-6 pounding at Oregon State, the Buffs were nicked by Kansas State (16-14), Oklahoma State (14-10), edged Iowa State (14-7), then got back on the wrong side of the score again, bowing to

Nebraska (21-3), Oklahoma (14-11), Missouri (16-7) and Kansas (10-7). But the Buffs, competitive in every game to the end, finished on a high note dazzling Air Force with 292 yards of kick returns including a 54-yard punt runback by Ted Somerville and a 91-yard kickoff return by Bill Symons to outpoint the Falcons, 28-23.

1965

Within two seasons, Crowder had returned the Buffaloes to respectability. What probably was the finest crop of sophomores in his 11-year tenure brightened the 1965 outlook. It was a very good year. The Buffalo rookies were as good as expected. From the opening whistle of a 0-0 tie at Wisconsin they performed like veterans. The Badgers weren't exactly a Big Ten dynasty but they were a solid favorite over the young Buffs. Some clutch punting by Dick Anderson got CU out of early trouble and the Buffs actually dominated the last 20 minutes of the half. But Wisconsin took command after the intermission and it took two interceptions by Dennis Drummond and another by Anderson to save the tie. The Buffaloes weren't good enough yet to play erratically and still dominate a heavy underdog. That's how it went against little Fresno State and CU needed a break when a penalty nullified an apparent Bulldog first down deep in Buffalo country in the game's waning moments. CU's win was by a nailbiting 9-7. The penalty prevented an almost certain Fresno field goal which would have tripped the Buffs.

They learned their lesson and put away their next two opponents efficiently, blanking Kansas State, 36-0, with a 30-point second half, then using a 76-yard touchdown sprint by William Harris to dump Oklahoma State, 34-11. But the Buffs almost stumbled against Iowa State, requiring a shoestring disputed catch by George Lewark which set up Frank Rogers' 33-yard field goal with 10 seconds remaining to

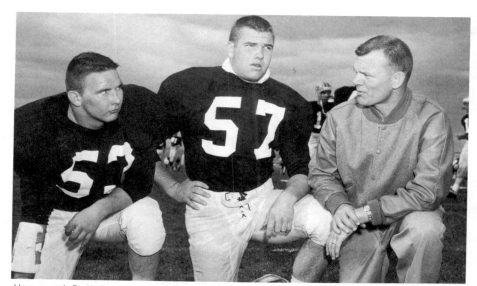

Line coach Rudy Feldman had a pair of aces in Larry Ferraro (53) and Steve Sidwell (57) in 1963.

Assistant Chet Franklin checked out three top end candidates in 1964 (l-r) Tad Polumbus, Bill Fairband and Sam Harris.

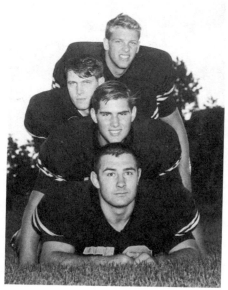

This hefty stack of tackles anchored the CU line in 1964. *Top to bottom,* Stan Irvine, Jerry McClurg, Bill Sabatino and Richard Redd.

Manning the middle defense for the Buffaloes in 1964 were guards Jack Parmater, Tom Kresnak and Dick Mankowski.

96

get a 10-10 tie with the Cyclones. CU's hopes at Nebraska were dashed by a demoralizing 95-yard touchdown pass by the Cornhuskers on a third-and-long gamble with CU trailing by only 10-6 in the first quarter. That killer collapsed CU as Nebraska went on to win easily, 38-13.

Freshman coach Dan Stavely posed with two top rookies in 1964 Wilmer Cooks (33) and William Harris (43).

Gomer Jones had replaced Wilkinson at Oklahoma and the Sooners had slipped back to the rest of the pack. Safety Hale Irwin, who would later gain fame as a golfer with a pair of U.S. National Open victories, supplied three key plays to lead a 13-0 CU win at Norman. Eastes Banks scored a TD and Rogers booted two field goals but it was Irwin's two interceptions plus a big tackle at the goal line as the half ended which kept the Buffaloes alive despite OU's statistical superiority. Any illusion the 3-1-1 Buffs had about moving up from last to first in a single season were ended by a 20-7 setback by Missouri. The Tigers had the best quarterback in the league, Gary Lane, and his running and passing were too much for the Buffaloes.

McCall showed he belonged with the best the next week in a 21-14 win over Kansas, setting up the first TD with a 20-yard keeper then passing for the other two, both to Lewark on 31 and 28-yarders. In the now-traditional season closer with Air Force, the Buffaloes got 12 points from handyman Rogers, the Big Eight's leading scorer that fall, on a pair of field goals plus a 58-yard TD reception from McCall. The 6-2-2 record was the best since the 1961 championship season. CU, after three straight years on the bottom, had moved all the way up to third place. If there were ever any doubts that Crowder wasn't the right man they were

Bernie McCall, the starting quarterback in 1964-5-6, takes aim against Oklahoma State.

Bill Fairband convoys Ted Somerville on a 54-yard punt return against Air Force in 1964.

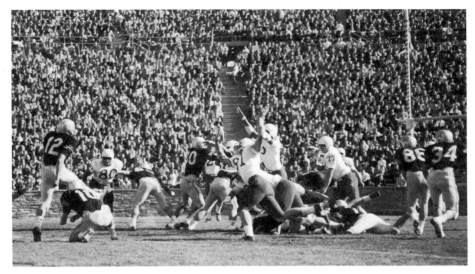

Frank Rogers kicks a field goal out of Hale Irwin's hold in 1964 against Nebraska.

Eddie Crowder with two ex-Lakewood high aces, George Lewark (40) and Kirk Tracy (65) in 1965.

Pueblo contributed three top hands in 1965. Grad assistant Loren Schweninger (also from that city) is shown with Dick Taylor (84), Ray LeMasters (88) and Rich Redd (79).

Middle guard Ron Scott (68) buries a Fresno State runner with the help of Sam Harris (80) in 1965.

long gone by the end of 1965. And the slender ex-Sooner was just getting started.

1966

The Buffaloes came ever so close to a vintage season in 1966. Only five points separated the Buffs from a perfect Big Eight record: the only two losses were to Oklahoma State (11-10) and Nebraska (21-19). CU raced past the other five conference foes by an average of more than two TDs. 30 lettermen were back. Only three rookies, defensive back Steve Tracy, tackle Mike Montler and end Mike Schnitker, figured to crack the top 22. All three were

blue-chippers. That's the way Crowder's staff was recruiting.

But first came a dose of humility. The Buffs sputtered in the home opener and were upset 24-3 by Miami, not a particularly highly regarded foe. The Buffaloes then had to rebound at Baylor against a team which had shocked nationally-ranked Syracuse in its previous game. CU's defense shackled Baylor quarterback Terry Southall as ends Bill Fairband and Schnitker harassed the Bears' ace passer all night long. Big fullback Wilmer Cooks, as good a short yardage fullback as any who ever played for CU, bent the Baylor line for 73 yards and a touchdown and slotback John Farler quick-stepped 23 yards for another in a tense 13-7 victory. The game-saving play came from reserve linebacker Steve Graves whose diving end zone interception stopped a Baylor bid in the final minute of play. Cooks and Farler continued their power running in a 10-0 win over Kansas State. The defensive play of the game was a diving interception by Schnitker to stop the Wildcats' most serious threat of the afternoon.

At Oklahoma State the Buffaloes stumbled and lost 11-10 when the Cowboys punctured a CU prevent defense to drive 69 yards in the closing minutes then won it with a 2-point conversion. At this point the Buffaloes needed an offensive shot in the arm. They'd averaged less than 10 points in each of the first four games and were a

disappointing 2-2-0. They got it from a brittle speedster, Dan Kelly, who had broken an arm then a foot to miss most of the previous two seasons. Crowder liked his quickness and gave him a shot at Iowa State. Kelly responded sensationally, squirting for 156 yards and three TDs as he ran the option flawlessly. His passing was just as impressive. He threw for 86 yards. That fiery performance left Iowa State in a 41-21 shambles. And his return to action gave Crowder a solid one-two punch at quarterback with Kelly and McCall and an outstanding inside-outside combination with Cooks.

Mike Schnitker won the Lee Willard Award, presented by the former CU star, as the outstanding freshman in 1965. *Photo in background shows John Wooten in action.*

But if Dal Ward had had an Oklahoma problem in the 1950's, Crowder developed an even bigger monster in Nebraska. In 11 starts against the Cornhuskers, he won only once. And it wasn't in 1966 although it should have been. With Kelly and Cooks having their own way, the Buffs forged a 19-6 lead with 13 minutes left. After stopping a Husker drive at the goal line the Buffs quickly got out of trouble when Kelly broke loose for 15 yards on a keeper. But CU stalled and had to punt, then went into a prevent defense to keep Nebraska's strong-armed Bob Churchich from hitting a bomb. Churchich never tried. Instead, he threw beneath the back-pedaling CU secondary repeatedly to take the Cornhuskers to two late touchdowns and a 21-19 triumph. CU could have iced the game long before the Husker rally, but Bill Fairband couldn't hang on to an easy interception as he stepped in front of a flat pass with no one between him and the goal. It was too easy. He took his eyes off the ball and dropped it. That was all Nebraska needed. It was crying time again in Boulder.

Now the Buffaloes got an unusual break of their own to nip an explosive Oklahoma team, 24-21. The Sooners had detonated three long touchdown runs to lead the stronger but slower Buffs, 21-17, midway through the fourth quarter. Sooner coach Chuck Fairbanks, ever the meticulous master of detail, carried not only a punting specialist but a deep-snapping center specialist for punting situations. The two specialists came out to kick the Buffaloes into a hole from which they couldn't recover. But the snap went high over the kicker's head. Dick And-

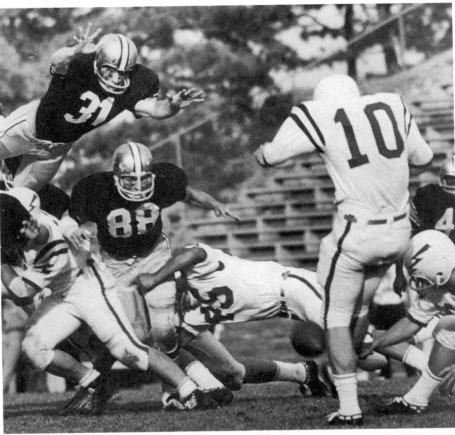

Dick Anderson (31) flies high to block an Air Force field goal try and preserve CU's 10-9 victory in 1966. Tackle Larry Donley (74) and end Mike Schnitker (88) pour through, too, as Charles Greer (45) protects against a fake.

erson covered it at the Sooner 18 and Cooks bulled into the end zone three plays later for the winning TD. CU breezed the next two times out. Isaac Howard's 99-yard interception return broke up a tight game as the Buffaloes whipped Missouri in Columbia for the first time since 1930, 26-0. Kelly was shelved with another broken bone, this one in his hand, so McCall stepped in

and total-offense for 201 yards in a 35-18 decision at Kansas.

An expected breeze against Air Force turned into a 10-9 thriller as the Buffs needed big plays both ways then breaks to pull it out late. Schnitker and Anderson blocked a Falcon field goal try which would have meant the winning points. Then a quick whistle cancelled an Air Force fumble recovery at

John Farler boots the winning field goal out of Bernie McCall's hold in the 10-9 win over Air Force in 1966.

Speedy Dan Kelly's run-pass options sparked CU's offense in 1966.

The CU co-captains in 1966 were a pair of standouts, Hale Irwin (10) and John Beard (60).

snared his first of many Anderson TD passes for a 35-yard score to trigger a 34-0 rout of Iowa State as Charlie Greer, CU's top punt returner, ran one back after several near misses in earlier games. Crowder's finest crew to that date was now ready to enter the heart of the Big Eight schedule with the four toughest teams coming up on consecutive weekends. Muscular Missouri was first and, for a change, CU won the physical battle, completely dominating the Tigers and preventing them from starting a scrimmage play beyond midfield until their last possession. Missouri jolted the Buffs with a 75-yard breakaway on the third play of the game before the CU defense took command in a 23-9 triumph. CU's domination was shown by a 20-5 advantage in first downs and 309-149 in total offense.

Again in the next game, the CU defense provided the impetus for a rare victory at Lincoln, 21-16, despite being shoved around all day by a Nebraska offense which netted 402 yards to CU's 182. But the CU secondary made the difference as Dick Anderson and Mike Veeder collaborated on an interception and lateral for a 50-yard TD late in the first half and Jeff Raymond applied the clincher with a 76-yard interception runback in the fourth quarter. In between, Anderson blocked an extra point to maintain an early CU lead.

The CU season had, by now, turned into a full-fledged fall festival. The Buffaloes were 5-0 and ranked third in the nation. Eddie Crowder's team was the talk of the country. Boulder's bartend-

their 41 to apparently kill CU's last chance. Given new life the Buffaloes drove to the Falcon 17 where the gritty Farler pounded a 34-yard field goal just over the upright.

The 7-3-0 season moved the Buffaloes to second place in the Big Eight. They were considered for a Sun Bowl berth but turned it down. The staggering finish against Air Force had dulled the enthusiasm for a post-season game. Without the dynamic little Kelly the CU attack was uncertain.

And now those splendid sophomores of 1965 were seniors. They'd brought CU back from oblivion. The workhorse McCall was gone. But waiting in the wings was a young quarterback whose prep achievements at Boulder high had CU coaches and fans quivering with anticipation. Would he be as good as advertised? Bobby Anderson was. No CU quarterback, before or after, would have more impact on the Buffalo program.

1967

Any doubts about Dick Anderson's younger brother were quickly dispelled in the 1967 opener against Baylor. Bobby Anderson merely ran for 83 yards, completed 11 (of 21) passes for 129 more, and scored three touchdowns. A pair of classmates, Kerry Mottl and Frank Bosch, anchored the defense along with junior Rocky Mar-

tin. Mottl's two interceptions were especially instrumental in the 27-7 victory. At Oregon a week later, the other half of the Anderson tandem took over as Dick got two of six CU interceptions to help secure a 17-13 chiller. Bobby didn't exactly take a back seat, bolting 18 yards for one TD and passing to Mike Pruitt for a 58-yard encore. The decisive points came on Farler's 30-yard field goal.

End Monte Huber, Bobby's arch high school rival from Ft. Collins,

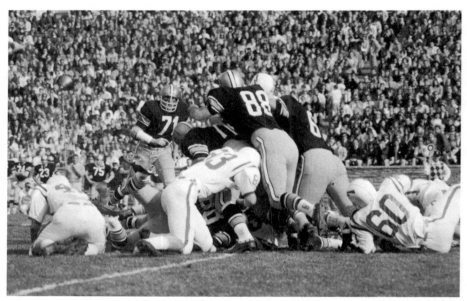

CU's 1966 team featured a rock solid defense. Here, Bill Sabatino, Mike Schnitker and Ron Scott surround an Air Force runner.

ers laid in an extra supply of ice and glasses for the Homecoming weekend with Oklahoma State. Unfortunately, the Cowboys spoiled the party, 10-7, relegating the hard drinking afterward to memory-erasing gulps. CU helped OSU more than it did itself, jumping offside on a third down play in which the Cowboys failed to make a first down. Following the penalty which gave them one, they rolled the remainder of the way for a 69-yard scoring drive. A violent windstorm came up suddenly, scattering the CU band's music sheets and the CU offense which threatened three times in the first half but failed to score. OSU extended its lead to 10-0 in the third period before the Buffs finally scored. Then CU apparently got a potential game-winning break when a fourth down snap sailed far over an OSU punter's head. But the Buffs had a

Charles Greer (45) was a solid 3-year regular for Eddie Crowder, a tough defender and fine punt returner.

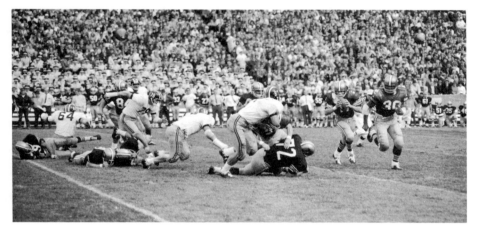

Wilmer Cooks (30) leads Bobby Anderson (11) against Missouri in 1967 as Bill Csikos (72) blocks.

punt return called and the line peeled back to block instead of making their normal rush and the punter retrieved the ball and followed the CU linemen upfield for 29 yards and a first down which helped them run out the clock. Such are the things that try Buffaloes' souls! The Buffs tumbled out of the top ten straight into a 23-0 humiliation at Oklahoma a week later. And Kansas' heavy underdogs almost dunked CU in Boulder, springing a surprise fourth down pass from punt formation to take a first period 8-0 lead which held up until Cooks' one-yard plunge capped a 46-yard third quarter comeback for a 12-8 triumph.

There were still two games remaining but bowl people are nervous types who want to arrange the best games possible and there were no calendar restrictions then so the Buffs quickly

accepted a Bluebonnet Bowl bid after the KU victory. If it was not a major bowl it was nevertheless a bowl and CU was not in the position of being choosy. The opponent would be the same Miami team which had spoiled the Buffs' opener a year earlier.

The remaining opponents provided only token resistance to the steamed up CU team. The Buffaloes buried Kansas State, 40-6, but lost its star end Schnitker with a knee injury. CU piled

up 473 yards and outgained K-State, 25-4. And the 33-0 finale over Air Force was also costly. Bobby Anderson went down with a badly sprained ankle in the first half. Dan Kelly filled in brilliantly, scoring a TD and passing for another to complete the easy win. Fortunately for CU, Anderson would have a month in which to heal. He would need it. Bobby's ankle was still tender when the Houston classic kicked off. But he was able to play.

In contrast to the 1961 bowl experience, this one had only minor problems, the main one being a brief player revolt involving four regulars who refused to practice when chief assistant Feldman (Crowder was on a speaking trip and unable to fly back because of bad weather) ordered the opening practice to begin despite a 6-inch snowfall and frigid temperatures. However, the head coach returned and soothed the situation. The next crisis occurred when Bobby Anderson, still unable to run hard, slept in and missed the bus to Rice Stadium. But the CU sophomore star awakened, hailed a cab and beat the bus to the game then wrote a happy ending to his sleepy beginning by becoming the game's outstanding player. Such are the trials and tribulations and, occasionally,

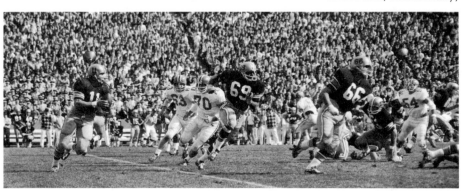

Guards Bart Bortles (66) and Eugene Johnson (69) lead Bobby Anderson against Oklahoma State in 1967.

Monte Huber was a fine receiver and an excellent runner who set records as Bobby Anderson's prime target.

Wilmer Cooks (30) takes a handoff from Bobby Anderson and follows William Harris (43) into the hole against Missouri in 1967.

happy endings of a football hero.

Kelly started the game but couldn't get the Buffs moving consistently. Miami took a 14-10 halftime lead. Crowder started Anderson in the second half and CU promptly drove 80 yards for a brief 17-14 lead but trailed again, 21-17, with time running out. Then with stubby slotback Tom Corson leveling two Miami defenders, one at the line of scrimmage and the other downfield, Anderson bolted 38 yards to put CU ahead. Ike Howard's interception and hometown Wilmer Cooks' short plunge wrapped up a 31-21 win.

1968

More good times were anticipated in 1968 despite the loss of 24 seniors, including eight 3-year regulars who had pulled CU from the 1962 ruins. But the return of Bobby Anderson and 23 other lettermen figured to keep the dropoff in quality minimal. "Let Bobby Do It" had become the CU battle cry.

And the stocky sparkplug picked right up where he left off - he was an opening day terror for three years, scoring 10 touchdowns in those three games - punching out three scores against Oregon as long punt returns by Pat Murphy and Mike Bynum helped CU to a 28-7 win. The Buffs came up with a 10-0 bummer at California but found a fullback replacement for Cooks a week later as sophomore Ward Walsh blasted for two touchdowns in a 28-18 no-sweat decision over Iowa State. Missouri was next and the Tigers turned on the Buffs viciously, atoning for their 1967 humiliation with a 27-14 win, bottling up CU's proud running game. A pair of Anderson bombs, 66 yards to Mike Pruett and 80 to Steve Engel, kept the Buffs within shouting distance but not much closer. The Buffaloes then got well with their favorite pain prescription, Kansas State, bludgeoning the Wildcats, 37-14, as Bobby unleashed his strong, if not deadly, right arm for three touchdown passes and 282 total yards. A disappointing 3-2-0 after the first half of the season, the Buffaloes got untracked early against Oklahoma, taking a 34-6 lead soon after the half. But the Sooners stunned the Buffs with three quick touchdowns which had CU gasping for breath until Anderson fought his way out of a trio of tacklers and bulled to a key first down to set up an insurance score in the 41-27 free-for-all which saw OU net 508 yards and CU 440.

But the finish exposed some fatal CU defensive flaws and the final four foes took advantage of them to score a shocking 141 points and send the Buffaloes reeling to four straight losses and the first sub-.500 (4-6-0) record in five years. First Kansas' burly John Riggins powered the Jayhawkers to a rain-soaked 27-14 decision at Lawrence in a game which had championship implications. Then OSU buried the Buffs at Stillwater, 34-17, despite Anderson's greatest game to that time. Bobby's 207 rushing yards and 146 more through the air added up to 353 total offense yards, only eight yards short of the Big Eight record. After Nebraska continued to cool down the Buffs, 22-6, Air Force ran wild in a crushing 58-35 finale as the Falcons' tortured Crowder's men with the same option attack which had served Eddie so well. Needless to say, the CU chief overhauled his defensive staff before the next fall. Eddie was never a patient man. His troops, both officers and enlisted men, got the message: batten down the bunkers and fine tune the artillery. Get ready for war!

Rain dampened picture day in 1967 as Dave Bartelt (32), Wilmer Cooks (30), Larry Plantz (21), Dick Anderson (with towel) and Vic Hokanson (70) waited in the runway.

This trio led CU's Liberty Bowl champions in 1969. With Eddie Crowder, they are Bobby Anderson (11), Mike Pruett (84) and Bill Collins (60).

Jeff Raymond's moment of glory was a 76-yard interception return which gave CU a 21-16 upset of Nebraska in 1967.

The Buffs would return 38 lettermen. The 1968 fadeout kept everyone from getting excited about 1969. But Eddie was. And the fans soon followed suit.

1969

Anderson topped even his previous amazing opening day standards, scoring four times in a 35-14 getaway against Tulsa that wasn't as easy as the score indicated. The first half was a 14-14 deadlock. The defense played a big role in this one. Interceptions by Eric Harris and Pat Murphy (2) set up three of Bobby's TDs.

However, powerful Penn State jolted the Buffs in a Pennsylvania meeting, unleashing a pair of sophomore terrors named Lydell Mitchell and Franco Harris en route to a 27-3 laugher. Obviously, Anderson was the key to

Opposing offenses saw a lot of Rocky Martin's massive forearms in 1967-8.

the CU attack. Stop him, which the Nittany Lions did effectively, and the CU offense was toothless. The Buffs needed to change gears and Crowder came up with the answer, a daring early-season experiment in which Bobby moved to tailback, a position he had never played in college or high school, and rookie Paul Arendt, an excellent passer, took over at quarterback. The gamble paid off quickly. Favored Indiana, bolstered by the seniors who two years earlier had extended mighty Ohio State in the Rose Bowl, was the unsuspecting victim. Despite a 24-inch snow which was still falling at the kickoff, the quick switch worked magnificently on the muddy field. Anderson ran like he was on pavement, mushing for 161 yards and three TDs. Arendt, playing with the coolness which, coupled with his off-field life style, earned him the nickname "Pearl Street Paul," threw for 103 yards and ambled for 72 more - running wasn't his forte. CU won going away,

Mike Montler came from Columbus, Ohio via the Marines to become a CU All-American.

CU unveiled a 5-story facility housing the press box and Flatirons Club in 1968.

30-7, and in the process uncovered a new defensive star, tackle Bill Brundige who almost single-handedly hogtied the Hoosiers with 12 tackles. Like Andy, Brundige didn't mind the mud.

The backfield now set with its new tandem, the Buffaloes bounced Iowa State, 14-0, with Anderson scoring on a 69-yard run and Arendt adding the second TD with a 5-yard rollout.

For the second straight week, Brundige was awesome, combining with a bloodthirsty rookie end out of the service named Herb Orvis to destroy the Cyclones. The pair was unstoppable as CU made 19 tackles behind the line of scrimmage, seven by Brundige. Then came a sensational shootout between All-Americans Anderson and Oklahoma's Steve Owens, who would win the Heisman Trophy in 1969. In a see-saw battle which would have done credit to a Super Bowl, the Sooners escaped 42-30 when the Buffaloes narrowly missed recovering an onside kick late in the game after Anderson's spectacular cart-wheeling touchdown had pulled the Buffs to 35-30. Anderson finished with 123 yards and three touchdowns. Owens got 109 and four TDs. But it was the insertion of junior quarterback Jimmy Bratten which brought the CU attack to life. The blond Californian darted for 107 keeper yards after replacing a struggling Arendt.

A leaping game-saving interception by Phil Irwin was the clincher as three more touchdowns by Anderson let CU

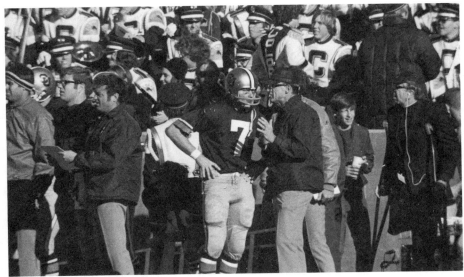

Eddie Crowder briefs QB Ken Johnson on the sidelines while assistants Jim Mora, Steve Sidwell and Irv Brown view the action in this 1969 sideline scene. Team chaplain Father Charles Forsythe is at the right.

trip Missouri in another offensive show, 31-24. But Anderson received a painful hip pointer and his hobbling efforts couldn't prevent a 20-7 upset at Nebraska. Neither Bratten nor Arendt could take up the slack for CU's wounded leader, throwing four interceptions. Still not fully recovered, Anderson managed to pound 12 yards with a minute left and Jim Cooch's interception stopped a furious Kansas counter-attack in a 17-14 victory.

Aerial heroics by Arendt and end Bob Masten helped get the Buffs into

positon for the fourth quarter rally. Irwin, following in the footsteps of his older brother, again came up with a key interception, this time in the end zone, to blunt an Oklahoma State comeback which almost toppled the Buffs. CU surprised the Cowboys with an Anderson-Engel reverse which returned the opening kickoff 99 yards. But OSU fought back to take a 14-10 third quarter lead before a long CU drive, highlighted by a great catch of a Bratten pass at the three by Masten, set up the winning TD with only 1:23 remaining. The Cowboys rode downfield swiftly with the kickoff, however, and reached the three where a wide-open receiver dropped a perfect pass in the end zone before Irwin came up with his game-saver.

The regular season ended with still another scoring spectacular as the Buffaloes outlasted a Kansas State team, suddenly contenders under Vince Gibson, 45-32. Both teams came out winging, each scoring a touchdown in the opening two minutes: CU on a 44-yard Bratten-Anderson bomb on the game's second scrimmage play and K-State with a 77-yard strike on its first play. Bratten threw for 251 yards and K-State's Lynn Dickey fired an amazing 63 passes, hitting 28 for 439 yards. At the end it took some outstanding theatrics from CU punter, Dick Robert, who fell dramatically to the ground after a K-State defender barely brushed him while trying to block a punt which would have given the Wildcats possession to mount a game-winning try any-

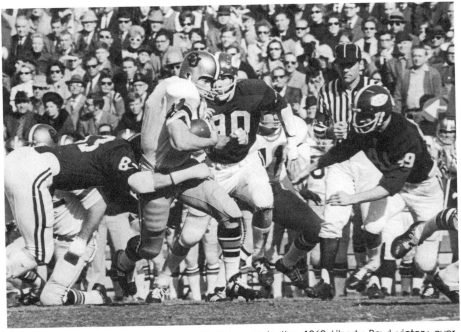

Bobby Anderson's greatest day as a Buffalo was in the 1969 Liberty Bowl victory over Alabama.

way. CU led at the time by only 35-30 and there was plenty of time left for the Wildcats to launch a counterattack. Robert's dive produced a roughing penalty and the Buffs went in to score the clinching TD in an aerial explosion which reminded Boulderites of the annual Fourth of July fireworks show. The two teams were battling for a Liberty Bowl bid. When the firing had finished, nearly 1000 yards and 77 points had ignited the scoreboard.

Anderson's opening touchdown, his 17th of the season, established a new CU season record. The old mark was 16 by Byron White in 1937. Anderson's superb CU career led to his No. 11 being retired at the end of the season. Only two others received similar treatment in CU's first century of competition: Rhodes Scholar All-Americans White's "24" and Romig's "67".

CU's opponent at Memphis would be Alabama, getting the berth because of its reputation rather than a 6-4-0 record. But Bear Bryant was the acknowledged guru of the gridiron and Alabama never missed a bowl during his long tenure. He might have been regretting his acceptance early in the Liberty Bowl contest. CU threatened an early runaway, bolting to a quick 17-0 lead behind the running of Anderson and Walsh and continuing it 31-19 at the half on a 91-yard Steve Engel kickoff return in which he took a handoff from Masten then got two key blocks from the rugged tight end to go all the

Ward Walsh (41), a fine blocker and runner, twists for yardage against Tulsa in 1969.

way. But the amazing Alabamans refused to fold and crept in front 33-31 after three quarters. Then Anderson, who was magnificent with 254 yards and three touchdowns, destroyed the Crimson Tide hopes as he thundered for 52 of the 53 yards in CU's march to the TD which sent the Buffs to a going-away 47-33 triumph.

Crowder's team had now won two bowl games in three years. His program was in full stride. Seniors were being replaced by equally-gifted newcomers every season. Only two things would keep the Buffaloes out of the Big Eight throne room: the monster programs at Oklahoma and Nebraska. Their annual presence at the top of the conference would frustrate Crowder and the rest of the league. Even when his 1971 team finished third in the nation, those two big, bad Big Eight brothers would finish in front of CU. It was discouraging, to say the least, and it was only a matter of time before Eddie got discouraged. But first there were more good days ahead. Now reaching eligibility after a transfer year from a Texas junior college was a slender speedster who would become the greatest gamebreaker in CU history.

1970

Forty lettermen from 1969's outstanding team returned in 1970. Anderson and his supporting cast of seniors were gone. Still, the Buffaloes looked solid. Trouble signs heralding an up-

and-down season came early as CU opened with an unimpressive 16-9 win at Indiana. The Buffaloes would be a bully-type team, one which would win by big scores then lose all too frequently in the close games. CU and its followers awaited the invasion of mighty Penn State, proud owners of the nation's longest undefeated streak, 34 games. The Nittany Lions had pulverized the Buffaloes a year earlier and CU hadn't forgotten. They were ready for this nationally-televised meeting.

What the Buffaloes also had was a new top gun, that flexible flyer from Texas, Clifford Branch, lightning fast with great maneuvering ability. The unsuspecting visitors never knew what hit them. Pat Murphy intercepted a pass on the first play of the game to launch a 40-yard TD drive. The Buffs got a followup field goal from a recovered fumble two minutes later. A Jim Cooch pickoff put the Buffs into field position for a third straight score and a 20-7 halftime lead. Then Branch, who was to thrill CU fans with his breakaway bursts for the next two seasons, streaked 97 yards with the third quarter kickoff. The final score was 41-13 and Franco Harris was not the best fullback on the field. That man was CU's John Tarver, who stormed to three touchdowns.

Unfortunately, that was the high water mark of 1970. The Buffs promptly squandered scoring opportunities at Kansas State then permitted

Big Bill Brundige was an All-American defensive tackle in 1969.

the Wildcats to win the game with a short pass which covered 75 yards on the play after a CU linebacker missed an easy fumble recovery. Even then the Buffs had a chance to tie on a late Tarver touchdown but their reliable placekicker, Dave Haney, shaded his PAT attempt wide. The Buffs came down to earth quickly, 21-20.

Then the roller coaster ride began in earnest. Steve Dal Porto broke loose for a 57-yard touchdown on the first play of the game and Branch flew 72 and 62 yards on punt returns and had an 80-yarder called back. The stunned victim was Iowa State, 61-10. The familiar turnaround took place immediately against Oklahoma. In a surprise move, Sooner coach Chuck Fairbanks switched his team to the wishbone offense just before the CU game. The formation baffled the Buffaloes. OU powered to a 17-7 first half lead then held on for a 23-15 win. CU tumbled again, this time to Missouri, once more falling far behind early, 17-0 in the first quarter. CU's brightest star in this one was Branch, suspected of having bad hands but disproving that rap by hauling down seven Arendt passes for 158 yards. The Buffaloes almost caught up but fumbles and penalties stopped serious last half drives and Mizzou pulled away, 30-16.

Jon Keyworth starred at several positions in 1970-2-3. From halfback he slashes for yardage against Kansas in 1970.

Then came another verse of a sad song. Nebraska dealt the Buffaloes still another downer, 29-13. Back to back plays after CU had gained momentum with a TD to creep within 15-13 of the Huskers in the fourth period were the difference. First, Branch's knee was ruled to have scraped the ground as he slipped beginning an apparent 2-point conversion carry which would have tied the game. Then on the kickoff, Cornhusker Jeff Kinney exploited careless kickoff coverage, pounding 70 yards deep into CU territory to start a 2-TD Nebraska finish.

The Buffs then righted themselves and swept past their final three foes with disdain, hammering Kansas 45-29 with Branch returning the opening kickoff 100 yards; Oklahoma State on a good defensive show, 30-6; and Air Force's Sugar Bowl-bound Falcons, 49-19. In that closing earthquake, the Buffs spotted Air Force an early touchdown on a long fumble return then swallowed up the embryo fliers with a 438-yard first half which produced a 35-7 intermission bulge. CU took out its frustrations on the outclassed Falcons who crashed and burned before the Buffs' 675 yards, highest single game total in the nation that season.

The furious finish earned CU a return trip to the Liberty Bowl. But the Buffs made a serious mistake. They accepted the bid on the assumption Arkansas or Mississippi would be their opponent. Instead, a relative unknown, Tulane, agreed to purchase 10,000 tickets and with that guarantee got the invitation. CU took the Green Wave lightly. Even though the Buffaloes would be without Bratten, who had injured a knee against Air Force, the Buffs were a solid favorite. They played miserably and Tulane played with the inspiration of an underdog sensing an upset. The Buffs went down, 17-3. It

A close-knit (and cropped) 1970 CU defense included these burr-cut Buffaloes. L-R, Rich Varriano, Phil Irwin, Herb Orvis and Dave Capra.

was their only game of 1970 in single figures. It left them with a 6-5-0 record. Very disappointing and completely unexpected. A murmur of discontent wafted over the Flatirons. The natives were restless. But Crowder, who'd sprung Branch loose in 1970, had another ace up his sleeve. Or, make that aces. Another fine rookie crop, led by quarterback Ken Johnson and tailback Charlie Davis, was ready to strut its stuff.

1971

If the Buffs thought they had a tough early opponent in Penn State the preceding year, that challenge was nothing to the prospect of facing both Louisiana State and Ohio State on the road in the first three weeks of 1971. But the Buffs were up to the assignment. Crowder had a good nucleus of 19 seniors. What wasn't expected was the surprising maturity of a sophomore cast which included 49 players. In the Baton Rouge opener, Johnson ran the CU offense flawlessly, running and passing expertly. Davis rushed for 174 yards, most by a Big Eight rookie in a decade, and caught two TD passes from Johnson. Junior John Stearns ran back two interceptions for 88 yards. And when LSU showed signs of regaining its poise, Branch sped 75 yards with a punt. All the while, big Tarver was grinding out 92 yards up the middle. When the last rebel scream of agony had died down, CU had tamed the Tigers, 31-21.

CU returned home to play its first

Two of the unsung heroes in CU's athletic history, equipment manager Lee Akins and athletic business secretary, Alice Clyncke received official citations of merit from assistant athletic director Fred Casotti in 1970.

game on a half-million dollars' worth of AstroTurf with Wyoming the sacrificial lamb at the unveiling of the new surface. Ironically, a 20-inch snowfall which stopped two hours before the kickoff, and which might have caused cancellation had the natural grass field still been in place, was easily removed by plows and trucks working all night and morning. Johnson was out with a broken bone in his hand but his backup, little Joe Duenas worked just as effectively against the Cowboys, scoring three touchdowns in a 56-13 runaway.

A week later at Columbus before

the largest crowd, 85,538 ever to watch a CU game, Branch worked his disappearing act again, surfacing in the end zone after a 68-yard punt return. A clutch 39-yard keeper by Johnson, who went all the way after the week's layoff, moved CU to a 20-7 lead with 3:50 left and the Buffs held off a Buckeye comeback to win, 20-14. CU's unsung defensive heroes were middle guard Bud Magrum and tackle Carl Taibi who made 20 and 10 tackles, respectively. Next the Buffs catapulted past Kansas State, 31-21, as Johnson threw for a CU record 276 passing yards, three to

Pat Murphy earned All-American honors as a defensive back in 1970.

Don Popplewell was an All-American center in 1970.

The incomparable Clifford Branch stretches for a pass at picture day in 1970.

Branch for 94 and a touchdown. The incomparable Clifford turned on the faucet with a 59-yard first quarter TD but it was Johnson's accurate arm which triggered a CU late surge after the Wildcats had gone in front, 21-17.

A Stearns attempt to run from a fourth down punting situation was stopped cold by an aroused Iowa State team which smelled upset after taking over on downs deep in CU territory and the game tied, 14-14, in the final

Bud Magrum was a tough ex-Marine and an even tougher middle guard in 1971-2.

period. But big defensive plays by Magrum, John Stavely and Brian Foster stopped the Cyclone threat and Branch capped a CU counterattack, scoring untouched on an end around which sealed a 24-14 triumph. Now 5-0 and nationally ranked CU moved on to Norman and got a 45-17 lesson from Fairbanks' Sooners. Little Duenas again came on in relief for the ailing-again Johnson and sparked the Buffaloes past Missouri, 27-7, pitching out with perfect timing to spring Tarver for 35 and 24-yard TDs as the big fullback had a 106-yard game. But Nebraska and rain and cold and disaster awaited CU at Lincoln.

The Cornhuskers had a future Heisman Trophy winner in Johnny Rodgers and CU had Branch. Both were superstars. But Nebraska had a better supporting cast. CU was never in this one, going down quietly, 31-7. Branch's 19-yard TD reception was

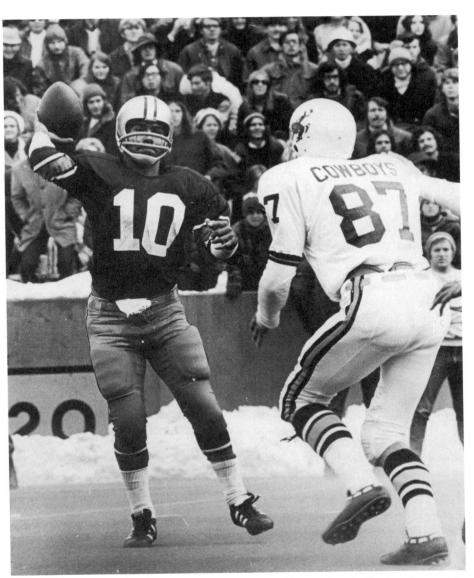

Little Joe Duenas earned Big Eight "back-of-the-week" honors for a brilliant performance against Wyoming in 1971.

All-American end Herb Orvis destroys an Oklahoma State running play in 1969.

CU's only bright spot. The Buffaloes had tested the Big Eight monsters and graded out "D-" both times. They had three games left in which to re-establish their reputation, soiled but not destroyed by the losses to two of the nation's top teams.

They did it with a flourish. Branch's 85-yard end-around broke up a tight game at Kansas in the fourth quarter to spark a closing salvo and a 35-14 win after the Jayhawks had shocked the Buffs by intercepting a pitchout in the end zone during CU's first series. Next against Oklahoma State, Davis exploded for 342 yards in 34 carries, by far the biggest game in Big Eight history. Branch wasn't a quiet bystander, either. He began the scoring with a 64-yard sprint off a trick play. Before the day was dark, CU had amassed 676 yards. In the finale, Branch closed out an unforgettable regular season career with still another amazing afternoon, returning a punt 65 yards and swinging 34 more on a reverse for two of CU's seven touchdowns in a 53-17 wipeout of Air Force. Davis continued his late-season surge with 202 yards. The closing charge of three straight one-sided victories earned the Buffaloes a repeat appearance in the Bluebonnet Bowl.

Unlike the year before, there was no sleeper waiting for the Buffaloes in Houston. The opponent would be Houston's Cougars playing before its home crowd on its home field in the Houston Astro-Dome. There was a definite Houston look to the CU starting lineup, too. Davis, center Bill McDonald and end J.V. Cain were all from the host city and Branch was from the vicinity too, by way of nearby Wharton JC. The Buffaloes won a thriller, 29-17, with a great goal line stand to thwart a Cougar drive which threatened to erase a slim 21-17 CU lead late in the game. The clutch play of the season came on the following series. Stearns, who had failed on a similar gamble at Iowa State earlier in the season, again ran from punt formation deep in the end zone. The line of scrimmage was the 10 and the first down marker was at the 19. Stearns carried a tackler out of bounds at the 22. The Buffs went on to score and wrap up a 29-17 triumph. Branch was used as a decoy most of the game with Davis getting the heavy duty and dancing for 202 yards and two touchdowns. But the little lightning bug still played an instrumental role in CU's drive to the final touchdown, drawing a 32-yard interference penalty to move

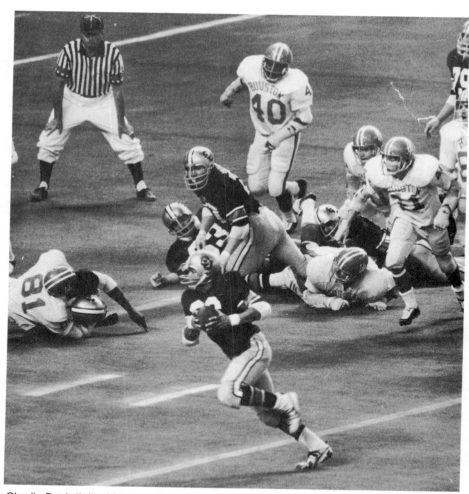

Charlie Davis thrilled his hometown fans as he shredded the Houston defense in the 1971 Bluebonnet Bowl. Davis was voted the game's outstanding player.

CU never had a tougher tight end than Bob Masten (1969-70-71) who excelled as a blocker, runner and receiver.

John Stearns was the "Bad Dude" and a sterling safety man and punter in 1970-1-2.

the ball into position for the vital CU touchdown.

Branch finished his 22-game career with unbelievable statistics: 31 rushes for 354 yards (11.4 avg.), 36 pass receptions for 665 yards (18.5 avg.), 44 punt returns for 733 yards (16.7 avg.), 30 kickoff returns for 755 yards (25.2 avg.), 16 touchdowns and a 2-point conversion for 98 points. Those figures added up to 2507 yards in the 141 times Branch got the ball, a remarkable 17.8 average. Nebraska's Rodgers may have been a future Heisman winner, but to many observers the nation's most dynamic player was Clifford Branch. Davis didn't have a bad rookie campaign, either, setting a new CU rushing record with 1386 yards in 219 carries, a flashy 6.3 average. But the top per-carry average in the Big Eight that fall was Branch's 26.1 mark on 235 yards in only nine rushes.

CU's upset of Houston came on New Year's Eve. The following day, Nebraska slaughtered Alabama and Oklahoma butchered Auburn to cap a tremendous Big Eight bowl performance. And when the national rankings came out the following week, it was a Big Eight sweep: 1. Nebraska; 2. Oklahoma; 3. Colorado. Losing to the conference monsters had been painful but ultimately rewarding. CU looked good enough against the perennial Big Eight leaders to complete the first sweep of the national ratings by a conference in history. Prosperity was back. Crowder was never more popular. The future looked even greater. Remember, that 1971 squad had contained 49 sophomores. But bright futures seem to bring bad times to CU coaches. Nearly at the top, Crowder's career would soon begin a downward spiral.

1972

No one would have guessed that Crowder's coaching days at CU were numbered as 1972 approached. Boulder was afire with enthusiasm. A veteran team coming off the superlative 1971 finish brought out the silver, gold and black everywhere. To top it off, a national football publication, albeit a relatively small one, picked the Buffaloes to finish first in the nation. If CU boosters needed any encouragement that was more than enough to send them over the edge and into a Nebraska-like frenzy. Fanatics with buckets of gold paint looked for University Hill buildings to redecorate. Toy buffaloes sprang up in every Boulder

Ken Johnson directed the CU offense brilliantly in 1971.

store. Some called it "Gold Fever", others "Gold Rush" and others whatever their wild imaginations conjured. There were gold buffaloes, gold footballs, gold clothes, gold everything. Boulder took on the appearance of a sandwich bun dipped in mustard!

But there was a familiar saying around Big Eight press and radio circles: Colorado is most dangerous when underestimated and most likely to fail when rated highly. Over the years it had been right more often than not. The 1972 team, possibly the most talent-laden in history, would go down as one of the most disappointing. And, in the process, break the hearts of the first pre-season sold-out Folsom Stadium in history.

The CU machine sputtered from the opening kickoff. Johnson, Davis and the rest of the offense which had been so productive the preceding fall moved only sporadically. The Buffs had to rely on a stingy defense sparked by Eddie Shoen's 48-yard interception return to nip an outmanned California team, 20-10, in the opener. Another steal, this one by Cullen Bryant for a 21-yard score, set off a 4-touchdown flurry in the last 10 minutes and made a 56-14 win over Cincinnati sound more impressive than it really was. CU's offense finally got untracked with a 24-point second quarter in a 38-6 decision at Minnesota. End J.V. Cain, who had been ineligible for the first two games while an NCAA investigation cleared him of minor charges, caught three passes for 57 yards and added 42 more on a pair of end-around carries to pace the victory at Minneapolis.

Unimpressive as they were, the three straight wins sent the Buffaloes to a No. 3 national ranking. They were ripe for a fall because they weren't as good as that perfect record indicated. The bubble broke at Stillwater as the Cowboys, in a repeat of their 1967 upset, turned off the CU lights, 31-6. The Buff offense still wasn't in sync. Johnson had missed practice all week because of the death of his father. Jon Keyworth, a big, versatile player, suffered a hip injury early. The Buffaloes contributed to the loss as much as OSU, fumbling 10 times, and losing three to halt themselves repeatedly.

That nightmare behind them, the Buffs snapped back to win the next three games. But again it was not a smooth, cohesive stretch. Mark Cooney lumbered 69 yards with a deflected pass and John Stearns set up another score with an 18-yard pickoff return. Those big defensive plays keyed a 38-17 win at Kansas State. CU unveiled a new star, crazy-legged Steve Haggerty, in a 34-22 conquest of Iowa State. Haggerty dazzled the Cyclones with a 78-yard punt return then a 41-yard reception, both for TDs. Johnson was on target again with 15 completions for 197 yards. Davis was busy, too, churning for 135 yards and two touchdowns. But the most sensational play of the game was a 57-yard field goal by Fred Lima, a Chilean by way of Los Angeles, who barefooted the longest placement in Big Eight history.

Against Oklahoma in Boulder, the Buffaloes finally showed the type of 60-minute performance everyone had been awaiting. The Sooners were undefeated and top-ranked nationally and took a quick 7-0 lead. Then sophomore Gary Campbell tightroped down the sideline 35 yards and over the flag. But Lima blew the extra point and slunk to the sidelines to be measured for goat's horns. However, Keyworth came to the rescue with a sensational, leaping catch at the goal line to give CU a 13-7 lead in the third period and Lima acquitted himself with two fourth-quarter field goals and the Buffs hung on, 20-14.

But prosperity lasted only six days. On the seventh, Missouri drove 39 yards in the final 51 seconds to kick a field goal at the gun for a 20-17 upset. The Buffs had just gotten a horrible break which cost them the game when

Cliff Branch (23) makes one of his patented punt returns in 1971 against Iowa State as Randy Geist (15), John Stavely (55), and Brian Foster (18) support.

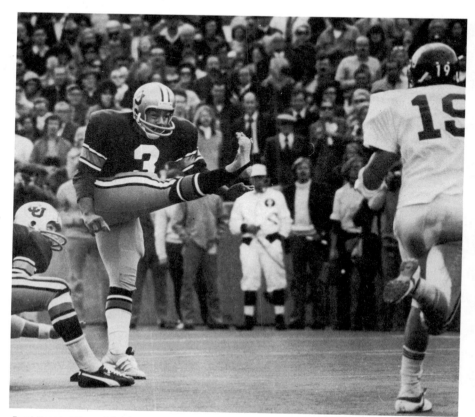

Fred Lima's 57-yard field goal set a Big Eight record in 1972. Ken Johnson holds.

Cullen Bryant capped a brilliant 3-year career as he made All-American in 1972.

an official ruled that a CU lineman had grazed a Tiger quarterback's facemask as a host of Buffs blasted the ball loose for an apparent fumble recovery at the Tiger 21. The penalty gave Missouri new life and, moments later, the Tigers marched to victory while CU was carried to a morgue.

When David Humm and Johnny Rodgers riddled the Buffs in a 33-10 triumph in Boulder the Buffaloes were all the way down, and almost out. Then, for the third year in a row, they bounced back from disappointment to blast Kansas, 33-8, and Air Force, 38-7. Shoen, whose interception had triggered the opening win of the season closed out the year with two thefts against the Falcons and Stearns contributed an 82-yard runback with his 16th career interception, a new CU record and just one short of the Big Eight mark.

Despite the disappointing 8-3-0 record CU had no trouble getting a variety of post-season bids, choosing the Gator Bowl in Florida. But that one was another disaster just like the 1970 debacle against Tulane. Like that game, CU got only a field goal in bowing, 24-3, to Auburn. The favored Buffs seemed to lose heart and Auburn became inspired when a wide-open Keyworth dropped a sure touchdown pass from Johnson early in the second

period of the then-scoreless game.

The 8-4-0 season was hard to take: for the Buffaloes, for the fans and most of all, for Crowder. It had begun with high hopes, staggered through much of the fall, then crashed in flames at the end. There was loud grumbling now. It had a definite impact on the CU coach, who had doubled as athletic director since 1965 and toiled overtime doing both jobs excellently. The quick turnoff by CU fans, many of them long-time loyalists, discouraged Eddie. He had done an amazing job of taking the Buffaloes from the bottom to near the top. His administrative leadership had produced a stadium enlargement and addition of a team building plus a new all-weather track and adjoining baseball field. That, plus five bowl appearances in the last six years, should have made the fans more considerate of the 1972 disappointment. But reason isn't necessarily a characteristic of football fans. And CU's were typical. Crowder never seemed to regain his brisk, authoritative command presence after that season. Close friends think he may have even decided to call 1973 his final coaching year well before the season started although he gave that indication to no one. Always a cold, almost-detached type in front of his team, Crowder seldom tried to arouse his teams emotionally. Some close to the program felt that the presence of enthusiastic Jerry Claiborne, for 1971-only Crowder's defensive coordinator, had added that one missing dimension to Eddie's program. But Claiborne left after that season to become Maryland's head coach and no other coach filled that role satisfactorily in Crowder's final two years.

1973

Nevertheless, there was good reason for optimism going into 1973. Those talented 1971 sophomores, led by Johnson and Davis, would be seasoned seniors. It was a deep, strong squad. But it never came together. Crowder and Johnson had disagreements almost immediately and the 2-year regular quickly dropped to the third team behind sophomores Clyde Crutchmer and David Williams, good but green newcomers. Davis also had an unhappy senior campaign and barely edged out sophomore Billy Waddy for rushing honors. There was fine young talent on this squad with still another all-time great, Dave Logan, in the rookie ranks. But, for some reason, possibly Crowder's frustrations, the chemistry

never worked.

As in 1971, the Buffs opened at Louisiana State. This time there was no upset. The Tigers tied up the CU offense for a 17-6 victory in a defensive struggle. Waddy and Logan then took over the spotlight in a 28-25 squeaker at Wisconsin. Waddy, an ex-prep quarterback, was especially impressive, passing for a 14-yard TD to Logan, running 76 yards for another, then contributing runs of 11, 16 and 14 yards to a winning fourth-quarter touchdown which he scored from 17 yards out. Wisconsin almost came back, reaching the CU 16 where Rich Bland's interception saved the Buffs. The win understandably buoyed hopes for a comeback campaign. There were no finer sophomores in the Big Eight than Waddy and Logan.

When the Buffs stampeded past Baylor (52-28) and Air Force (38-17), then nipped Iowa State (23-16) on a 73-yard surprise pass from Waddy to quarterback Williams in a steady rain at Ames, the CU picture brightened considerably. But Oklahoma broke CU's momentum with an early 96-yard interception return and went on to bury the Buffs, 34-7, and begin a torturous finish which saw the Buffaloes lose five of the last six games. The team didn't die immediately, using a Whitney Paul fumble recovery with 2:07 remaining and the passing and running of

Gary Campbell's touchdown dash into the northeast corner of the end zone sparked CU's dramatic 1972 upset of No. 1 Oklahoma.

Crutchmer to nip Missouri at the wire, 17-13. Crutchmer hit Cain for 19, sprinted 40 yards to the 17, pinpointed Haggerty at the four then handed off to brawny fullback Jim Kelleher for the TD in an electrifying 76-yard drive which required only those four plays and needed just 46 seconds.

But then came four frustrating games which the Buffs could have won but didn't. First Nebraska held off a CU comeback, which threatened to overhaul an early 28-3 deficit to win, 28-16. Kansas out-slogged the Buffs in the mud at Lawrence as CU lost a chance for a possible winning Lima field goal in the final minute when Waddy lost the ball at the KU 35 after apparently making a first down. The final score was, 17-15. The Buffs finished their tailspin at home and that didn't help, either. Oklahoma State overcame a quick 10-0 CU lead then bruised the Buffs, 38-24. The final shot was administered by not-so-lowly-anymore Kansas State which also overcame an early CU 14-0 lead to win on a field goal with five seconds left, 17-14.

As this late season slump gathered momentum, Crowder began to feel the fury of the fans who unrolled "Goodbye, Eddie" signs in the stands at the final game, toilet-papered his house and even stuck a "For Sale" sign in his front yard late one night. It wasn't a pleasant November for him. He had been a popular and successful man all his football life which began when he was the star quarterback on a state championship high school team at Muskogee, Oklahoma, then a brilliant quarterback at Oklahoma and after that, first class coaching jobs under Wilkinson and Blaik and finally his triumphant takeover at CU.

He was perplexed at the change in his fortunes. He had led CU to the top ranks of college football, taken his teams to five bowls in 11 seasons and turned down a sixth bid in 1966. But the prevailing attitude in the state was, "But what have you done for us lately?" Crowder wasn't willing to deal with this type of confrontation. After some quiet time at a mountain retreat away from the turmoil, he announced his resignation in mid-December, remaining as director of athletics, a position which never provided a proper outlet for his energy and intellect. So perhaps the most dynamic influence on CU athletics in the last half of the first century of intercollegiate competition quietly hung up his coaching cap and whistle.

There was little public mourning.

Realistically, 11 years on the job is almost a lifetime for a football coach. Take away those first two rebuilding 2-8-0 seasons and Eddie had an outstanding 63-33-2 record, good enough for long life at many institutions. But he had elevated CU hopes too highly: anything except championships or very-near misses had become unsatisfactory. The 5-6-0 of 1973 was totally unacceptable. So Crowder rode quietly into the shadows of the athletic directorship. His unrest would continue in that post although he would continue to lead from that chair for another decade. It was a path two of his closest coaching friends also took: Frank Broyles at Arkansas and Darrell Royal at Texas.

And so a strange search began. "Name" possibilities were reluctant to touch the CU job. They were suspicious of the school's priorities regarding football. After all, Crowder had been one of the top coaches in the country for several years. Something not obvious from the distance must be wrong, they reasoned. And another

shadow hung over the CU campus. It was the continued presence of Eddie as athletic director. A lot of potential candidates weren't wild about the prospect of a football mind as sharp as Eddie's looking over their shoulders. There was a flurry of rumors about such well-known coaches as Frank Kush of Arizona State and Terry Donahue of UCLA. But they were happy where they were and weren't interested in the CU job.

When things settled down, there were two leading candidates: Bill Mallory of Miami (Ohio) and Jim Sweeney of Washington State. Mallory was a sound, conservative disciple of the Woody Hayes school. He had just finished a brilliant year at Miami where his team had gone undefeated, whipping Florida in the Tangerine Bowl. It was the greatest season in the 85-year history of the midwestern school known as the "Cradle of Coaches" because of the emergence of such top men as Paul Brown, Ara Parseghian, Sid Gillman,

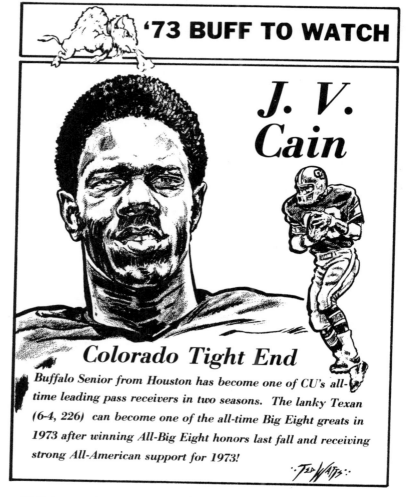

'73 BUFF TO WATCH

J. V. Cain

Colorado Tight End

Buffalo Senior from Houston has become one of CU's all-time leading pass receivers in two seasons. The lanky Texan (6-4, 226) can become one of the all-time Big Eight greats in 1973 after winning All-Big Eight honors last fall and receiving strong All-American support for 1973!

J.V. Cain was a tremendous tight end for the Buffaloes in 1971- 2-3 and an NFL star for St. Louis until a heart condition ended his life in 1979.

Eddie Crowder walks off the field as CU coach for the final time after a closing loss to Kansas State in 1973. With him is Wildcat coach Vince Gibson.

Hayes, Weeb Ewbank, Paul Dietzel, Johnny Pont and Bo Schembechler from that starting place. Mallory's 5-year record at Miami was an imposing 39-12-0. He was the odds-on favorite, especially in the one mind that counted, Eddie Crowder's.

But Sweeney had support. The free-wheeling Irishman whose coaching and life styles were exactly alike, was a fine coach. Crowder considered hiring him and even led Sweeney to believe he would get the job. But Eddie's failure to do so probably was based on his distrust of the passing game as a primary attack, Sweeney's approach to offensive football. CU's only venture into that area had been the Bud Davis disaster of 1962, a season filled with footballs and futility. Ironically, Sweeney would have probably brought with him one of his Washington State aides, Jack Elway. It was no big deal then, but Elway had a young son named John who would later become a household name at both Stanford and Denver. Had Crowder hired Sweeney, young Elway very possibly might have become a Buffalo and CU's path undoubtedly would have taken a different turn.

MALLORY

But, after a week's period in which Mallory played his cards coyly, he took the job on his own terms, disregarding Crowder's recommendations that he retain two top recruiters, Jim Mora, who had been working on the state's top quarterback, Jeff Knapple, and Steve Ortmayer, who had been shadow-ing Terry Miller, the best prep running back in Colorado. Mallory insisted on bringing a complete staff so Mora went to UCLA and took Knapple with him and Miller defected to Oklahoma State. A forlorn figure far back in the pack who never even got an interview with Eddie was ex-CU assistant Don James who had moved on in 1971 to become a success at Kent State and, after being ignored for the CU job, became one of the top coaches in the nation at Washington.

But the important thing in 1974 was that Crowder wanted Mallory, liked his no-nonsense approach to the game and finally got him. However, the same chemistry, or lack of it, which had damaged Crowder's last two teams had the same effect on Eddie and his new man. The two men had completely different personalities. Crowder was shrewd and smooth, especially in his public appearances. Mallory was almost brutally blunt in his dealings with press and public. Bill had much better rapport with his players than Eddie. And his coaching philosophy was basic and uncomplicated in contrast to Eddie's frequent experimentations and changes in strategy. It looked like it would be a good blend. But it wasn't. Eddie was impatient with Mallory's recruiting tactics. The new man was never at the same level as a recruiter as Crowder. There were other differences but the basic problem between the two men was their inability to communicate.

There was one positive about the change, though. Mallory inherited a super crop of returnees from Crowder. Eighteen members of the three classes Bill took over in 1974 played in the NFL.

The new CU headmaster was a dedicated coach who wasted very little of his time thinking about anything other than football. He promised his all-out effort, emphasizing dedication and endless energy. He brought in a staff entirely from his former conference, the Mid-American. It was a good, hard-working group. Mallory made an immediate hit in his early public appearances. The difference between he and Eddie captivated the crowds who came to hear him. He was a fire-breathing shouter who pounded tables and battered blackboards when he got warmed to his task. It was a refreshing change from the always-cool Crowder. CU partisans hoped he could instill some of that passion in the Buffaloes.

1974

No CU coach ever faced a tougher brace of opening games. In fact, the first two - at LSU and at Michigan - may have influenced Crowder's decision to retire. Eddie knew he had to get away fast in 1975 or the howls would begin quickly and, this time, probably from some of the power brokers inside and outside the university administration. Nobody in his right mind gave the Buffaloes much chance to win at those two deathtraps. And there was one thing certain about Eddie Crowder: he was always in his right mind.

A new coach could absorb losses in those two games and still escape undamaged because he'd still be on his first-year honeymoon. And sure enough, Mallory's Buffaloes got shellacked: 42-14 at Baton Rouge and 31-0 at Ann Arbor. The shutout by Michigan was CU's first in 66 games. Still nobody faulted Bill. The defeats had been almost taken for granted. Then Bill got things moving, coming from 11 points down with 18 minutes left to upset Wisconsin, 24-21; outlasting Air Force, 28-27, in the final game of that series, despite 13 penalties; and toppling Iowa State, 34-7, behind Waddy's 145 rushing yards and a 51-yard punt return TD by the versatile Logan.

But Oklahoma introduced the new coach to the Big Eight facts of life, humiliating the Buffaloes, 49-14, after leading 42-0 going into the fourth quarter. There was too much Sooner strength for the Buffaloes, especially that of a pipe-legged halfback named Joe Washington, who scored four TDs including one in which he staggered backward the last 10 yards while dragging a tackler. To Mallory's credit, he brought the Buffs back the next week to almost upset Missouri. But a 4-play, 80-yard fourth period drive, almost a carbon copy of CU's winning march the year before, pulled it out for the Tigers, 30-24. Nebraska then threatened to blow away the Buffaloes at Lincoln, building a 31-0 lead before the Buffs, who always fought hard for Mallory, came back, scoring twice and almost getting a third to make the final count a respectable 31-15.

The Buffs did catch Kansas at the finish when Melvin Johnson raced 94 yards with a kickoff and Tom Mackenzie kicked a pressurized 24-yard field goal with 5:03 left for the winning points, 17-16. The Buffaloes then played their finest 60 minutes of the season, shattering Oklahoma State's

Bill Mallory became CU's 16th head coach in 1974.

Bill Mallory was always wired for action.

bowl-bound Cowboys, 37-20, in a televised game at Stillwater. CU then finished with a 33-19 relapse at Kansas State as the Wildcats got great running and passing from its fine quarterback, Steve Grogan. That upset skidded Mallory's first Buffalo edition to 5-6-0, same as the year before. But this had been a clawing, never-say-die team which had responded well to the new coach. Despite the sub-.500 campaign, Mallory had passed his opening test. He had proven he could hold his own in the Big Eight. And he could look forward to 1975. His staff would have a full year behind them. He'd have his first group of recruits available. He and his squad would be much more comfortable with a year behind them. And, most importantly of all, Wyoming and Wichita State would replace LSU and Michigan on the schedule!

1975

The Buffs slipped past better-than-expected California in the opener, 34-27 as Mike McCoy returned a punt 61 yards and David Williams threw a 45-yard TD strike to Emery Moorehead, and later, cut 12 yards on a fourth-quarter keeper to break a 27-27 tie. Wyoming wasn't as easy as anticipated either, as mistakes - the main one a clip which negated a 108-yard kickoff

In the era of the Afro, no one did it better than defensive ace Mike Spivey (1974-5-6).

return by McCoy - frustrated a 513-yard offensive afternoon. CU's defense, led by middle guard Charlie Johnson, paced a 27-10 victory, limiting the Cowboys to only 40 rushing yards. McCoy got to keep a 99-yard kickoff runback as the Buffs frolicked past hapless Wichita State, 52-0, to take a perfect 3-0 record to Oklahoma.

James Mayberry was CU's most valuable player in 1978. He's shown with coach Bill Mallory and an armful of awards.

Mallory got the familiar Sooner treatment as he contributed an unlucky decision of his own in a 21-20 heartbreaker. Trailing 21-14 late in the game, the Buffaloes drove 68 yards flawlessly, scoring on a Williams backdoor pass to Waddy for the final eight with 1:19 remaining. Correctly deciding that a tie could very well mean an Orange Bowl bid down the line, Mallory ordered a PAT kick. There were raised eyebrows in the CU rooting section. All fans everywhere like a coach who gambles for the win at a time like that. To CU's horror, Mackenzie, who had converted 16 straight attempts, hooked this one far to the left. It actually was a good decision by the CU coach except that the kick failed. The Buffaloes finished just a game behind OU and Nebraska. A tie would have brought them even with the Sooners and might have made a difference in the Nebraska game. But the world loves a gambler and Bill Mallory didn't gamble so he took a lot of heat despite a gutty performance against a Sooner team that extended its winning streak to 33 games.

A different torture awaited CU at Miami a week later: the heat, humidity and a serious case of food poisoning which sidelined six Buff regulars. Still

the Buffaloes survived, 23-10, then kept winning, 31-20, against Missouri. Tough Troy Archer, a great defensive end Mallory had recruited out of junior college a year earlier, launched a comeback against the Tigers when his smashing tackle produced a fumble and a quick CU turnaround after Missouri had taken a 17-3 lead. Archer's defensive mates kept it going. Brian Cabral launched another TD drive with another fumble recovery and Tom Tesone set up still another with a 47-yard punt runback boosted 15 yards further by a roughing penalty. The Buffs were also beginning to get some fine running by dancing Tony Reed, a JC transfer who was just beginning to understand Mallory's style of running, which was upfield.

At Nebraska though, the world caved in on the Buffaloes after Williams' opening 74-yard touchdown jaunt. The score came almost effortlessly as the CU quarterback faked a pitchout, cut inside the end and outran the Nebraska secondary.

Williams' sortie had the same effect as tickling a cobra. The Cornhuskers struck back savagely, helped greatly by six CU fumbles and two interceptions. The Buffs were finished by the half, 42-

Jeff Geiser was an outstanding Buff linebacker who became an equally excellent college coach.

Defensive backs didn't come any better than Rod Perry (1973-4).

7, and the score rose to 63-7 in the third quarter before Nebraska relented to yield two meaningless touchdowns. The final score was 63-21. Truly, a game to forget.

And CU did, recovering for four straight closing wins: over Iowa State (28-27), Oklahoma State (17-7), Kansas (24-21) and Kansas State (33-7). The closing surge produced a Bluebonnet Bowl bid much to the delight of CU fans who relished the speed with which Mallory had gotten the Buffs back to the post-season parade. The opponent would be Texas, a fine team featuring an all-time great, fullback Earl Campbell. But the Longhorns had crippled quarterbacks so the game was a tossup. What happened was more like two games. CU won the first one, 21-7, pushing Texas all over the field in the first half. The Longhorns then came out after intermission even more decisively, recovering a fumble and blocking a kick then booting a 55-yard field goal to move ahead in the first 11 minutes of the third quarter to win going away, 38-21. The second-half collapse was unexplainable. The same thing had happened in the second quarter at Ne-

braska. Both times the Buffs had come unglued after impressive beginnings. Would this be an omen of things to come? It would not. The Buffaloes were ready to contribute greatly to the state's celebration of its 100th birthday in 1976.

1976

The CU prospect was bright in 1976 despite the loss of 11 seniors who were drafted into the NFL, three (Troy Archer, Mark Koncar and Pete Brock) in the first round and three more (Dave Logan, Mike McCoy and Steve Young)

Woody Shelton presents Dal Ward with keys to a new Cadillac at his retirement dinner in 1975.

Rugged tackle Mark Koncar was a CU All-American in 1975.

injury when he was hit late after kicking an opening 47-yard field goal. Austin also went down early with a knee problem but recovered in time to start against lowly Drake but yielded the starting job to Knapple for the rest of the season, leaving with the Buffaloes hung up in a 10-10 first half tie. Knapple was impressive this time, moving the Buffs quickly in front with a good drive then exploding the offense with three touchdowns in the first five minutes of the second half to salt away a 45-24 win.

CU couldn't keep it going before a capacity crowd in Boulder after Mark Zetterberg's four first half field goals which gave the Buffs a 12-7 intermission lead over Nebraska. But Howard Ballage, whose 37-yard punt return had set up one of the field goals, dropped one to put the Cornhuskers in position for a go-ahead touchdown. The Nebraska defense muffled CU's attack in the final 30 minutes and Nebraska won, 24-12. Then came one of the most unbelievable finishes in Big Eight history as the hopelessly-beaten Buffaloes scored 14 points in 18 seconds with time nearly gone to beat Oklahoma State, 21-10. The weird sequence began when Knapple threw desperately into a flock of Cowboy defenders on fourth down at the OSU 18 with the Buffs trailing, 10-6. A Cowboy easily intercepted the pass - a knockdown would have sufficed - but instead of kneeling for a touchback he tried to run out of

in the third. The Buffs had 12 regulars returning and lettermen at 21 starting positions so there was no reason to brood about the Bluebonnet Bowl fadeout. Adding encouragement was a not-too-menacing non-conference schedule. Mallory rolled up his sleeves, driving the squad hard in spring and pre-season drills. He's been around long enough to know a good thing when he saw it.

The biggest void was caused by the graduation of quarterback David Williams. His 1975 backup, Jeff Austin, edged out Knapple (who had seen the light and come back home after two years at UCLA) for the starting assignment in the opener at Texas Tech. But Austin bombed out quickly against the Red Raiders, throwing four interceptions in the first half to put the Buffs in a hole from which they never recovered. Only the zig-zag, upstream maneuvering of Reed, who dug out 107 tough yards, highlighted the 24-7 defeat.

James was still putting in his program at Washington and the Buffaloes ground out a 21-3 win at Seattle, as Austin, getting a second chance, guided the Buffs to a pair of 80-yard drives. The home opener was a 33-3 triumph over Miami but it cost CU the services of its fine placekicker, Pete Dadiotis, who went out for the season with a knee

CU's 1975 Bluebonnet Bowl team had two outstanding ends in Dave Logan (88) and Don Hasselbeck (89).

the end zone. CU wide receiver Steve Gaunty reacted swiftly, stripping the ball away and Waddy fell on it inside the one. Kelleher scored on the first play with the clock showing 43 seconds left. Following the kickoff, OSU threw a flat pass which linebacker Frank Patrick intercepted and rambled 25 yards into the end zone.

The electrifying finish resurrected the Buffaloes who followed up with a 33-14 win over Iowa State to set up a critical Folsom Stadium collision with Oklahoma. This time the Buffaloes found the right combination. It was a third-quarter 70-yard bomb from a scrambling Knapple to the wide-open Waddy which turned the momentum around with Oklahoma leading 31-20. The CU defense dominated the fourth period, setting up a pair of Kelleher lunges for a 42-31 win. Knapple, primarily a passing threat, showed some fancy footwork in his finest game as a Buffalo, cutting inside for a vital 21-yard gallop for one touchdown and using the same maneuver to go 28 yards for another.

The Buffs could smell a title. Only also-rans Missouri, Kansas and K-State were left. A sweep would give CU the championship. They didn't come close, losing to Missouri as the Tigers poured cold water on a CU dream for still another time, stopping Knapple and plodding to a 16-7 upset. CU then rallied with an easy 40-17 win over inept Kansas then outlasted a fired-up Kansas State team, 35-28. CU's fate was in the hands of Oklahoma on the following

David Williams (1973-4-5) was one of CU's finest all-around quarterbacks.

All-American center Pete Brock (1973-4-5) was the first of three brothers to play at CU.

Emery Moorehead was a versatile halfback in 1974-5-6 and made good as a tight end in the NFL.

Mike McCoy was a defensive stalwart in 1974-5.

Charlie Johnson (1975-6) had no peer as a nose guard.

Breakaway Billy Waddy (1973-6) scoots for daylight.

Thanksgiving Day. If the Sooners whipped Nebraska, they'd finish in a 3-way tie with CU and OSU with the Buffs getting the bowl bid on the strength of wins over both teams. A Nebraska win would send the Huskers, who had defeated CU. Oklahoma pulled it out at the gun with a short pass followed by a lateral to David Overstreet who sailed into the end zone, pulling the Buffaloes to Miami with him.

The Orange Bowl opponent was Ohio State, led by Mallory's former mentor, Woody Hayes. It was a bruising battle but Hayes had the best weapons. CU took an early 10-0 lead on a 26-yard field goal by Zetterberg and an 11-yard Knapple-Moorehead TD following a 40-yard sprint by Waddy. From then on, however, it was all Ohio State as the Buckeyes threw a blanket over the CU offense in the final three quarters to win, 27-10.

The story of 1976 was much the same as 1975 except the Buffaloes broke down in a major bowl this time. There were thrilling wins, disappointing defeats and a faded finish. The tom-toms of the CU backers began tapping out a familiar tune: Mallory couldn't win the big game - like Ward and Crowder, he could come close only to fail. Or, when the victory over OU was mentioned, couldn't win enough big games. The natives were restless once again. The pressure was on the CU coach. And it is difficult to escape once the howling of the wolves begins.

There is something eerily fatal about a CU coach having a big season. Bunny Oakes was fired two years after taking the Buffs to the Cotton Bowl. Jim Yeager went down three campaigns after his finest fall. Dal Ward was gone in two seasons after winning the Orange Bowl. And beleaguered Eddie Crowder

threw in the towel two years after finishing third in the nation. Mallory continued the fatal pattern. He would be gone in two years, too.

1977

Bill's major problem was recruiting. He was a solid field coach. But he and his staff couldn't live up to the high Crowder standards for bringing in raw material. A steady deterioration in squad strength began to show in 1977 despite a seemingly-sound 7-3-1 record. But that mark was misleading. Three of the victims were pushovers Kent State (42-0), New Mexico (42-7), and Army (31-0) following a shaky start against an underdog Stanford team coached for the first time by a newcomer named Bill Walsh. The Cardinals flashed a talented rookie named Darrin Nelson and it

122

Brian Cabral returns an interception to preserve a victory over Stanford in 1977.

Tony Reed (19) covered a lot of ground for Bill Mallory in 1975-6.

took an end zone interception by Brian Cabral to preserve a 27-21 decision.

The Buffs lost their best tailback, Mike Kozlowski with a punctured lung against Kent State, a loss which would hurt when the tough last half of the schedule came up. New Mexico offered no resistance and a 59-yard Ballage TD followed by Mark Haynes' 97-yard interception guided the Buffs. In a steady downpour at West Point, Stu Walker's fumble recovery at the 16-yard line stirred up his stumbling mates who led by only 15-13 at that point but scored twice in the final six minutes to win, 29-13.

CU's five straight victories, although the opposition was far from formidable, lifted the Buffaloes to third place, nationally. It should be remembered that pollsters rely primarily on won-lost records for their rankings, dis-

regarding the quality of a team's schedule. In this case, CU didn't belong that high and soon exposed itself, staggering home with only two wins and a tie over three inferior opponents in the last six games. Kansas sounded a warning as the Jayhawkers rallied from a 17-3 deficit to get a 17-17 tie, narrowly missing winning when they mishandled a pitchout while already in position for a deciding field goal. In fairness to the Buffaloes, they lost the heart of their defense in this game when Cabral was lost for the season with a serious knee injury.

A near-fatal head injury to linebacker Tom Perry overshadowed a 33-15 loss at Nebraska as emergency surgery in Omaha removed a blood clot and saved his life. It was almost deja vu. As had been the case in the Buffs previous appearance in Lincoln, they took early command with a 15-3 lead then

helped revive the Cornhuskers with two turnovers. Missouri continued Mallory's miseries with three second half touchdowns after fumbling on three of their first four possessions to give the Buffs an early 14-0 lead which turned into a 24-14 loss.

It took a gritty performance by a freshman quarterback, Larry Lillo, to save a 12-7 win at Iowa State. CU's first two signalcallers, Knapple and Pete Cyphers, went out with injuries with the Buffs nursing that narrow lead. Lillo, who had scarcely practiced at that position and who was playing in his first game, ran the team flawlessly, handling the ball perfectly then hitting a short first down pass to let the Buffs run out the clock.

CU took its show on the road and it closed in barely more than 30 minutes before a national television audience,

Defensive tackle Ruben Vaughan (1975-8) talked a good game and played an even better one.

52-14, at Oklahoma. Their defense shattered by injuries, the Buffs took a brutal beating, yielding 35 points in a 10-minute period during the second and third quarters. The Buffs then closed out the disappointing fall with a 23-0 victory over Kansas State as James Mayberry, latest in a line of fine CU fullbacks, ripped out 174 yards in a record 40 carries. The happy-go-lucky senior closed out his final season with 1299 yards, second only to Davis' 1386 in 1971. But that was small consolation for CU fans.

Mallory was getting it from all quarters now. Crowder and other CU officials were nervous about the future. The CU ranks were thinning because of the inadequate replacements coming in. To compound his problem, the out-spoken CU coach had antagonized many Boulder boosters with an ugly confrontation during a weekly meeting. He had already upset the press with a peculiar policy two years earlier in which reporters were banned from the dressing room following a CU defeat but permitted in after a victory. That ruptured his already shaky relations with the covering scribes.

Mallory didn't get any breaks in the press after that and by 1978 he needed all the help he could get. None came, least of all from his team which did him in with another fadeaway in 1978. Like Oakes, three decades earlier, Mallory was a private person who trusted only a few intimate friends and suspected everyone else. He could survive these characteristics as long as his teams played well. Good teams can always cover up any coach's flaws. But Mallory's sin wasn't his personality. That was a minor discord. The late season collapses in 1977 and 1978 were what did him in.

1978

The Buffs ran roughshod over five straight opening foes, limiting each to a single touchdown and running up a rousing 135-35 composite score. Here's the way it went: Oregon (24-7), Miami (17-7), San Jose State (22-7), Northwestern (55-7) and Kansas (17-7). Once again, Oklahoma State brought the Buffaloes to earth, 24-20, as a last-ditch CU rally failed on a wind-blown incomplete pass with the receiver in the open. Then came the crusher. A 100-yard kickoff return by Ballage and a 43-yard fumble return by Tim Roberts gave the Buffs a sudden 14-3 first

Jeff Knapple's pinpoint passing led CU to the Orange Bowl in 1976.

again, for two touchdowns which, with one from QB Bill Solomon, got the Buffs off the deck. It was a fine tribute to Mallory that his team would still battle despite the gloomy season and the big Missouri third quarter lead.

But the reprieve didn't last long. Powerful Billy Sims led Oklahoma's wishbone past the Buffs, 28-7, the first of three straight closing losses. Next was a dismal 20-10 loss on a dismal day at Kansas State. Then Iowa State, trying successfully for a bowl bid, wrote a melancholy finish on Mallory's CU career as his coaching ally from Ohio State days, Earle Bruce, got his only win in five tries against Bill's teams. It was Iowa State's first win in Boulder since 1963 and it closed the book on Mallory. It was true that injuries had wrecked the team. But injuries are part of football and Mallory's undoing came primarily because he didn't have adequate replacements for the wounded. And gathering material is a coach's first responsibility.

period lead over Nebraska.

But the Cornhuskers were accustomed to early CU leads and came back relentlessly to tie the score at the half, then buried the Buffaloes with a 42-point second half. The turnaround was just as unbelievable as the one at Lincoln in 1975. CU's demoralized legions poured abuse on Mallory who was now fair game for every armchair quarterback in the state. His demise was by now a foregone conclusion.

But Bill's teams may have been confused by sudden turns of events and overwhelmed by others but they never quit. His Buffaloes fired one closing salvo, a tremendous comeback at Missouri in which they scored three times in the final 20 minutes to win, 28-27. CU got a big break in this one when, with the Tigers leading 27-7 in the third period a wide open receiver dropped a sure touchdown pass which would have put the game out of reach. Instead, CU detonated a young fullback named Eddie Ford, who was never heard of

Howard Ballage was a fine runner and kick returner for Bill Mallory in 1976-7-8.

Burly Matt Miller anchored CU's defense in 1976-7-8.

Mallory's record for five years was 35-21-1, not bad on the surface. But his five seasons were dotted with easy non-conference opponents plus the also-rans in the Big Eight. Bill was fired on November 21, 1978, three days after the final game. He went out like a man, setting his jaw and stalking out of his stadium office without comment. He remained in Boulder for a year then took the head job at Northern Illinois where he quickly produced a small col-

lege bowl team. From there he went to Indiana where he became the hit of the Hoosier state with his facelift on that downtrodden Big Ten school's program. Mallory had made many mistakes, mostly off the field, at Colorado. But he learned his lessons well and used his experience to become a fine major college coach. It was only a case of his becoming as effective off the field as he was on it.

During the next decade his football

fortunes would far outstrip CU's. Keeping horses was his hobby. He loved to ride for relaxation and he rode out of town in style, with two year's salary tucked in his saddlebags and headed not for a western sunset but toward an eastern sunrise. Like the morning sun, his coaching career would rise out of the darkness. But Coloradoans were glad to see him go. They looked forward to a new Messiah. They got one but his message didn't take. The next six years

Fullback James Mayberry leads Mike Kozlowski (21) on a sweep at Oklahoma.

would be the worst stretch in CU's first century. Buffalo teams would win only 14 games during that span. Mallory had won that many in his first two seasons. The dark days were directly ahead.

The Chuck Fairbanks nightmare years were up next. CU fans would wake up screaming on countless early Sunday mornings during the next three falls. Crowder would begin to twist on his mattress, too. It is very important that athletic directors hire good football and basketball coaches. Unfortunately, Eddie didn't hire head coaches nearly as well as he had recruited football players. His career as an administrator would spiral downward with the football program. Not as quickly but nevertheless to the same dead end. But not until the most bizarre episode in CU history, or

any other schools, for that matter. It took part mostly in the courtroom not the playing field and it would result in a costly setback for CU and Crowder.

Eddie backed himself into a corner almost immediately when he publicly stated that he would come up with a big name coach to succeed Mallory. And such names as UCLA's Terry Donahue, Nebraska's Tom Osborne and, from further out of reach, such luminaries as Crowder's aging idol, Bud Wilkinson of the St. Louis Cardinals, and the top-ranked coach in the NFL, Miami's Don Shula. Crowder felt certain he could lure someone of this calibre, if not one of these four. His chief allies in his search were a pair of powerful friends who played large roles in Eddie's CU program, Denver oilman Jack Vickers

and Bob Six, president of Continental Air Lines and a resident of Denver until he moved his headquarters to Los Angeles several years earlier.

Six liked the way a young Donahue had moved UCLA quickly to the top. The tough-acting, rough talking super-executive, regarded by many as the outstanding individual in the air line industry, supported the Los Angeles school second only to CU. His summer jobs for football players at Continental locations were a key source of NCAA-approved vacation employment for college athletes. The promise of them was an important recruiting tool, especially for the Californians to whom CU now looked for its basic source of man-power. But Donahue was happy at UCLA. Six pushed him hard. Crowder liked him too. But after talks with both men, Donahue elected to stay put.

Now Eddie went after Wilkinson. But the ex-Oklahoma legend had just completed his first season in St. Louis. The Cardinals had given him an opportunity to get back into coaching at the professional level. Bud felt an obligation to stay. Shula was a shot in the dark but he was probably the football coach in America whom Crowder most admired. However, successful pro coaches aren't inclined to step down to a college job. An occasional Lou Holtz might defect after an unhappy season. But not the Don Shulas of the world. Suddenly, Eddie learned that Osborne might be interested. He was, to the extent of making a public visit to Boulder with his wife to check out the situation and to get an inside look at CU facilities, and more importantly, CU administrative attitudes toward football.

Osborne a totally honorable man, was serious about the possibilities of the move. But he is also a practical man. A delegation of Nebraskans met him at the airport upon his return and sweetened the Cornhusker pot considerably. That, plus the knowledge that Nebraska's program was light years ahead of CU's, led him to withdraw. Now Crowder was down to what has always been the best source of replacements, the field of college assistants. There is no better training for a college head coaching job than to have been a player on a major college team, then an assistant in one or more top college programs. CU's history certainly reveals that this is the best place to look. Folsom, Oakes, Ward, Grandelius and Crowder had come from that background. Mallory had not. Neither would the next man.

As Crowder stepped back to look into the ranks of top assistants, the name of Monte Kiffin surfaced quickly. Kiffin had been a fine lineman at Nebraska, assisted there after graduation and was currently a top hand at Arkansas. Kiffin had strong endorsements from Osborne and from Razorback athletic director Frank Broyles, a longtime Crowder friend whose success as a coach and director had earned Eddie's great admiration. Kiffin seemed to be on track for the job. Suddenly, he was derailed.

Eddie made a routine call to former Oklahoma coach and then the head man at the New England Patriots about an unrelated subject. When Fairbanks hinted he might be interested in returning to the college ranks, Crowder exploded into action as only Eddie could explode into action. He had his big name now! He'd pull out all the stops to get Fairbanks, who had won a fine reputation for superb jobs at both

Laval Short (92) chokes off an Oklahoma running threat in 1978.

Eddie Crowder managed the CU athletic program with great effectiveness from 1965-84.

Norman and Boston. Fairbanks definitely was interested. Vickers, also a longtime friend of Chucks, entered into the picture, serving as a middleman between the two. The deal was worked out quickly and to the satisfaction of all parties concerned: CU, Crowder and Fairbanks.

There was only one omission: the New England Patriots' volatile owner, Billy Sullivan. Not to worry, Fairbanks assured Crowder, he and the Pats owner were the best of friends and Sullivan's approval would be automatic. After all, nobody stopped football coaches from jumping ship. Contracts protected coaches not the organizations who wrote them. That settled, CU moved quickly. The *Boulder Camera* sports editor Dan Creedon, a CU grad, hinted of such a move in a December 12 column. On the following Monday morning, Dave Nelson, like Creedon a CU grad

with an intense and loyal feeling for the school, broke a front page story in the Rocky Mountain News stating that Fairbanks had accepted the job. Then all hell broke loose that night!

The plan was magnificent. It would be a public relations coup! New England was closing out the regular NFL season against Miami in the Orange Bowl. It was a Monday Night TV game which meant the largest possible sports audience. Fairbanks would visit with Sullivan, who was already in Miami, and tell him about his move. His buddy Billy would congenially give Chuck his blessing and best wishes. The announcement would be made on ABC-TV that night. Dramatically, the Fairbanks move to CU would be beamed into millions of homes.

Unfortunately, things were not what they seemed. Sullivan did not give his blessing. Instead, he angrily informed

the top mouth on the national telecast, Howard Cosell, that CU and Fairbanks had plotted the move without his knowledge and that he would not release Chuck from his New England contract and that furthermore, Fairbanks was suspended and would not be allowed to coach the Pats in the game. In a terse editorial comment before the game following a brief interview with Sullivan, Cosell blasted CU for tampering and named Jack Vickers and a relatively uninvolved Boulder business man named Everett Williams as two of the chief conspirators. That bomb dropped, Cosell and his broadcast mates turned their attention to the game, a Miami rout of the Pats which further enraged Sullivan.

Crowder and his CU allies turned to each other ashenly and muttered something like, "What hath Chuck wrought?" Then they gathered themselves and vowed to get Chuck, whatever the cost. The price was high, unbelievably high.

A Boston judge immediately granted an injunction preventing Fairbanks from taking the CU job. A 3-month court fight followed. CU's legal fees topped $100,000. The Buffalo barristers lost. The Boston judge awarded Sullivan a $200,000 settlement from CU and ordered Fairbanks to surrender $110,000 to the Pats from a deferred income account. That settled, Fairbanks limped into Boulder in early April. He had hastily formed a staff with ex-Florida coach Doug Dickey acting as temporary head man during the three months Chuck was bottled up in Boston. Spring practice was ready to begin. It had been an embarrassing and expensive ordeal. But the Buffaloes finally had the man they wanted. Regardless of the cost, Chuck would prove to be worth it. Never, anywhere in the sports world, was there a worse assumption. If CU partisans had thought they'd undergone every type of torture possible on and off the football field, they hadn't seen anything yet!

FAIRBANKS
1979 - 80 - 81

The less said about Fairbanks' three seasons the better. The Buffs were 7-26-0 during that time. Horror followed horror. Did the Buffs bottom out when they lost two straight games to lowly Drake in 1979 and 1980? Or was it in the 1980 opener at UCLA when they trailed at the half, 56-0? Or was it in that same season when they swept Davis' 1961 team out of the record books by four points in permitting 282 points? Or was it in an 82-42 defeat by Oklahoma before the home fans in 1980, the most points given up by a CU team since Colorado Mines' 103 in the second game of the first century in 1890? Or was it an 0-59 Nebraska -0-49 Oklahoma parlay in 1981? If selecting a single low-water mark during 1979-80-81 was too difficult to determine, there was no doubt about this: that 3-year period was, by a figurative mile, the worst in CU's first 100 seasons.

For the record, here were the results of Chuck's three teams: (home games in CAPS): *1979:* 19 OREGON 33, 0 LSU 44, 9 DRAKE 13, 17 Indiana 16, 24 Oklahoma 49, 7 MISSOURI 13, 10 Nebraska 38, 10 Iowa State 24, 20 OKLAHOMA STATE 21, 31 Kansas

Chuck Fairbanks' brief CU coaching career produced few happy moments for him or the Buffaloes.

17, 21 KANSAS STATE 6. *1980:* 14 UCLA 56, 20 Lsu 23, 7 INDIANA 49, 42 OKLAHOMA 82, 22 DRAKE 41, 7 Missouri 45, 7 NEBRASKA 45, 17 IOWA STATE 9, 7 Oklahoma State 42, 3 KANSAS 42, 14 Kansas State 17; *1981:* 45 TEXAS TECH 27, 10 WASHINGTON STATE 14, 20 BRIGHAM YOUNG 41, 7 UCLA 27, 0 Nebraska 59, 11 OKLAHOMA STATE 10, 10 Iowa State 17, 0 Oklahoma 49, 14 MISSOURI 30, 0 Kansas 27, 24 KANSAS STATE 21.

Despite the steady barrage of batterings, there were bright moments. The Buffs finished 1979 with two straight wins after a 1-8-0 start as quarterback Bill Solomon threw four TD passes and scored one himself. Sophomore back Walter Stanley had the most sensational debut in CU history against Texas Tech in 1981, catching touchdown passes for 87 and 74 yards, returning a punt 70 yards for a third TD and rushing for 28 yards in four carries. (Unfortunately,

ineligibility then troubles with CU regulations made 1981 his only season with the Buffaloes.) Quarterback Randy Essington had 345 passing yards for three TDs in that same opener. (Sadly, Essington's career was ended before the finish of the 1982 season by a blood condition.)

And a tremendous comeback which beat Oklahoma State at the gun in 1981 when sophomore Steve Vogel, seeing his first college action, replaced the injured Essington with 1:28 remaining in the game, CU trailing 10-3 with first-and-15 at its four-yard-line and out of timeouts. Vogel drove the Buffaloes 96 yards, hitting the touchdown pass to Brad Parker then a winning 2-point conversion to Derek Singleton. The game meant nothing in comparison to the 1961 finish against KU which was for the Big Eight crown. But it was to rate as the most improbable finish ever in Boulder.

There was one singular tragedy in

Stan Brock was the youngest of three Brock brothers to play for CU and he joined his older brother Pete as an All-American in 1979.

Mark Haynes was an all-star high school quarterback who became an All-American defensive back at CU in 1979.

Lance Olander steps over guard Art Johnson for yardage in 1979.

1981 which far overshadowed the CU record and dimmed any highlight of the season. Sophomore Singleton, well on the way to a tremendous career, contracted meningitis the week after that winning PAT catch, made what appeared to be a full recovery then suffered a relapse and died January 1, 1982. That terrible tragedy seemed to typify the cloud which had hung low over the CU scene for three years.

Even the seemingly unperturbable Fairbanks buckled under the avalanche of negatives. But he didn't go down in flames. Instead, he parachuted into a gold mine which made him a wealthy man as he resigned suddenly June 1, 1982 to take a job as coach of the New York Generals in a newly-formed professional league. Always a shrewd operator, Chuck reportedly got a 10% share of the franchise which sold two years later for $10 million. CU was not as fortunate. It had endured Mallory's faltering finish then Fairbanks' no-start, wasting several hundred thousand dollars in settling with Mallory and the Patriots.

The CU program had become the laughing stock of the nation. Crowder's well-earned reputation as one of the country's finest directors had been tarnished badly. The CU program was deep in debt. And, to top it off, the football program was charged with 132 rules infractions over a 10-year period involving the Crowder, Mallory and Fairbanks regimes and handed a one-year-slap-on-the-wrist ban on TV appearances. Surely, the Buffs were at the bottom. Not so! There would be more

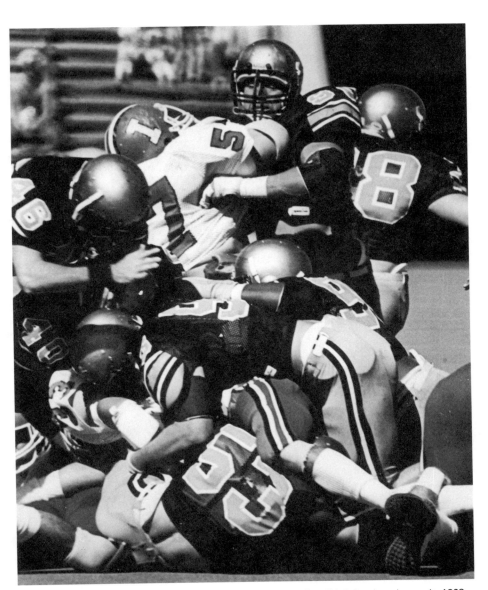

Pete Perry puts a headlock on an Indiana runner to top off a CU defensive charge in 1980.

Fairbanks views the scoreboard with concern as assistant Buck Nystrom expresses the same feeling.

nosedives before the program finally surfaced again. For instance, a 1-10 record in 1984 that was just as pathetic as the one in 1981.

But at least the Fairbanks nightmare was over. Once again, Eddie Crowder was searching for a football coach. And, once again, the hunt would take some bizarre turns before a surprising underdog got the nod. Fairbanks' sudden resignation had caught Crowder by surprise even though rumors of his departure for the New Jersey pro team had been circulating for at least a week. But the tight-lipped coach never really confided in anyone at CU and there was no real reason to believe the rumors. After all, they could have been wishful thinking.

As Eddie sorted out possible candi-

dates in his mind one name kept surfacing, that of Drake coach Chuck Shelton. Actually, Shelton's name had come up quickly following the 1981 season when Eddie briefly considered firing Fairbanks. The Drake coach had shown Crowder well-prepared teams in the Bulldogs' upsets of Fairbanks' CU teams in 1979 and 1980. Shelton was an excellent prospect, a coach who had compiled a solid record at Drake and who appeared ready to move into a major college job. Eddie liked the way his Drake teams had played against CU. He had checked out Shelton in December and gotten some good recommendations. This time there was no talk from him about a big name coach. He didn't have much time to search - the 1982 season was less than three months away. The more Eddie thought about the field of possible candidates, the better he liked Shelton.

Shelton flew in from Des Moines for his CU interviews two days after Fairbanks' resignation. He impressed everyone with his down to earth style of thinking, talking and acting. He was characterized by a member of a committee as a "good old boy." The feeling was that he would be a refreshing change from the cold, aloof Fairbanks. Crowder's feeling was that he would be a tough, no-nonsense head man much like Mallory but with a better public personality. He wouldn't be a sparkler but he'd be good. Eddie was impressed sufficiently to keep the latest Chuck in Boulder for three full days, at least double the normal visit. Shelton saw everyone, some people twice. Eddie had him in tow constantly. It appeared certain that Shelton would get the job.

But there was a hitch. His playing and coaching background, almost completely at the small college level, made some people nervous. CU president Arnold Weber was included in this group. A shrewd judge of people, Weber cautioned Eddie to be careful about hiring Chuck. It would make Eddie, who was already vulnerable, even more vulnerable if Shelton bombed out like Fairbanks. Weber liked Eddie Crowder, admired his intelligence and his athletic connections, liked being around him even though Eddie's department had produced nothing but problems for the CU leader.

Other close friends of Eddie's, whose opinions he respected, also suggested that hiring a coach from tiny Drake might not be a worthwhile gamble. Eddie listened and pondered but he was not inclined to change his mind. He did invite BYU's Lavelle Edwards, who had done an outstanding job of building that school into a nationally respected power, to Boulder for an interview. In contrast to Shelton's 72-hour stopover, Edwards was in town less than a day. He was only mildly interested in leaving his solid position at Brigham Young and probably was more interested in seeing what CU was offering in comparison to what he was getting at BYU, a school well off the beaten track and probably not paying Edwards what he was worth. At any rate, the talks never got serious and Edwards left Boulder a non-candidate.

Now there was the possibility that Eddie might even consider stepping back in on an interim basis because

Derek Singleton (43) takes a handoff from Steve Vogel and heads downfield behind Willie Beebe (47) and Doug Krahenbuhl (66).

Derek Singleton rips for good yardage against Texas Tech in the 1981 opener.

Ray Cone (60) and Guy Egging (37) form a convoy as Steve Vogel (13) looks for an open receiver against Texas Tech in 1981.

Walter Stanley steams goalward during a super Saturday against Texas Tech in 1981.

ent at few of his interviews but the CU director was getting a constant feedback and it was all good. Even though he had started from far back, McCartney closed ground with each meeting. Shelton's early lead faded fast as soon as the Michigan-Drake comparisons developed. There was never a feeling that the Drake coach wasn't a good man. It was simply a case of McCartney having a better background, both as a player and as a coach.

After a 36-hour visit, he flew back to Michigan with the job in his pocket. Before he accepted it though, he would seek Schembechler's advice and discuss the opportunity with his family. A devout Catholic who had renewed his religious dedication following a Missouri career as a free-spirited collegian, McCartney was a devoted family man on the order of Mallory. Hesitant about his chances upon his arrival, he quickly caught the feeling he was gaining ground but still appeared almost shocked that he had become a serious candidate, possibly even the favorite, after less than 24 hours on the scene. His trip back to Ann Arbor was not critical to his decision. Major college head jobs don't grow on trees and nobody knew this better than the 41-year-old who had toiled rather obscurely for 19 years.

Ron Brown was a fine runner and receiver in 1981-3-4-5.

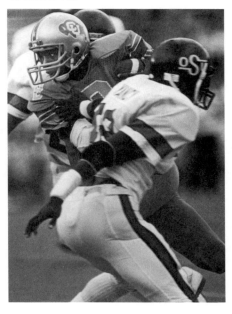

there wasn't time for a thorough search. But Weber and other CU authorities quickly squelched that option. So Eddie looked for a third prospect and came up with Bill McCartney, a member of the Michigan staff for the past eight years, the last five as defensive co-ordinator. McCartney had established a reputation as one of the Big Ten's finest defensive coaches. He wasn't unfamiliar with the Big Eight, having played on some of Dan Devine's excellent Missouri teams. He had, in fact, played in Folsom Stadium in 1961 when he was the starting Missouri center in the game which decided the Big Eight championship.

But he was still a longshot, obviously chosen for an interview to make the selection process more diversified. Shelton was still the odds-on favorite. But Crowder was wavering. As the search headed toward its second week, Shelton was losing momentum. The

Drake coach realized it and pressed Crowder for a decision - to no avail. Eddie wanted to check out McCartney who was getting glowing recommendations from Michigan's Bo Schembechler and other midwestern coaches.

McCartney arrived in Boulder June 8, seven days into the search. Despite not getting the attention from Eddie that Shelton did, he impressed everyone he talked to: the faculty athletic committee, administrators, the regents and, gradually, Crowder. The personable visitor from Michigan with the finely-tuned defensive mind lodged behind a linebacker's nose, played his interview cards well. Without coming right out and saying so, he let everyone know that his background was Michigan and not Drake. There was a mountain of difference between the two schools' and McCartney quietly made certain that everyone realized it. Crowder was pres-

McCARTNEY
1982

McCartney wasted no time accepting the job after returning to Michigan. So the search was over in eight days. It had been an interesting and unusual race. If a horse track announcer had

After a rough start, Bill McCartney was all smiles as his CU program began paying dividends.

described it, it would have sounded like this: Shelton showed great early speed but faded at the finish; Edwards made a brief run early but quit; McCartney came from far back with a bristling stretch drive and won going away.

The new CU coach faced a formidable assignment. The CU program was in near ruins. Fairbanks' late start on the job and his failure to generate any real high school recruitment followed by the usual desperation dip into the junior college ranks had decimated the program. There was very little time for McCartney to assemble a staff, get acquainted with his players and prepare for the season. Almost incredibly, his first meeting with his new squad came on the first day of fall practice. To say the odds were stacked against the new coach and the Buffaloes in 1982 is putting it mildly. There was almost no chance for success that fall or in the near future.

McCartney faced a gigantic rebuilding job and he knew it. Fortunately, so did everyone else at CU and he was given every opportunity to make his program produce. But first there was his trial by fire and the flames were often brutal for the next three seasons as his teams won only seven games. But he doggedly bit into problem after problem and discouragement after discour-

agement, digging deeply into his religious roots, often to the dismay of CU administrators, for strength and encouragement. He was an outspoken crusader, maybe even a Don Quixote attacking a windmill.

Whatever, he kept pushing forward, at times almost excruciatingly slowly. But if the progress was painful it was real. He assembled a good staff. As an assistant at Michigan he had been acknowledged as an outstanding recruiter. Not a handsome Sonny Grandelius type, he was probably the most convincing speaker in modern CU coaching history, both eloquent and convincing but, above all, fervent. McCartney could captivate an individual or a group and, in particular, the parents of a high school senior. It is doubtful that anyone at CU realized he had this talent when he was being recruited. But he had it magnificently and it was the one ability that led the way to an ultimate CU revival.

His first game was a disappointment. An equally unheralded California

team, with a new coach in Joe Kapp who had never coached before, was the opponent in Boulder. It rained on McCartney's parade. The day was totally soggy and so was the CU performance in a rare season opener which featured two new head coaches. Three turnovers deep in CU territory led to a 21-3 halftime lead for the visitors. The Buffs tried hard, pulling to 24-17 after three quarters. But two interceptions and seven fumbles, three of them lost, kept them on the ropes most of the afternoon. Although his entire college background under Schembechler and Devine had been run-oriented, he went to a passing game with his under-manned Buffaloes who threw 38 times, completing 21 to give some encouragement for an offense.

The Buffaloes had a fine passer in Essington, a pair of fireplug halfbacks who could run, Richard Johnson and Guy Egging, a fine tight end in Dave Hestera and some tough defenders including linebacker Ray Cone and backs Jeff Donaldson and Clyde Rig-

Dave Hestera was still another in a great line of CU tight ends in 1981-2-3.

Placekicker Tom Field's accurate toe produced 190 points from 1979 to 1983.

streak. The Cowboys from the WAC conference had other ideas. But it would take some encouragement from McCartney's men to implement them.

The game began exactly as anticipated. A very nervous Wyoming team fumbled deep in its own territory the first three times it got the ball. CU covered all three. But the Buffaloes failed to capitalize on their opportunities, getting only a Field goal. Taking heart from CU's offensive ineptness, the Cowboys collected themselves and handed the Buffs a sound whipping, 24-10. In fairness to the Buff offense, quarterback Randy Essington missed the game because of the blood condition which would shorten his career and sophomore Steve Vogel threw three interceptions in a shaky start. Wyoming, meanwhile, baffled the CU defense with a weapon which the Buffs would use to excellent advantage four seasons later, the wishbone, to dig out 373 yards and thoroughly dominate the game.

It was a humiliating experience for CU. Wyoming had won only one of its three previous starts. CU teams had toyed with their northern neighbors in recent years: 56-13 in 1971 and 27-10 in 1975. But times had changed. Those teams had been coached by seasoned men like Crowder and Mallory. And those CU teams were laden with talent. This one was not. And it was led by a young, inexperienced coach who had

gins. But not much else and no depth at all. If the present looked dark, the future was even darker. Off their getaway performance against a poor California team, the Buffaloes appeared to be in a tunnel which not only had no light at the end but might not even have an end.

But CU quickly found a team in worse shape, Washington State, which had lost its top two halfbacks with preseason injuries. The Cougars had very little offense without these two regulars. CU didn't have much more. But Tom Field, who would become a record-breaking placekicker, sidewheeled four field goals and McCartney won the game and lost his maiden, 12-0. It was not a resounding victory but it was a victory. And it came over a Cougar team which had upset the Buffs in Boulder a year earlier. There was hope. The next opponent would be another relatively weak team, Wyoming. CU fans anticipated a 2-game winning

Lee Rouson, a fine running back in 1981-2-3-4, leaves a Washington State defender in his wake.

Coach Mac gets a happy ride after a big CU victory.

same receiver. With the ball at Nebraska's 24, the squatty little Johnson, shorter than his listed 5-9, burrowed beneath a scrimmage tangle to break free for an electrifying TD.

And suddenly the surprised Huskers were in a battle. But Nebraska teams seldom lose their poise and this one didn't, putting CU's upstarts back in place by scoring the next three times it got the ball, the last two TDs beginning with interceptions. The rally of Mac's men gave CU fans heart. The Buffaloes were puny but plucky. And there were some fine individuals wearing the silver, gold, and blue which had been added to the CU color combination the previous year. Linebacker Ray Cone, a superconfident defensive leader, was the best man on the field that day, making 11 unassisted tackles and getting in on eight more.

One significant point had occurred at this stage of McCartney's career. He publicly proclaimed that his number one target would be Nebraska, wasting no words in labeling the Cornhuskers as CU's Public Enemy No. 1 and going on record that beating the midland monsters would be his primary objective in all of his CU tomorrows. There were many who considered his statements foolhardy. Why needle Nebraska, they reasoned. The Cornhuskers were intimidating enough without being further agitated by a feisty young coach still in his formative years. But Mac was a crusader and Nebraska quickly became his obsession. And the series picked up momentum after two decades of CU torture.

The Buffaloes gathered themselves to gain a nervewracking (for both teams) 25-25 tie at Oklahoma State with defensive backfield standout Victory Scott's three interceptions, two for TDs, providing the spark. The Buffaloes led practically all the way in this one, 13-0 at the quarter, 16-7 at the half and 22-10 with less than five minutes to play. But suddenly OSU exploded with two touchdowns to move ahead, 25-22, with 1:24 remaining. CU's defense had snatched defeat from the jaws of victory. But not quite. There was exactly enough time left to come back and Essington did, hitting Don Holmes for 22 yards to midfield then Dave Hestera for 24 to the OSU 32 from where Field drilled a dramatic 49-yard bulls-eye with no time showing on the scoreboard.

CU's elation didn't last long as the Buffs came tumbling back to earth with

literally been catapulted from the assistant ranks just three months earlier. The road back to respectability would be long and hard. If anyone had doubted that fact, the Wyoming Cowboys drove it home emphatically on this gray September afternoon in Boulder.

There was no relief on the horizon. Nationally-ranked UCLA and Nebraska were next. The Los Angeles-based Bruins punished the Buffs, 34-6, and Nebraska did it too, 40-14. Despite these topheavy defeats there were rays of light. Mac's men (that shortened handle quickly became McCartney's moniker) played fiercely while they were fresh. But there simply were not enough top hands to sustain a 60-minute effort.

Against UCLA, CU fought back with two Field goals to trail by only 10-6 late in the first half. But the Uclans detonated a 50-yard bomb in the final minute to take the heart out of the Buffs who never reached midfield after the rest break. CU extended Nebraska even further a week later, erupting for two third period touchdowns to pull to within 20-14 after a pair of high-stepping Cornhusker tailbacks, Roger Craig and Mike Rozier, had propelled the visitors to a 20-0 halftime bulge and an apparent easy victory. But Essington, able to play again because of transfusions which added a clotting factor to his blood, nailed Johnson for a 37-yard TD then came right back to get his team rolling again with an identical gain to the

three straight clubbings at the hands of Iowa State (31-14), Oklahoma (45-10) and Missouri (35-14). The offense continued to sputter against Iowa State. Aside from a sudden 2-play, 84-yard thrust to tie the score 14-14 at the half, the Buffaloes were impotent. The first TD came when Scott blocked a punt which opportunistic linebacker Dan McMillen scooped up and vaulted 13 yards into the end zone to make the score, 7-7. After the Cyclones had moved back in front, the Buffs drew even again when Essington hit Hestera for 37 yards on first down and butterball Johnson squirted loose for the remaining 47. But that was it for the CU offense. The Buffs crossed midfield only twice in the second half and were stopped by interceptions both times.

The Buffaloes had a surprise for Oklahoma, too. Johnson, by now one of the most sensational backs in the Big Eight, bolted 17 yards to give CU an early 7-3 lead which they nursed to a 10-10 halftime lead. But, like Nebraska earlier, the Sooners awakened during intermission to score with their first five possessions of the second half to put the game away.

Missouri, a tormenter for its alumnus McCartney, in Mac's beginning years, took heed of the Nebraska and Oklahoma early problems with the Buffs, and defused CU quickly, leading 35-0 at the half. But the ever-dangerous Little Richard struck again, racing 83 yards for one of CU's touchdowns. Sophomore Vogel had his best passing day, hitting 13 of 28 for 200 yards and a TD (the clotting problem had ended Essington's college career earlier as further transfusions of the clotting agent were ruled out by administrators and physicians.)

Despite the turmoil at quarterback, Richard Johnson remained a constant positive all fall and he reached new heights against Kansas, scoring four touchdowns as the Buffaloes blasted the Jayhawks, 28-3. The upset developed almost immediately as Vogel hit Johnson with a screen pass on the second play of the game and the squatty speedster fled 77 yards to the end zone. Before the final gun, Johnson added 13, five and two-yard TDs and the ever-present secondary nemesis, Cone, had driven KU runners to the ground 15 times.

But the season closed on a sour note as CU traveled to Kansas State rated as an even choice. K-State, however, had supreme motivation - a bid to the Inde-

Bill McCartney queries a CU back after a play misfired.

pendence Bowl with a victory. A Wildcat team had never been to a post-season game before and didn't pass up this opportunity, belting CU 33-10 as they took a quick 14-0 lead and didn't let up. CU was its own worst enemy in this contest. Trailing only 17-10 at the half, the Buffaloes stopped themselves the first four times they got the ball after the intermission: on a blocked punt, fumble and two interceptions.

So McCartney's first season ended 2-8-1. The fall had been filled with rays of hopes and clouds of despair. But the new coach, a fanatic who split his reading time between his playbook and the

bible, had caught the fancy of his public. A sharp contrast to the silent, and self-centered Fairbanks, Mac was a dedicated crusader (there is no better term to describe him) who gave the promise of unyielding, and courageous (if not always polished) effort. He had quickly established that few miracles would come with his program. (It takes great talent to produce gridiron miracles and the new man simply did not have it, and would not for several years until his recruiting ability took effect.) But he was fresh and clean and enthusiastic and almost wholesome in his approach to the CU problem.

Colorado fans liked that and, accordingly, were prepared to stand behind their new leader. He would often test their patience with his unbending insistence that his players live up to his rules, an attitude which would cost the CU program several talented men during the next decade. But, though some of his dismissals were extremely painful to his plans, he stood by them and ultimately won the respect of CU fans. (It should be remembered that most fans are immediately ready to sacrifice principles for victory and it requires a coach of resolute character to withstand the temptation to relax a rule when the right player is involved.) The road ahead would be rough and tough and discouraging. But Bill McCartney was an eternal optimist. Everybody loves a good guy and Mac was a good guy. And, most importantly, still on his CU honeymoon. It is a tribute to his

Victor Scott provided blanket coverage in the CU secondary in 1980-1-2-3.

personal public stature that he enjoyed the longest honeymoon in CU, and possibly college football, history.

1983

The Buffaloes got a schedule break in 1983. The first three opponents were beatable. CU would have the benefit of a year's exposure to Mac and his staff. And vice versa. Vogel was coming into his own as an excellent passer though not a running threat. Lee Roúson was developing into an excellent power runner. Tom Field was the finest place-kicker in CU history. Defensively, there was a talented trio of backs available in Victor Scott, Clyde Riggins and Jeff Donaldson. The lines were thin but

Chris Symington (71) and Junior Ili (63) were a pair of stalwarts up front in 1983.

flecked with solid returning starters like center Steve Heron, tackle John Firm and tight end Dave Hestera on the offense and linebacker Terry Irvin and tackle Vince Rafferty on defense. And there were already some fine sopho-more prospects showing up in line-backers Barry Remington and Dan McMillen, wide receiver Loy Alexander and center Eric Coyle. This precarious mixture of veterans and rookies, was not deep enough to produce great con-fidence in the season but sufficient to create hope for the future.

CU's first three opponents were Michigan State, still in a rebuilding pro-gram; Colorado State, a second division WAC club; and Oregon State, a peren-nial west coast doormat. The fourth was

midwestern goliath Notre Dame. But even the Irish were in an unusual down period under Gerry Faust. September held hope for the Buffaloes.

But the CU players weren't yet ready to sustain an upset effort to final victory against a superior foe. The Buf-faloes outplayed Michigan State at East Lansing for three periods, leading 10-6 going into the fourth. Then the Spartans moved ahead 16-10 midway through that final period and got a game-clinching break when the usually sure-handed Victor Scott fumbled the 16-10 kickoff at the 12 to enable Michigan State to put the game out of reach. On the plus side for CU was the pinpoint passing of Vogel whose arm produced 228 aerial yards.

The highly-publicized renewal of the CU-CSU grid series - the two teams hadn't met since 1958 - was no contest. The Rams were no match for the Buffs who punched out three straight long scoring drives midway through the first half to take a 24-3 intermission lead, then coasted home, 31-3. CU intro-duced another stubby member of the Johnson family in this one, 5-5 Daryl, younger brother of the departed Richard. The latest Johnson jackrabbit zipped 32 yards for CU's third TD in a carbon copy of his older brother. The Buffaloes piled up 386 yards, best to that point for a McCartney team.

Oregon State was almost as easy. The Buffaloes handled them the same way, scoring the first three times they

got the ball as Vogel hit Ron Brown for a 50-yard bomb to set up a 2-yard John-son plunge then nailed Brown with a 62-yard scoring throw. In between those two, Donaldson ran back an interception 44 yards. Those big plays took the heart out of the visiting Beav-ers quickly. CU led at the half, 24-0, and the final score was 38-14. Rouson slashed for 106 yards and Vogel was 8-13-167 passing and the game was a laugher all the way.

The first meeting with Notre Dame was predictably painful. The Irish, not a polished crew under the by-now belea-gured Faust, had too much muscle for the Buffs and prevailed, 27-3, pounding out 334 rushing yards and 160 more through the air. CU didn't help its own cause, either, crossing midfield four times in five second half possessions but failing to score. Field's 43-yard field goal early in the game was CU's only score as a record Folsom Stadium crowd of 52,692 never got much chance to cheer.

McCartney's alma mater did it to him for the second straight year as Mis-souri brutalized the Buffs in Boulder, 59-20. It wasn't as close as the score indicated. The Tigers took a 31-0 first half lead and stretched it to 59-6 before calling off the dogs. Iowa State con-tinued CU's woes on a wet afternoon in Ames, 22-10. The Buffs trailed 19-10 at the half but came away empty after reaching a first down at the Cyclone nine entering the fourth period. Field's placekick for a consolation three points sailed wide and CU never threatened again as the Cyclones got out of reach with a late field goal.

The Nebraska game was unexplain-able. CU played the Cornhuskers to a standstill for 30 minutes, scoring late to trail by only 14-12 at the half. Then Nebraska exploded a record-breaking 48 points in the third period to stun the Buffaloes, 69-19. The Husker holocaust was aided by a nightmarish CU perfor-mance during that 15-minute period. The Cornhuskers served notice there would be no nonsense quickly, going 67 yards in their first two plays after the kickoff. Then CU turned the ball over on its next five possessions: on a fourth down gamble at its 24, two fumbles, an interception and another fourth down failure. When Nebraska finished their firestorm with a 48-yard drive following a CU punt, the Huskers had broken the Big Eight mark for points in a quarter. They also broke CU's hearts with that unbelievable parade to the end zone.

Nebraska's barrage overshadowed Johnson's 81 rushing yards, Vogel's 170 through the air and pair of field goals by Field.

A blitzing Oklahoma State didn't give CU any opportunities for recovery a week later. The Cowboys, not as nationally recognized as their Norman neighbors but always a problem for CU teams, ripped out 30 points in the second quarter and added seven more in the third before backup quarterback Derek Marshall injected some life into CU with a 56-yard strike to Alexander and a 22-yard TD run. The promising newcomer threw for 274 yards to give some hope for the future. But injuries blunted much of his career and the promise he showed on this afternoon failed to develop.

Still another sophomore, halfback Chris McLemore, fueled CU to a 34-23 upset of Kansas, scoring three touchdowns on two short runs and a 75-yard breakaway. In his first CU start, Marshall was impressive, running the offense flawlessly and completing 11 of 22 passes for 148 yards. KU's aerial wizard, Frank Seurer, riddled the CU secondary for 394 yards on 23 of 52 but the Buffalo defenders fought back with five interceptions to neutralize his efforts.

McCartney seemed to always get his men ready for the monster teams and once again CU fought bravely before bowing to Oklahoma, 41-28 at Norman. When the Sooners broke to a 34-0 second quarter lead, it looked like another landslide loss for the Buffs. Then Vogel hit Alexander for a 7-yard score just before intermission. A pair of second half touchdowns by McLemore and an 11-yard Vogel-Brown score pulled the Buffs to within 13 points with time running out. CU had one more shot left and actually nursed a longshot chance to win as they drove deep in the closing minutes. The Buffs were at the Sooner three on fourth and goal but McLemore was stopped inches from the end zone after taking a short Vogel pass. Had the Buffs scored, recovered an onside kick then somehow scored again - and they had completely taken away the Sooner momentum in the second half - they might have managed a miracle. But an inch was as bad as a mile on their goal line try. CU was getting closer to respectability. But it was still more than a year away.

The Buffs closed the season with a 38-21 comeback against traditionally inept Kansas State, trying desperately to

give the game away in the first half but failing when the Wildcats refused to take advantage of four interceptions, fumbling the ball right back as many times. The Wildcats lost six straight fumbles during the game. Despite those problems, they led the Buffs 21-7 at the half. K-State was fumbling but CU was stumbling and things looked dark for the Buffs. Then the accommodating Wildcats quickly took care of CU's problems, fumbling the first two times they had the ball in the third period. The Buffs struck quickly with each

break. First Johnson bolted 13 yards in a 2-play drive from the 26. Then Vogel hit Rouson for 28 yards on the first play after the next recovery. Just like that the score was tied at 21 and CU dominated the rest of the game as Scott's 71-yard interception return produced the final points.

The CU record was 4-7-0. It could have been 6-5-0 with more productive play against Michigan State and Iowa State. But the Buffaloes were still an in-and-out team: inconsistent during the games and unpredictable from week to

Linebacker Dan McMillen (1982-5) always had his eye on the ball.

In one of the most poignant Folsom Stadium moments in history, Ed Reinhardt made this dramatic return with his parents in 1985 following his brain injury in the Oregon game a year earlier.

week. But they always fought fiercely and the fans recognized their efforts and suffered silently with them. Better times were coming, they predicted painfully and often unconvincingly. And they were. But not for another year.

1984

1984 was a repeat of 1980, a wretched 1-10-0 campaign. All that kept the Buffs from the school's first winless season since that only one in 1890 was a botched field goal from point blank range by Iowa State in the final two minutes of play. There were defeats of all types during 1984. First a 24-21 handwringer to Michigan State when placekicker Larry Eckel missed a 32-yard attempt for a tie on the final play of the game. CU that afternoon unleashed a fine-looking sophomore end in Ed Reinhardt who made a sensational debut, catching 10 passes for 142 yards and two touchdowns.

Next came another near-miss. Alexander, all alone at the five, dropped a perfect Vogel pass with time running out and CU trailing Oregon by what would be the final score, 27-20. Minutes before that, Reinhardt had gone down with a serious brain injury after catching his fourth pass for a 19-yard gain to move the Buffs into Oregon territory. Tackled, but not savagely, by two Oregon defenders, Reinhardt suffered a blood clot in his brain and

required lifesaving surgery immediately. The resulting disability and long rehabilitation period, which was still moving ahead as this was written, cast a pall over the CU season from which the team never completely recovered. It was a tragedy similar to the one involving Derek Singleton in 1981, taking away a fine young man who would have become a leader both on and off the playing field.

Tragedies seemed to stalk CU football teams during the last two decades of the first century. Polie Poitier, a sophomore defensive back, died within 24 hours after collapsing during pre-season drills in 1974, a victim of sickle cell anemia. Tricaptain and linebacker Tom Perry's life was saved by emergency brain surgery following an injury in 1977 at Nebraska but he never played again. Singleton died of meningitis after being stricken in mid-season of 1981. Reinhardt was now the fourth victim as he faced the remainder of his life with serious disabilities following his injury.

The Buffs tried hard to bury their feelings about their unconscious teammate but were not ready to play a foe of Notre Dame's physical superiority. Priorities were important to McCartney and the CU coach spent most of the week at Reinhardt's bedside. Predictably, CU was devastated at South Bend, 55-14. UCLA, an even better team than Notre Dame, had first half problems

with the Buffs but scored 17 straight points in the third period and went on to a 33-16 win. Once again, Missouri was merciless to McCartney, savaging CU 52-7 at Columbia, rolling to a 45-0 lead before sophomore fullback Eric McCarty broke loose for a 40-yard TD late in the third quarter.

The Buffaloes were 0-5 and reeling from those three straight lopsided losses. After coming close in their first two games, CU had suddenly become a disaster looking weakly for a weekly place to land. But the Buffs were rescued by the errant Iowa State field goal attempt and two Vogel-Brown bombs for 43 and 85-yard touchdowns which erased a 12-6 Iowa State halftime lead. CU nursed its 23-12 margin into the fourth period when Iowa State suddenly erupted for nine points and were once again deep in CU territory. The Buffs stiffened at the nine-yard line but all the Cyclones needed was a chip shot field goal to go in front with 2:17 remaining to play. The kick was wide to the right and CU somehow had averted a winless season.

The Buffs surprised Nebraska with a 7-3 halftime lead on Vogel's 16-yard TD pass to Alexander on the first play of the second quarter. In a psychological move, McCartney had scrapped his team's bland blue jerseys for this game and outfitted them in the black ones which had marked the Grandelius, Crowder and Mallory seasons. The sartorial surprise worked for three quarters. But Nebraska finally saw red instead of black and punched out three fourth-quarter touchdowns to win, 24-7. The Buffs were blue in black during the second half, failing to reach midfield in their last six possessions.

In a weird game at Stillwater marked by two safeties, two field goals, a missed PAT attempt and a successful 2-pointer, Oklahoma State made a first-quarter touchdown hold up for a 20-14 victory. CU had the longest play of the game, an 80-yard bomb from Craig Keenan to Brown in the second period. But it was not enough. OSU led at the quarters: 8-0, 15-8, 17-11 and, finally, 20-14.

The Buffaloes were running out of Saturdays but they almost upset Kansas, failing to hold leads of 10-0 in the first quarter and 24-13 in the first five minutes of the second half. Two touchdown passes by a fine KU quarterback, Mike Norseth, propelled the Jayhawkers to a fourth-quarter victory, 28-27. That was the last gasp for the Buffaloes. They buckled before Oklahoma,

42-17, and Kansas State, 38-6. In the Wildcat loss, the Buffaloes suffered a fitting final embarrassment which typified the season. After sophomore quarterback Chuck Page had directed a 73-yard drive for CU's only score, bringing them to within 24-6 early in the fourth period, CU attempted an onside kick which K-State almost insolently returned for a touchdown as a Manhattan crowd enjoying a rare afternoon of victory bellylaughed at CU's final fiasco.

The disaster over, McCartney picked up the pieces, smiled bravely, consulted the good book and hit the recruiting trail. He also did some serious soul-searching about his offensive plan. Clearly it needed some improvement. He'd been forced to use a pro-type pass-oriented attack because of no effective running threat from his quarterbacks.

The CU headmaster, semi-desperate, found a wishbone and snapped it. He got the big piece. The Buffaloes had a burly, great young fullback and an athletic new quarterback. They were the major pieces of the wishbone fragment he held in his hand entering spring drills. They would be the primary reasons for the start of the CU comeback which McCartney was now ready to launch after three years of frustration. Slowly and steadily the CU commander had quietly rebuilt the Buffalo program. It now had some muscles and he was ready to flex them.

1985

There were no great expectations as 1985 began. But there was an aura of mystery to the CU battle plan. In the spring, McCartney had abandoned his pass-oriented attack, switching unexpectedly to the wishbone alignment made famous by Oklahoma. The wishbone was a one-dimension offense with almost total emphasis on running, basically with two parts: a powerful fullback battering straight up the middle, with or without the ball, on every play, and a quick quarterback operating the option, with fleet trailing halfbacks ready to break outside. Passing was an afterthought in the wishbone scheme although, occasionally, a tight end might slip downfield to surprise the secondary.

There were many skeptics who doubted the wisdom of a basically undermanned team like CU moving to a limited offense like the wishbone. The wishbone is good for great teams like the Oklahomas who have the personnel to run out of any formation effectively,

or struggling teams without great striking power who can grind along on the ground thus controlling the ball and the clock and keeping the score respectable, they argued, adding that CU fit neither of these categories in McCartney's fourth year and would be more effective with a balanced attack.

But McCartney knew his squad better than anyone. He had the two basic requirements in a pair of highly-recruited sophomores, quarterback Mark Hatcher, a strong, fast runner with a suspect arm, and fullback

Anthony Weatherspoon, a bruising, power plunger who could move a defensive mass to dig out consistent short yardage and thus establish the inside threat which would open up the outside to Hatcher and some improved running backs, headed by the swift Brown, who had been switched there from wide receiver, and sophomore Sam Smith. Many observers were nervous about CU and its wishbone. Mac was not. The CU coach was a strong-willed man with tremendous faith in what he believed. He figured, correctly, that CU did not

Center Eric Coyle celebrates a CU touchdown against Oklahoma State in 1985.

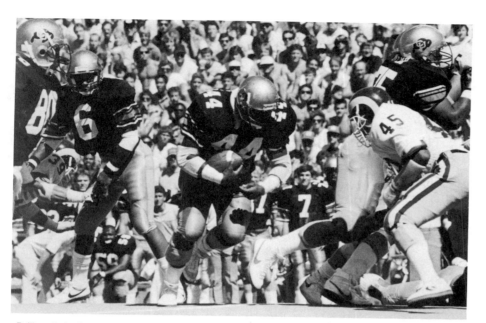

Fullback Anthony Weatherspoon (44) follows big Jim Webb (75) after this 1984 handoff from Mark Hatcher. Jon Embree (80) comes up to support the play.

The start was solid but not spectacular. The Buffaloes ground out a 23-10 win over still outmanned CSU, leading 16-3 at the half. But two drives were significant. With the inside-outside maneuvering of Weatherspoon and Hatcher working efficiently, if not sensationally, the Buffaloes pounded 80 yards in 12 plays in the first half then 88 in 15 in the fourth period. While the defense applauded from the sidelines, the CU offense totally controlled the game. The wishbone debut was a smashing success, even if it was smash football and not professional-type pyrotechnics.

But the turning point of the season, and probably of McCartney's CU coaching career, was supplied by the defense in a dramatic last-minute, last-ditch stand which preserved a 21-17 triumph over Oregon. The Buffaloes had hammered out a quick 14-0 first quarter lead only to see Oregon keep have the passing threat from Hatcher that they had previously with Essington and Vogel.

Therefore, they'd run 90 percent of the time and try to control the flow of a game that way. Passes can be spectacular when the right people catch them. But incomplete passes keep the clock stopped too frequently, extending the length of a game and putting great pressure on an overworked defense. Passing teams can spring an occasional upset. But they also contribute to a lot of lopsided losses. McCartney was tired of watching opponents roll up double figures while his teams completed an occasional bomb. His first three teams had yielded 1007 points, an average of 335 per season or nearly 31 per game. In 1962, Bud Davis had been chased out of Boulder after his team was punctured for 346 points. Only Fairbanks' 1980 horror, 451 points, exceeded CU's 1984 total of 364. Enough, snapped McCartney, whose defensive background had been his chief asset in pointing him toward a head job.

So the Buffaloes bored away from the wishbone, beginning a period in which CU began raising eyebrows with a steady succession of victories which drew praise at first from fans but then yawns as CU spectators fretted about an offense which took them back to the "three-yards-and-a-cloud-of-dust" era of the split T. But that was still ahead. In 1985, the wishbone was a magic formula which would heal CU's miseries.

Until a freak spring vacation injury in 1987 slowed him down, defensive tackle Curt Koch was an outstanding All-American candidate.

coming back and finally go in front 17-14 after three quarters. Now the wisdom of the wishbone conversion loomed large. It was panic time but CU didn't panic. There were no desperation passes as the Buffs took over at their 13 yard line. Instead, Hatcher guided a steady upfield surge, inside and outside and crunchingly effective. CU fans shivered with tension but they liked what was happening - a CU team was climbing off the deck and playing, tough old-fashioned football. There was that surprise pass to the tight end, however, as Hatcher hit Jon Embree for 28 yards to the Oregon 22 in the biggest play of the comeback drive which finished on the next play as Hatcher kept the ball and cut back for the final 22 yards. Amazingly, the Buffs had driven 87 yards in nine plays under the severest pressure to regain the lead, 21-17.

But Oregon wasn't through, either. They began an almost identical comeback, starting from their own 13 and reaching a first down at the CU five with 1:55 left to play. Then the defense stepped forward. David Tate blitzed for a tackle four yards behind the line. Lyle Pickens stopped a Duck receiver for a 2-yard gain and Dan McMillen did likewise on another short (4-yard) completion. With nine seconds left, Oregon took its final time out and called the play which would decide the game. So did CU defensive coordinator Lou Tepper on the other side of the field. Oregon predictably called a semi-rollout action pass from quarterback Chris Miller, as fine a clutch performer as McCartney's teams had seen and who would torture the Buffaloes to defeat in three of the four times he faced them. Tepper correctly guessed that Miller would roll to his right to give him the best passing position. So he ordered a blitz from the back side by strong safety Mickey Pruitt, a quick, deadly pursuer. Tepper's strategy was perfect. Pruitt buried Miller for a 14-yard loss and CU fans went crazy and the Buffs were 2-0 and sniffing success.

But powerful Ohio State forced a 36-13 tranquilizer down CU's throat the next Saturday, crushing the Buffaloes after Weatherspoon had opened the scoring with a 35-yard TD burst in the first quarter. There was one note of hope, however. Backup quarterback Rick Wheeler, a successful prep operator for Cherry Creek's annual powerhouses but regarded as too slow, too slender and not strong armed enough to be a top college signalcaller, got a chance

Mark Hatcher (1984-5-6-7) was CU's first outstanding wishbone quarterback in 1986.

late in the game and led the Buffs to a 16-play, 80-yard scoring drive, getting the TD himself with a 2-yard keeper. Good backup quarterbacks are extremely necessary and often difficult to develop. Wheeler looked like a winner, though not physically equipped to challenge Hatcher seriously for the starting job.

The Buffaloes recovered from the

Buckeye disappointment to win their next three straight over Arizona (14-13), Missouri (38-7) and Iowa State (40-6). A key interception at midfield by John Nairn started CU's drive to their winning touchdown, scored by Brown on a 7-yard run to cap an 11-play, 40-yard drive (there was that relentless short yardage power of the wishbone again.) But CU had to sweat

Barry Helton, CU's All-American punter in 1985-6 displays his oratory ability at a Disneyland dais during the 1986 Freedom Bowl festivities as coach Bill McCartney obviously approves.

But when the pile untangled after that last gain, he didn't get up. The CU fireman was gone for the season with a torn up knee and the Buffaloes had to go to Craig Keenan, who had begun the fall as number three man. Keenan played well, moving the Buffs on in for a TD which gave them a 7-0 lead. But with neither Hatcher nor Wheeler, the CU attack wasn't up to the job. Nebraska tied it at the half then sprang fullback Tom Rathman 84 yards in the closing seconds of the third quarter and won, 17-7. Nebraska dominated the statistics with advantages of 445-218 in total offense, 332-151 in rushing and 113-67 in passing. But CU's conservative attack kept the Buffaloes alive throughout the game as the Buffs continued to hammer away at the beefy Nebraska line with enough success to stay close. Nebraska,

out the win. Arizona had the longest placekicker in the nation, Max Zendejas, who had drilled 46 and 54 yard field goals earlier in this game. Now he tried a 61-yarder with 3:09 left. It had plenty of distance but drifted wide of the upright and CU held on for the win.

McCartney then got his first big bite of revenge against his former school. Hatcher hit Sam Smith with a short pass on the second snap of the game and the play covered 71 yards to the Missouri three and CU romped, 38-7. Hatcher ran for 151 yards and passed for 110 more to earn Big Eight "back of the week" honors while linebacker Darin Schubeck's 11 unassisted tackles earned him "lineman of the week" accolades from Sports Illustrated. The Buffaloes were beginning to impress people. Iowa State was another laugher but with a serious undertone. Hatcher fractured a small bone in his ankle on the third play of the game. But Wheeler came in and moved the Buffs meticulously and Barry Remington grabbed a Cyclone fumble in mid-air and took it 24 yards to ice the win early in the third quarter after CU had taken a 17-0 halftime lead.

At Lincoln, CU extended mighty Nebraska to the limit as Wheeler continued his amazing takeover, getting the Buffs going immediately as he ran for four yards, then eight, then hit Alexander for 12, then kept for seven more to take his team to the Cornhusker 37.

Jon Embree, an outstanding tight end in 1983-4-5-6 celebrates a Buff TD.

David Tate was an inspirational leader of the secondary in 1985-6-7.

QB Alan Strait was the first winner of the Jimmy Powell Memorial Scholarship in 1984. Mrs. Jean Powell presents the award as athletic director Bill Marolt and coach Bill McCartney watch.

frustrated more often than not by Oklahoma's wishbone, must have shuddered after this game thinking about having to face the formation twice annually from this point on.

Oklahoma State then caught CU in a downer as the best running back in the Big Eight, Thurman Thomas, scored twice and ran for 201 yards in a 14-11 Cowboy victory. The Buffaloes, directed by Keenan, could never get going after an early field goal by Eckel. At Lawrence a week later, Pruitt, whose last-minute heroics had saved the Oregon win, then came up with an opening-minute winner, intercepting a Kansas pass on the third play of the game and returning it 27 yards to the end zone to pave the way for a 14-3 victory in another struggling CU afternoon. CU's continuing offensive woes and an overpowering Oklahoma defense produced a 31-0 Sooner shutout at Norman in a game that was closer than that. CU trailed only 7-0 going into the final 19 seconds of the half when Oklahoma's brilliant quarterback Jamelle Holieway scored to give the

Sooners all the cushion they needed. CU could never cross midfield in this game, netting only 109 yards of total offense.

But the Buffaloes were the surprise team of the nation by now. No team in America had come as far as McCartney's wishbone warriors. From a hopeless 1-10 outfit they were suddenly prime contenders for a bowl bid. A victory over Kansas State would nail one down. CU did it easily as the offense and defense contributed equally for an almost effortless 30-0 whitewash of the woeful Wildcats. The Buffaloes had come back from 1-10 to 7-4. From a team which had been outscored 364-172 the previous season they now had built a 211-154 margin on the scoreboards. They got their post-season bid, to the Freedom Bowl in Anaheim, directly in the heart of their prime southern California recruiting territory. It was a double bonus for the McCartney program. In addition to playing perennial national power Washington, CU would have the opportunity to showcase its program to the area to

which they looked most for talent. The Buffs were back, dressed in black and featuring their own "Mac Attack" sparked by Hatcher, Weatherspoon and two score other Californians.

The game, unfortunately, was an almost-but-not-quite affair. It was a tight, tense battle. Washington, coached brilliantly for several seasons by ex-CU aide Don James, led at every quarter turn, 3-0, 10-7, 17-7 and finally 20-17. But CU had a great chance to win after a surprise pass from punt formation saw CU's All-American punter Barry Helton, an 8-man quarterback in high school at tiny Simla, hit Embree in the end zone with a 31-yard rainbow to bring CU to within four points with 3:52 left.

The Buffs, sensing the upset and on fire now, forced the Huskies to punt after three plays then began a relentless drive toward the end zone. With Weatherspoon and an underrated halfback named Mike Marquez doing the heavy work, the Buffs began at their 43 and marched steadily to a second-and-five at the seven. There was nothing fancy. No passes, just nine smashes up the middle or off tackle. The longest gain was 15 yards by Marquez to the 12. On second down from the seven, Marquez ripped right up the middle for five yards and an apparent first down. But the ball popped loose as he hit the ground. In a questionable call, much maligned by CU supporters, an official ruled it was a fumble recovered by Washington. That horrible break probably cost the Buffaloes the game. They never recovered, failing to advance beyond the Washington 42-yard-line in their last two possessions.

The defeat was understandably tough to take. The Buffaloes had played well enough to win, deserved to, in fact. The call on Marquez was a bummer but bad calls are part of the game and McCartney and his men took their disappointment without a whimper. Why not? They had just finished a nearly-miraculous season. Replacements were pouring in as the CU recruiting program, directed by Mac, was by now producing big dividends. The Buffaloes had gotten tremendous national exposure with their great comeback season. McCartney was voted "coach of the year" in the Big Eight and got serious national consideration. The CU football program was beginning to click on all cylinders. McCartney's slow but steady rebuilding job, suspect in many minds at the beginning, had worked.

O.C. Oliver's brilliant bursts sparked the Buffaloes in 1986.

that 3-0 lead. Not to worry, almost every Buff told himself during the intermission. But it was too late. The momentum would never swing back to them. A brilliant CSU aerial attack, orchestrated by former CU aide Kay Dalton, would see to that. The Rams scored 20 straight points after intermission before a meaningless CU touchdown drive, engineered by reserve quarterback Alan Strait, finished the scoring. The Buff offense never got untracked until the closing minutes. On its first eight possessions of the second half, CU netted only 24 yards.

If that opening nightmare wasn't sufficient to send CU into a state of shock, the next three games did. The defense buckled in the closing three minutes, allowing Oregon to rally for a touchdown and field goal to erase a 30-23 CU lead and win, 32-30. The Buffs had raced to a quick 10-0 lead in the first quarter and appeared to be en route to an easy victory. Even after an Oregon comeback had tied the score at 23-all late in the game, Mark Hatcher's clutch 55-yard breakaway had seemingly put the game away. But the Ducks drove 60 yards with the kickoff then recovered an onside kick at their 46 with 0:44 remaining and raced the clock to the 18 to get the winning 3-pointer with no time left.

There was no respite. The first two games had been expected to be CU breezes. The next two, against Ohio State and Arizona, would find the Buffs in an underdog role. At Columbus, the

CU was strong again, physically and mentally. The Buffaloes were ready to produce consistently in the classroom as well as on the gridiron. The program was sound. The leadership was solid, if not superb. Happy days were here again!

1986

Happy days, indeed! CU and its followers, dancing in the streets following the amazing comeback of 1985, went wallowing in the alleys after the opening game of 1986. The worst possible catastrophe happened to the Buffaloes: a loss to Colorado State in the opener. To make matters even more unbearable, it was not an accident. After a shaky start, the neighboring Rams lined up and kicked the daylights out of a flat, shaken CU team which was unable to recover and went down, 23-7.

The Buffaloes should have known

they'd be in for a battle. Even though it is a lopsided rivalry (CU had a 48-15-2 as the first century ended), CSU teams are always sky-high for CU. The Buffs, on the other hand, tend to take their upstate rivals for granted, depending upon superior ability rather than emotion. Physical superiority does not always prevail, as it did not this time.

The game began as expected. CU drove, almost effortlessly, 58 yards in nine plays to the CSU six with its second possession. But a mixup in the backfield produced a fumble on second down and CSU recovered then promptly drove to midfield and out of danger. More importantly, the Rams sensed they had a chance. And when they booted a 40-yard field goal on their next possession they knew they had a chance.

CU didn't score in the first half, losing an interception then missing a long field goal as it ended with CSU nursing

Defensive star Mickey Pruitt, who rang a few bells himself in 1984-5-6-7 walks off the field with trainer Dave Burton after a collision.

Big Ten Buckeyes rolled to a 10-0 half-time lead and settled down for an easy triumph. But a 37-yard Dave DeLine field goal then a 19-yard scoring pass from Hatcher to Lance Carl tied the game with 5:21 left to play. The Buckeyes fought back with a drive deep into CU territory. The Buffs then stiffened at the 23 and when a third down pass was incomplete in the end zone, Ohio State faced a 40-yard field goal to win. However, CU was called for interference on the play, giving the Buckeyes a first down at the eight and they kicked a 19-yarder with 0:25 left to win, 13-10.

So the Buffs, now staggering with three straight losses - two of them in the final 30 seconds - now faced an Arizona team still bristling from the CU upset in Tucson a year earlier. The Wildcats dominated this game statistically, building a 434-246 total offense advantage, but CU took a 14-6 halftime lead on touchdowns set up by a 68-yard Hatcher-Jon Embree pass then a 30-yard interception runback to the six by Rodney Rogers. Leading 21-15 in the fourth quarter, the Buffs took a deliberate safety to get out of deep trouble. But Arizona struck suddenly with a breakaway following a short pass completion for a 67-yard TD to win, 24-21.

Downtrodden Missouri was next but the Buffs still had to struggle to snap their 4-game losing streak, 17-12. CU overcame an early 3-0 Missouri lead when Hatcher hit Mike Marquez for 30 yards then broke free for a 29-yard score on the next play. The Buffs stretched the lead to 14-3 as a fourth down gamble in which All-American punter Barry Helton, a former prep quarterback, passed successfully on fourth down to Mickey Pruitt for 17 yards from the CU 29 to launch an 11-play, 30-yard scoring drive. Missouri got a Big Eight record 62-yard field goal as the half ended but a countering 25-yarder by DeLine late in the third period gave the Buffs a safe 17-6 advantage.

Buoyed by their first win, the Buffaloes destroyed Iowa State, 31-3, with 17 first quarter points, triggered by a fumble recovery at the Cyclone 36 by David Tate then a 13-yard interception return to midfield by Barry Remington. This one was no contest as CU rolled up a 21-8 first down advantage and 339-191 in total offense. It was 24-3 at the half.

Fighting back with a 2-4 record, and probably the best team in the nation with that mark, the Buffaloes had a chance to salvage the season against third-ranked Nebraska. And they did, decisively, shocking the Cornhuskers, 20-10, with a solid defensive performance plus a pair of trick plays. The first was a deep reverse to ace wide receiver Jeff Campbell who sped 46 yards for a quick 7-0 lead. Big Curt Koch covered a Husker fumble at the Nebraska 45 and DeLine's 57-yard field goal sent the visitors reeling to a 10-0 halftime deficit.

The Cornhuskers got an easy TD after recovering Hatcher's fumble at the CU 14 in the third period but the Buffs countered quickly, pulling another ace out of their sleeve just three plays after the Husker score. Tiny running back O.C. Oliver took a pitchout from Hatcher and threw the first pass of his CU career to Lance Carl for a 52-yard touchdown to put the Buffs safely in front, 17-7. The bomb came on the first play of the fourth quarter. The two teams then traded field goals before Remington sealed the upset with an interception at the CU 23.

Barry Remington (1982-4-5-6) returns this interception against Washington in the 1986 Freedom Bowl to cap a brilliant CU career.

Rolling now, CU dumped Oklahoma State, 31-14, overcoming a 14-3 OSU halftime lead, and Kansas, 17-10, to stretch its comeback to five straight wins, longest streak for a CU team since 1978. The win at Stillwater was especially gratifying as the Buffs bounced back in the last half to completely dominate a tough Cowboy team. Hatcher's 23-yard bullseye to Oliver got the Buffs going and the rugged CU quarterback dove over from the one to send CU in front to stay. Late in the third period after hitting Carl with a 17-yard strike to the 16, backup QB Marc Walters got in on the kill with a 35-yard strike to Marquez to set up the third TD.

The win over KU was a struggle but never in doubt after the Buffs went 71 yards in 11 plays with their first possession. Another successful reverse, this one for a 34-yard Campbell score following a Darin Schubeck interception, gave the Buffs a 17-0 lead and the final score wasn't as close as it indicated.

Over .500 for the first time in 1986, CU now faced still another confrontation with awesome Oklahoma. A combination of Sooner defensive superiority and a generous CU offense snapped the Buff win streak, 28-0. The Sooners established command immediately with a 71-yard scoring march on their first possession. They then recovered a Weatherspoon fumble at the CU two for an easy second period TD which made it 14-0 at the half. The Buffs, held to 135 yards of total offense by a strangling

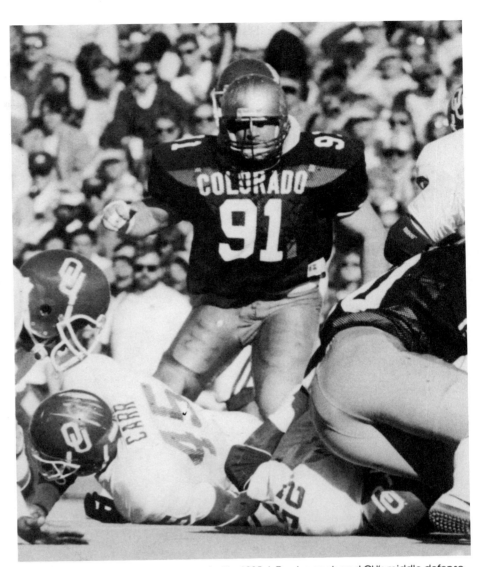

Kyle Rappold was CU's "trash compactor" in 1985-6-7 as he anchored CU's middle defense.

The weight room was an important part of Eric McCarty's preparation. Mark Larson was his strength coach.

Sooner defense, got beyond midfield only once. And then, at the 39, Hatcher didn't see a wide-open Embree and threw an interception into coverage to turn what should have been a touchdown into a turnover.

Still, it had been a gutty CU performance against the Sooners, like Nebraska third-ranked nationally going into the Boulder meeting. When the Buffs shattered Kansas State at Manhattan, 49-3, after a 28-3 halftime lead, the Bluebonnet Bowl beckoned with a fourth invitation to a CU team. Flushed with the furious finish which had produced six of seven wins in the Big Eight, the Buffs accepted gratefully.

But once again they were thwarted in their bid for a bowl victory. A solid Baylor defense completely throttled the CU wishbone to win, 21-9, limiting the Buffs to just 83 rushing yards, lowest

total during the CU wishbone recovery. The Buffs never got closer than 7-3 on a second-period DeLine field goal. Hatcher's 31-yard burst late in the third period with CU trailing, 21-3, only made the final score more respectable. The game was never in doubt. For the second straight season, McCartney's men went into the winter with the memory of a bowl defeat clouding what had been a gritty comeback campaign. And yet the disappointment was not overwhelming. CU was now strong physically. And it was looking forward to some support for the inconsistent Hatcher at quarterback from sophomore Sal Aunese, a highly-touted newcomer who had been forced to sit out his freshman season because of academic ineligibility created by a new NCAA rule, Proposition 48. Aunese was considered a better passer than

Hatcher and a more elusive runner. His presence would add balance to an offense which relied heavily on the crunching power of the wishbone.

1987

With 44 lettermen, including 16 starters, back for the 1987 campaign, CU was again, after a decade in the doldrums, a potential top twenty team. But McCartney had shown a propensity for stumbling starts (his teams had won only one of five previous openers) and he reached a new depth this time.

The Buffaloes were shocked by 2-touchdown underdog Oregon, 10-7. And, adding insult to injury, the Ducks did it with a Colorado youngster whom CU had turned down. Bill Musgrave, a pass-oriented quarterback from Grand Junction who didn't fit into CU's wishbone plans, decimated the Buffs with a 16-24 afternoon and 175 yards. It was an afternoon of utter frustration for CU, who came away empty on five penetrations inside the Oregon 30. Three fumbles and two interceptions stymied the CU attack in a game in which the Buffs always seemed on the verge of taking command but never did. Highly-touted sophomore J.J. Flannigan's bobble at the Oregon 35 on the last play of the third period, opened the door for a 52-yard Duck drive which finished with the winning 32-yard field goal. The Buffs had a 354-277 total offense bulge but out-turnovered Oregon, 5-1. That was the difference. CU would never recover from this beginning which would haunt the Buffs throughout the season.

Still there was hope. Aunese made an impressive debut in a 31-17 struggle over Stanford. But not before the unsung, and relatively unused since his 1985 injury at Nebraska, Wheeler had taken over for Hatcher, who went down with an ankle injury in the second quarter, and directed two scoring drives, getting both TDs himself, the second one propelling CU to a safe 2-TD lead and opening the door for Aunese's first appearance. The heralded sophomore promptly scrambled for runs of 6, 14 and 12 yards, displaying both strength and agility, to move the Buffs 57 yards to the Stanford 21 as the game ended.

Another Pac 10 team, Washington State, gave CU a full afternoon of thrills, threatening to upset the Buffs throughout the game before finally yielding, 26-17. Pruitt's 18-yard interception return touched off a second quarter rally which pulled the Buffs from a 7-3 deficit to a 19-7 halftime advantage. But the Cougars drew near at 19-17 in the fourth period and reached the CU 20 before throwing four straight incompletions. They got off the deck for one more shot as Flannigan fumbled and WSU recovered at the CU 24 for an 18-yard loss on the turnover. But the Buff defense braced and forced a 42-yard field goal which barely twisted to the left. That threat past, Aunese took the Buffs in for the clincher, scoring it on a 22-yard run to climax a great afternoon in which he replaced the re-injured Hatcher in the first period and went on to a 215-yard game with 185 rushing yards and one completion for 30 more.

The cool leadership of the CU sophomore got CU back on track. It was now obvious that he was ready to live up to his promise, giving CU a sudden wealth of quarterbacks with Hatcher, Wheeler and Walters also proven producers. But Colorado State was next and once again CU would have to go to the wire to beat its ever-

Linebacker Alfred Williams and linebacker Eric McCarty formed a real roadblock for CU opponents in 1987.

Sal Aunese's late-game heroics inspired the Buffaloes in 1987-8. He hands off to Mike Simmons here.

yards. As expected, the Buffaloes were superior on the ground, 250-69.

CU was favored over Oklahoma State but fell two touchdowns behind at the start of each half to put themselves into a hole they could never escape. The Buffs fell to the Cowboys, 42-17, as OSU unleashed a devastating offensive combination of quarterback Mike Gundy and tailback Barry Sanders. Gundy completed 21 of 28 passes and Sanders, in relief of the Cowboys' great Thurman Thomas, scored twice. The Buffaloes battled back from a quick 14-0 deficit to draw to 14-10 at the half. But fullback Mike Simmons fumbled on the first play of CU's first third quarter possession and on the second play the next time the Buffs had the ball to give the Cowboys easy opportunities to pull away again.

Fullback Erich Kissick then got the Buffaloes back on track with a 122-yard performance in a 35-10 rout of Kansas as five different Buffs (Aunese, Ferrando, Bieniemy, Hatcher and Kissick) took turns getting into the end zone.

But once again Oklahoma's defense choked CU's running game as the Sooners punched out a hard-fought 24-6 win at Norman. The Buffaloes netted only 178 yards on the ground and crossed midfield just three times. The Sooners, meanwhile, ground out 358 infantry yards to build a whopping 412-213 total offense lead over CU. Oklahoma led at the quarter turns, 10-0, 10-6 and 17-6. CU battled gamely despite their lack of a passing threat to counter their rushing failures. But, realistically, the Buffaloes were not yet at a talent and manpower level to consistently challenge the Oklahomas and Nebraskas of the football world. Not many schools in the country were. But McCartney had his sights set firmly on these two conference titans. The Buffaloes were building for better results in the future.

The McCartney Men stretched their record to 7-3 with blowouts of Iowa State (42-10), Missouri (27-10) and Kansas State (41-0). But that opening loss to Oregon and the recent losses to the two Oklahoma schools had erased any hopes for a bowl bid. Instead the Buffaloes would close out the campaign with what McCartney labeled "our own bowl game," a nationally televised Boulder meeting with Nebraska in the first game ever to finish under lights at Folsom Stadium. A temporary lighting system created and refined by an Iowa firm which specialized in transporting

battling brother school. The game didn't start out as a struggle as the Buffs broke quickly to a 26-0 lead and stretched it to 29-7 at the half. CU's opening barrage was set up by a Pruitt interception at the CSU 25, a 79-yard scoring bomb from Aunese to Drew Ferrando and a John Nairn interception and 20-yard return to the CSU 42. A furious CSU second half comeback then chilled CU, playing at Ft. Collins for the first time since 1957 (the first three games in the renewal of the series had been played in Boulder) although

the Rams never threatened seriously to win the game. The final score was 29-16 for still another of the "moral victories" claimed by a CSU team over the years. But the Buffaloes had the most points, as they usually did in this series, and that was what counted. Still it had not been an overpowering performance. Their last half rally had produced a surprising 467-389 total offense advantage for the Rams. CU's proud defense was not used to that type of treatment. In particular, the CSU aerial attack had punctured CU's secondary for 398

their equipment to unlighted stadiums made the happening possible.

The game may have been an incandescent success but it turned out to be a power failure for the Buffaloes. McCartney pulled out all the stops in this one, dressing his team in all-black uniforms. But they only contributed to the gloomy look of this late-November game which began at 2:00 P.M. and ended in total darkness. The Buffalo offense could not take advantage of early opportunities. CU moved into Cornhusker territory on its first three possessions but came away scoreless as a drive-ending penalty, blocked field goal and fumble ended the threats. Nebraska then countered, punching out 10 second quarter points and stretching its lead to 17-0 in the third period before the Buffs finally scored on Hatcher's 4-yard pass to George Hemingway. Hatcher's fine CU career ended on an even gloomier note as the Buff quarterback suffered a broken leg in the final quarter. Like Oklahoma, Nebraska throttled CU's running attack to just 147 yards, to pave the way to the victory. In contrast, Cornhusker running back Keith Jones bolted for 248 yards.

And so the frustrating, so-near-and-yet-so-far 1987 campaign ended with the Buffaloes at home during December's bowl season. McCartney and his coaching staff would take a hard look at their offensive plan during the winter. CU's wishbone was concentrated almost exclusively on rushing and the Buffaloes were not strong enough or quick enough to use the formation as effectively as Oklahoma. The wishbone wasn't designed for a consistent passing threat. So McCartney took a bold step, combining the wishbone's quick-hitting ground power with a deeper tailback threat from what appeared to be a Power-I formation but which Mac labeled the "I-Bone." It would be the first major offensive innovation since the I-formation was popularized by Southern California's John McKay two decades previously. It would still be rush-oriented. Most good offenses are. But it would give CU a legitimate running threat from a deep back and it would put the dropback pass back into the attack, a maneuver badly needed when the offense falls into a passing situation. The "I-Bone" would not be a dramatic success in 1988. But it would recycle the CU attack into a more balanced threat. And it would continue to improve as the Buffs got more comfortable with it. McCartney, heretofore

known as a defensive master, had come up with, at the least, a promising new formation. Now he had the manpower and the talent to make it work. CU continued to gather momentum. The school once again had a strong football program and, more importantly, it was a healthy one.

If the CU football situation seemed settled into a healthy and comfortable pattern after six years of McCartney's guidance, a strange and totally unexpected development threatened to unsettle it. Southern Methodist, a school which had been handed the NCAA's death sentence (two years' ban from competition plus other sanctions including the loss of several scholarships

and a severe limitation on the schedule when it was finally permitted to resume intercollegiate competition) beckoned to the CU coach to lead it out of the woods. After all, he had resurrected an almost moribund CU program. If anyone could do the job at Dallas, it was Mac.

McCartney was more than casually interested in the prospect of tackling this new challenge which made CU's situation in 1982 look like a Sunday School social. After all, SMU, though long a party haven for rich Texas playboys and playgirls, was affiliated with the Methodist church. And, as such, it was a private school not subject to the political pressures and limitations which

Keith English continued CU's outstanding punting tradition as he earned All-American honors in 1988.

had placed a harness on Mac's freedom to practice his strong Christian beliefs with his squads and, furthermore, his freedom to wear his religion on his sleeve, a tendency the devout Catholic was inclined to do. The SMU job would take the CU-imposed limitations off his back.

McCartney gave every indication he would accept the job, even to the extent of notifying his staff he would probably be leaving for Dallas. But he got derailed and by his own priorities. Since arriving in Boulder, Mac had constantly proclaimed the need for loyalty by the prep graduates of the state, a loyalty which should, he insisted, lean them toward the state schools like CU and CSU.

McCartney was big on loyalty, felt there wasn't enough in Colorado, especially among those fine high school athletes who so consistently went to out of state colleges. And he had a point. Colorado, peopled by a high percentage of non-natives, was a state with very few grass roots such as those which made the state universities of Nebraska, Oklahoma, Iowa, Texas and other more traditional states so attractive to their native sons.

McCartney's words now came back to block his defection to the southwest. CU president Gordon Gee, in a last-ditch effort to retain the highly popular coach, used the loyalty argument as his chief weapon. How could you, as one who believes so deeply in loyalty, jump ship when you still have three years left on your contract and especially when you were granted an extension midway through a 1-10 season in 1984, reasoned the CU president. Mac saw the light and bought Gee's point and agreed to remain on the job. An honorable man in a field which always includes a good share of mercenaries, Mac extracted no concessions to stay. He would remain at CU until the end of his contract which extended through the 1990 season.

CU partisans heaved a sigh of relief. Peace and prosperity, football-style, would continue to reign on the Boulder campus. McCartney would be present to continue CU's climb toward the top. For the first time in more than five decades there was a glimmer of hope that the CU program might not self-destruct. The clouds lifted and skies were bright once again.

1988

There was good reason for optimism going into the 1988 season. For one

"High Fives" by the "H-Bombs" Kanavis McGhee (96), Alfred Williams (94) and Arthur Walker (83) were a familiar defensive sight in 1988.

thing, despite the loss of 27 lettermen, where still were 35 returning. The CU program had become strong enough to produce some easy victories in which McCartney could use a lot of reserves, thus widening the range of the team's experience. Of the returnees, eight were offensive and five defensive regulars. But more importantly the Buffaloes had some offensive guns in halfbacks Eric Bieniemy and J.J. Flannigan, now proven breakaway threats. Even more importantly, Aunese had a full season behind him. He had become, by 1987's end, a legitimate Big Eight offensive standout. And behind Aunese, in the background, was still another bright young prospect, freshman Darian Hagan who would challenge Walters, still recovering from a serious knee injury, for the backup job. Still another rookie, redshirt freshman Charlie Johnson, gave the Buffs even more depth. Defensively, the Buffaloes looked forward to an extremely promising pair of sophomore linebackers, Alfred Williams and Kanavis McGhee, who would

join fellow Houstonite, tackle Arthur Walker, who already had a pair of fine seasons behind him. They would quickly become known as the "H-Bombs," one of the most feared defensive trios in the Big Eight in 1988.

CU's hopes, thus, were at a level unknown since the Buffs' Orange Bowl season of 1976. There were even whispers of CU finally having a team to challenge Nebraska and Oklahoma physically. That was almost too much to expect but McCartney, always the crusader, fueled the fire with his optimism. The CU coach openly predicted his Buffaloes would be in the Big Eight hunt all the way. Almost heresy: college head coaches are expected to cloak their evaluations in clouds of gloom. But McCartney was never a traditional head coach. Coming from an exclusively conservative run-oriented background at Missouri and Michigan, he had begun his career at CU with wildly-passing offenses. When that failed to produce, he quickly switched to the other extreme by converting to the wishbone, basically a no-pass attack and turned a 1-10 program into 7-5-0 within six months. And never during that topsy-turvy span had he publicly berated his poor teams. He was the eternal optimist, a man at least one veteran observer had labeled as the "Don Quixote of college football - always battling windmills and never realizing he couldn't defeat them." But McCartney was now nearing a position of power in which he could start whipping windmills like

Fresno State (45-3), Iowa (24-21), Oregon State (28-21) and Colorado State (27-23). Mac's merry men were, to say the least, very impressive in the first fortnight. An expected close game with Fresno State turned into a rout when the Buffaloes unlimbered their artillery for 35 second half points. In the process they displayed their promising rookie quarterback, Hagan, who debuted in the fourth quarter with electrifying runs of 11, 63 and 10 yards (for

by one national publication to be the No. 1 team in the country. But they were not that impressive on this sweltering Iowa afternoon. The Buffaloes threatened to turn the game into a stampede early, driving 74 and 50 yards for touchdowns in their first two possessions. But Iowa came back in the second quarter to tie it by halftime, 14-14. The Hawkeyes seemed to have the game wrapped up late in the fourth period, leading 21-17 and at second down at the CU seven with six minutes remaining.

But cornerback Dave McLoughan forced a fumble with a furious blindside blitz and Williams covered it at the 15. The death blow had been averted but the Buffaloes were still 85 yards from the touchdown which would win the game and CU had been able to get but one field goal since that first period flurry. Not to worry. Aunese was ready for his finest hour as a Buffalo. On third-and-nine, he hit Campbell with a 23-yard bulls-eye. The pair repeated for 13 more. Then Bieniemy, who had ripped out 118 yards in the opener, burrowed beneath the huge Iowa line for 22 and 10 yards. Aunese slid in from the one and suddenly CU had its second biggest victory of the McCartney years. Almost overlooked in the Aunese-orchestrated finish was Bieniemy's sensational 153-yard game, the first of many for the squatty little speedster that fall.

The Buffs figured to let down after that spectacular start, and they did. But they still had enough talent to escape a strong Oregon State upset bid after the Buffs had established a 16-7 halftime lead. Trailing 16-14, the Beavers kept chewing away and, after being stopped by CU at the one, came right back after a booming 64-yard Keith English punt to drive 69 yards in five thrusts and move ahead for the first time, 21-16. CU had an answer: Bieniemy. The stubby slasher promptly sped 66 yards to send the Buffs back in front, 22-21. Oregon State had one last effort left and they moved 35 yards following the kickoff, then from the CU 45 punted dead at the one with 5:21 remaining. They never got the ball back. CU pounded 99 yards in a merciless drive which used up every second and finished with a 10-yard score by Aunese at the gun. Bieniemy's late burst capped another big afternoon for the 5-6, 190 blockbuster. He alternately darted and drilled his way for 211 yards, his third straight game in triple figures.

Wide receiver Jeff Campbell (1986-7-8-9) was a high school hockey star who ran with a football like he was on ice skates.

those at Lincoln and Norman which had been spinning relentlessly since the conference had expanded to eight teams. At least, that was the outlook going into 1988.

The Buffaloes, indeed, came out whirling like windmills, rotating past

a TD) on his first three collegiate carries. No CU rookie ever made a more sensational start.

When the Buffs caught Iowa at the end for a resounding upset, CU had finally drawn the attention of the nation. The Hawkeyes had been picked

Riding that impressive 3-game win streak, the Buffaloes now faced another CSU ambush. The Rams were ready, as usual. And, as usual, the Buffaloes were not. In what was becoming a familiar scenario, the Buffs needed a large dose of luck coupled with great clutch play by both the defense and offense down the stretch to pull out a 27-23 nervewracker. CSU came out swinging, shocking the Buffs with 10 first period points before linebacker Don DeLuzio rallied his men with a 58-yard interception TD after CSU had stretched its lead to 13-0 early in the second quarter. Bieniemy then broke loose for 22 yards and another DeLuzio interception set up a late Ken Culbertson 28-yard field goal to send the Buffs into halftime with a nervous 17-13 lead.

CSU's upset bid picked up momentum after the rest period and the Rams seemed to have the victory secured, leading 23-20 with a fourth-and-one at the CU 29 and just four minutes left. But the Rams spurned both a field goal try or a rush and tried to pass. Big Williams roared through for a sack at the 36. The Buffs had life, although they had shown no signs of it until Williams' sack, and they had Aunese. The CU junior showed that his Iowa performance wasn't a one-time happening. He tore loose for six yards on fourth-and-two to start the winning drive. Then on third-and-ten, he pinpointed Campbell for 17 to the 33. After an interference penalty moved CU 15 yards closer, the Buffaloes stalled at the five. Facing third-and-goal there, Aunese floated a perfect touch pass to Mike Pritchard for another CU lifesaver. This was a game the Buffaloes should have lost but didn't. Heroics by DeLuzio, Williams and Aunese made the difference. CSU deserved a better fate. But they couldn't make a yard when it would have meant the game and CU had the poise to drive 64 yards under the most intense pressure to pull it out. The statistics showed CSU's domination of this one. The Rams had an amazing 453-280 in total yardage, Bieniemy was limited to just 66 yards. He'd made that many on his final carry against Oregon State.

Suddenly, the first big game of the Big Eight season, between undefeated Oklahoma State and the Buffaloes, occupied the Folsom Field - and national - spotlight. The Cowboys still had the Big Eight's best all-around quarterback in Gundy and by now Sanders was enroute to what would be a Heisman Trophy junior season. Once again,

the two were unstoppable, rallying OSU from an early 7-0 deficit to a 24-7 halftime advantage as the Buffaloes committed suicide with six turnovers.

The game began impressively for CU as the Buffs drove 75 yards with their first possession. OSU tied it immediately. CU almost hit a bomb on its first play after the Cowboy kickoff when Aunese barely overthrew Pritchard who was far behind the OSU secondary. From then on it was all Oklahoma State. With Sanders galloping through big holes for a total of 174 yards and Gundy perforating the CU secondary with 13-23-202 passing, the Cowboys put the game out of reach early in the third period when Sanders streaked 65 yards on the third play after CU had pulled to within 24-14 at the half. For the second straight game, Bieniemy was kept in check with 81 yards, only 41 of them after that explosive first period. This was a wild offensive game. When it was over, Oklahoma State had a 440-390 total offense lead. But CU's two fumbles and four interceptions and OSU's turnover-less performance, plus the running of Sanders behind a powerful line, turned an expected close game into a rout.

The Buffaloes didn't recover quickly from this devastating defeat. They got a quick, easy touchdown when safety Bruce Young recovered a fumbled Kansas reception at the KU 38 on the first play of the game. Later, when Aunese couldn't move the Buffs, Hagan came in and directed an 88-yard scoring drive, running for 38 of those yards in five carries, to give CU a hard-earned 14-6 halftime lead over a hapless but hustling Kansas outfit which was winless to that point. The Buffs rode the sturdy legs of Bieniemy to put the game out of range, 21-6, with a 15-play, 80-yard drive in the third period. Bieniemy carried 10 times for 55 of those yards, including a stretch of eight straight which took the Buffaloes 48 yards, from their 32 to the KU 20. CU's squatty slasher squirmed for 195 yards to get back in the groove.

Now came one of the most exciting games in the most spectacular Folsom Field setting in history. National television required a night game so CU brought in the portable lights from Iowa again as the Buffaloes squared off against 8th-ranked Oklahoma. The setting was perfect - a balmy late-October night and two fine football teams fighting for the Big Eight lead. The game wasn't a letdown, in doubt until the closing gun when Ken Culbertson's 62-

yard field goal attempt which would have given the Buffaloes a 17-17 tie barely drifted to the right and Oklahoma took a 17-14 win.

Oklahoma struck swiftly when freshman sensation Mike Gaddis broke 33 yards on the second play of the game and the Sooners went 80 yards in eight plays for a 7-0 lead with just 3:02 gone. The Buffs came right back, reaching Oklahoma's 17 and eight yard lines but had to settle for short Culbertson field goals both times. In that first drive, Aunese had run and passed for 61 of CU's 63 yards. The scrambling Samoan then hit Pritchard for a 52-yard bomb on the first play of CU's next possession to position the Buffs for the field goal.

DeLuzio then recovered an OU fumble at the CU 45 and the Buffs covered the 55 yards in two plays, Aunese hitting Campbell for the first 31 then springing Bieniemy for the final 24. Aunese found tight end John Perak alone in the end zone for a 2-point conversion and CU led, 14-7. But Sal's next pass was intercepted at the CU 28 and the Sooners scored in four plays to send the teams into halftime tied, 14-14.

The second half was a bitter defensive struggle. CU had the best chance to score in the third period. The Buffaloes began a steady drive from their 20. A double penalty nullified an apparent 31-yard CU gain to the Oklahoma 23 on a daring fourth down pass from punter Keith English to David Gibbs. Undaunted, CU kept right on moving, reaching a first down at the OU 24. But Aunese and Bieniemy missed connections on a pitchout and the Sooners recovered the fumble at the 28 to end the Buffs' most serious threat of the second half.

Three exchanges later, Oklahoma drove 71 yards to the CU five where the Buffs stiffened after a first down at the 11 and forced the Sooners to settle for a field goal. It would turn out to be the only score of the final 30 minutes and decide the game.

But the Buffs had one more chance. It came when Young dove on a Sooner fumble at the CU 46 with 2:17 left to play. On first down, Bieniemy took a pitchout from Aunese and sped 19 yards and out of bounds at the OU 35. But a holding penalty erased all but two of those yards and the Buffs had to start over. They kept coming. Aunese hit Perak over the middle for 10, Bieniemy dug out six more and Campbell reversed for six to the OU 40 for a first down. But two plays later the Sooners sacked Sal for an 8-yard loss, forcing Culbertson's desperation long range field goal attempt. When it barely went wide, Oklahoma had once again escaped a Boulder ambush, a tradition which had begun with Dal Ward's teams in 1950. Surprisingly, an aerial barrage had kept CU in the game. Aunese hit 8-18 for 184 yards as compared to OU's 19 passing yards. But the Sooners were supreme on the ground, 360-155, and that was the difference in this exciting nocturnal collision.

There was no great letdown this time although the Buffaloes spotted Iowa State a 6-0 lead before spanking the Cyclones, 24-14. Bieniemy, who had punched out 114 tough yards against Oklahoma's superb defense, was sensational in this one with 166 yards,

including a 46-yard TD which broke up a tense 10-6 struggle early in the fourth period. Again, Hagan had to spell Aunese when the CU star was shaken up in the first half. The CU rookie didn't scintillate but he kept the Buffs alive until Aunese returned in the second half.

Missouri was no problem for the Buffs, falling 45-8 at Columbia. The defense prevailed early as frosh cornerback Dion Figures blocked an opening Missouri field goal attempt to launch CU's first scoring drive from 56 yards out. Then safety Tim James swiped a Tiger throw and hauled it back 26 yards to start a 17-yard drive. It was 24-0 and out of reach at the half as Aunese played probably his finest all-around game despite bitter cold and sleeting conditions. The CU junior handled the wet

ball flawlessly (there were no CU turnovers) and hit 7-of-9 passes, all of them at critical times, for 92 yards. He ran for 59 more in eight carries. The Buffaloes turned loose still another fine runner in freshman Mark Reliford who sped for 114 yards in 12 carries to top the ever-reliable Bieniemy's 106.

Now 7-2 and still in the chase, the Buffaloes traveled to Lincoln for another visit to Nebraska's house of horrors where CU teams had won only once since 1963. More than that 1-11 won-lost record, the Buffaloes had suffered a steady series of humiliations in Lincoln. During that 12-game span, Cornhusker teams outscored CU, 453-142. The average score was 38-12. Included were a 63-21 humiliation of Bill Mallory, a 59-0 flogging of Chuck Fairbanks and a 69-19 massacre of McCartney. Lincoln was a place for CU teams to avoid.

But not in 1988. This meeting would be a battle in which the Cornhuskers would be fortunate to escape with a 7-0 win. To triumph by that slender margin, Nebraska needed a Bieniemy injury which took him out of action for but one play after the first quarter, an unbelievable fumble by Flannigan when the CU speedster was in the open at the Husker 19 enroute to an untouched 43-yard touchdown run, a fumble by Bieniemy after he had plowed 12 yards for an apparent first down at the Nebraska 12, and a fumbled snap by Aunese on fourth-and-one at the Nebraska 27 late in the game.

With Bieniemy out for all but that second quarter fumble at the 12, Flannigan finally had the kind of game CU fans had been expecting ever since his highly-publicized arrival on campus in 1986. The lean speedster, who had never learned to run upfield like Bieniemy thus neutralizing his great speed, netted 133 yards in 27 carries. But what would have been a tremendous performance was blighted by that unexplainable second period fumble. Nebraska's Ken Clark got 165 yards, including the touchdown which capped a 9-play, 59 yard drive late in the third quarter. Clark came up with the biggest play of the game in that one, slashing for 10 yards to the CU seven on a fourth-and-two from the 17.

If Flannigan was the second best tailback on the field at Lincoln, he was number one the following Saturday in Boulder as CU finished the regular season with a 56-14 wipeout of Kansas

All-Big Eight center Erik Norgard anchored the offensive line in 1988.

Every move J.J. Flannigan made in 1987-8-9 sent the Folsom Field crowd into a familiar chant.

State. The CU junior, who triggered a crowd chant of "J-J...FLANNIGAN" after every Boulder carry, crossed the goal line three times in the opening quarter. After linebacker Michael Jones' interception at midfield, JJ scored from the 16. And following end Lamarr Gray's fumble recovery at the CU 44, he rambled 25 to the three and into the end zone, fumbling as he crossed the goal with fullback Erich Kissick falling on it for the TD. JJ capped his first period pyrotechnics with an 11-yard score. It was 35-7 at the half as CU clinched a bowl bid, to either the Freedom or Gator, with its closing cascade of points. JJ's 151 yards, on 20 carries, sparked a 555-yard CU assault, the highest total offense ever by a McCartney machine. Reliford added 125 in his second 100-plus game in November. Unfortunately, the frosh flash got in disciplinary trouble in the next game,

got into even more trouble the following summer and was gone via the transfer route by the 1989 campaign.

CU opted for a second Freedom Bowl appearance over the Florida trip to the Gator because of the chance to appear once again in its prime southern California recruiting area. The opponent would be Brigham Young, which had backed into the bowl off its previous post-season successes plus an early season record which overshadowed 57-28 and 41-17 floggings by Utah and Miami in its last two starts of an 8-4 campaign.

The Buffaloes were a solid favorite. BYU, as always, relied on its passing game. CU had better personnel and better balance. But the Buffaloes also had a bowl problem. CU teams had failed in five straight post-season appearances since Eddie Crowder's crew had knocked off Houston in 1971 to earn that

third-place national finish. To compound the CU problem, McCartney had come out of the Bo Schembechler regime and the renowned Michigan mentor was nearly always at his worst in the December and January classics.

But all that was history and history does not necessarily have to repeat. But it did. When the Buffaloes used a Michael Jones fumble recovery at midfield on BYU's opening series then covered 49 yards in six plays for a 7-0 lead in barely more than two minutes, the oddsmakers seemed correct in installing CU as 10-point favorites. And the Buffs looked even better as they promptly sacked BYU on third down and started their second possession at midfield after the Cougar punt. But they failed to capitalize on a chance perhaps to put the game away early and BYU took heart and fought back to a 7-7 tie. The Buffaloes stayed in front for nearly

CU's stubby sparkplug Eric Bieniemy is consoled by assistant coach Oliver Lucas after the Buffs lost a heartbreaker to Oklahoma in 1988.

the entire 60 minutes but the leads were always precarious. The quarter turns were 7-7, 14-7 and 14-14. Freshman Pat Blottiaux' 19-yard field goal sent the Buffs in front, 17-14, early in the final quarter.

But Brigham Young wouldn't fold. The Cougars came right back with a 79-yard drive to tie the game with a 31-yard field goal. Aunese couldn't get the Buffs into the end zone in the second half and he had been replaced by Hagan in the final period. The CU rookie wasn't up to the pressure created by the 17-17 tie with four minutes remaining. On second-and-six at the Buff 27, he rolled right to pass and had more than enough running room for the first down but pulled up beyond the line of scrimmage and threw incomplete to Pritchard. After the 5-yard penalty, he then threw an air ball which was intercepted at the CU 45. When CU drew an unsportsmanlike conduct penalty on the play, Brigham Young suddenly was in control of the game with a first down at the 32 and plenty of time, 3:14, remaining. The Cougars surprised the Buffs with two running plays for a first down to grind down the clock. On fourth down with 0:35 left, they kicked a 35-yard field goal for a 20-17 upset. Once again, CU was frustrated in December. McCartney was now 0-3 in bowl appearances, moving ahead of Mallory by a game in an undesired competition involving negative bowl appearances. Mallory had failed in his only two tries, in 1975 and 1976.

To add to the CU frustration, the Buffs, as anticipated, had dominated the ground game, rushing to a 273-152 advantage. But a combination of costly CU penalties and a 168-64 BYU passing bulge plus clutch Cougar play at the finish produced the turnaround. And once again the Buffaloes crept back to Boulder to anguish over their final performance.

But the shadows of December didn't darken the picture for long. There was continued optimism for the CU future. The outlook was solid. Bowl games aside, McCartney had wreaked a near miracle in bringing the Buffaloes from that 1-10 season in 1984 to three post-season appearances in the four years since then and, more importantly, muscling up to Oklahoma and Nebraska in 1988. CU was now on a physical level with those two gridiron goliaths. And the Buffaloes now had outstanding players at the skill positions: Aunese and Hagan at quarterback, Bieniemy and Flannigan at running backs, Campbell, Pritchard and M.J. Nelson as prime receivers, Perak as a rugged tight end and, most important of all, savage defenders led by the H-Bombs - Williams, Walker and McGhee.

Everything was rosy once again in Boulder. There would be 40 lettermen, 18 of them starters, returning in 1989 to launch CU's centennial season of football. Personnel was no longer a problem for McCartney and his staff. The Buffaloes were strong and talented and deep. If there was any cloud on the horizon it was a schedule which included five teams - Texas, Illinois, Washington, Oklahoma and Nebraska - who were among the nation's elite. But September was eight months down the road. For the present, CU could look to its recent accomplishments with a comforting glance at its returning strength and regard the future with confidence.

Don DeLuzio was an intimidating linebacker in 1985-6-8.

These members of the 1961 CU Big Eight champions returned for a reunion at the CSU game. *L-R, standing:* athletic director Bill Marolt, John Lockwood, Walt Klinker, Ted Somerville, Reed Johnson, Ed Coleman, Ralph Heck, Jerry McClurg, Ken Vardell, Bob McCullough, Dave Young, Jerry Hillebrand, Larry Cundall, Joe Romig, Jim Hold, John Denvir, trainer Lloyd Williams, John Meadows, assistant coach Bob Ghilotti, manager Gordon Swanson; *kneeling:* Loren Schweninger, Dave Vivian, Jim Raisis, Pat Young, Claude Crabb, Bill Harris, Gale Weidner, Dean Lahr, Jim Perkins, Ken Blair, C Club president Frank Bernardi.

This trio of sports writers, Leonard Cahn of the Rocky Mountain News (*inset*), Frank Haraway of the Denver Post, and Dan Creedon of the Boulder Camera (*right*) are the all-time longevity leaders in covering CU football.

The University of Colorado All-Century Football Team

CU's All-Century team lined up for this photo at the half of the 1989 Nebraska game. *L-R, standing:* Pete Brock, Dick Anderson, Carroll Hardy, Bobby Anderson, John Stearns, Gale Weidner, Boyd Dowler, Dave Logan, Mark Haynes, John Wooten, Kayo Lam, Billy Waddy, George Pruitt (for his son Mike), Buzz Jordan (for his father Zack), Hatfield Chilson, Herb Orvis; *kneeling:* Cliff Branch, Fern St. Cyr (for her son Eric Bieniemy), Joe Romig, athletic director Bill Marolt, Byron White, Carol Furrey (for her father Lee Willard), Bob Stransky, Hale Irwin, Pete Franklin (for his father Walt), Frank McGlone (for his brother Bill). **MB**

Bobby Anderson, QB/TB (1967-68-69)

One of three players to have his number (11) retired at Colorado, Bobby had a stellar career in which he established 18 game, season or career records at CU, many of which still stand. He owns the CU career bests in total offense (5,017 yards), points (212) and touchdowns (40).

Dick Anderson, DB (1965-66-67)

An all-state fullback on outstanding Boulder High teams, Dick was converted to safety where he became one of the Big Eight's top defensive backs. He doubled as punter, averaging 40.4 yards his senior year. Dick was an All-American 1967 and then went on to a brilliant nine-year career with the NFL Miami Dolphins.

Eric Bieniemy, TB (1987-88-89)

The only current member of the team to make the All-Century Team. Eric is already the school's fourth leading rusher and sixth leading scorer.

Cliff Branch, WR/KR (1970-71)

Easily one of the most exciting players in CU history. An integral part of CU's No. 3 ranked team in 1971, Branch touched the ball 141 times in his CU career for 2,707 yards, or 19-plus yards every time he had the pigskin. He scored 16 touchdowns in his career, including eight via kick returns. Cliff went on to have a brilliant NFL career with the Oakland Raiders.

Pete Brock, OC (1973-74-76)

Pete anchored the offensive line that helped CU finish 11th in total offense nationally in 1975 (415-plus yards per game). He garnered All-American honors in 1975, and then went on to have an 11-year NFL career with the New England Patriots.

Hatfield Chilson, B (1923-24-25-26)

Hatfield "Chilly" Chilson was a dynamic tailback for CU under coach Myron Witham. He could run, pass and play defense and was the man around whom the offense revolved during those years. He was one of the nation's first jump passers and earned national recognition with that unique style. Chilly was one of the leaders of the 1924 team which shutout eight regular season opponents then broke even in two post-season games in Hawaii.

Boyd Dowler, QB (1956-57-58)

One of the most versatile performers ever to wear CU's colors, Boyd's appearance as a sophomore in 1956 gave Coach Dal Ward the opportunity to convert to a multiple offense in which Dowler was the blocking back and prime receiver in the single wing (as well as the quarterback in the T-formation). He was also a tremendous punter for the Buffaloes. Boyd then went on to star with the NFL's Green Bay Packers.

Walt Franklin, C/E (1917-19-20-21)
The late Walt Franklin was one of CU's truly tremendous All-around athletes, starring in football, baseball and golf in addition to being the Rocky Mountain Conference heavyweight boxing champion. Franklin played center and end for the Buffaloes during his gridiron career and then served with distinction as CU's graduate manager of athletics until 1940.

Carroll Hardy, HB (1951-52-53-54)
There are many who rate Carroll Hardy at the same level as Byron White as the most gifted back ever to play for CU. Hardy could do everything: run, pass, punt and play defense; and he did it all in outstanding fashion. But it was as a runner that Hardy, a 9.8 sprinter, excelled. His slashes inside and outside end highlighted Dal Ward's single-wing attack. Hardy set a single-game rushing record which stood for 17 years. Carroll had an outstanding season with the San Francisco '49ers before concentrating on a major league baseball career in which he played outfield for Cleveland and Boston.

Mark Haynes, CB (1976-77-78-79)
One of the top 10 tacklers at Colorado, as his 256 career stops ranks third among all defensive backs. He was an All-American in 1979, when CU's pass defense was ninth in the nation, allowing only 97 yards per game. He owns the school record for fumble recoveries (eight). Mark went on to become an all-pro with the NFL's New York Giants and Denver Broncos.

Hale Irwin, (DB (1964-65-66)
Hale knows golf, but Hale knew football, too. He was a two-time all-Big Eight pick at defensive back, as he had nine career interceptions. He was one of the players who helped turn CU's football fortunes back around from the losing ways of the early 1960's. Hale still owns numerous golf records at CU, and went on to enjoy a fabulous PGA Tour career.

Zack Jordan, HB/P (1950-51-52)
The late Zack Jordan was CU's first great tailback in the Big Seven. He was an excellent runner, an outstanding passer and the nation's best punter during his three-year career as a Buff. The Buffalo offense revolved around this do-everything back as his class led CU into Big Seven prominence and established Dal Ward's Buffs as a constant title threat. Jordan was also a fine shortstop on Frank Prentup's CU baseball teams.

William Lam, B (1933-34-35)
William "Kayo" Lam was the first CU gridder to play in the Shrine East-West game, the nation's top post-season all-star game after a brilliant career. The scrappy little battler was an outstanding runner who set a national rushing record in 1935 when he ran for 1,043 yards on 145 carries. He also led the country in all-around yardage that season. He remained on as CU's business manager of athletics from 1940-70.

Dave Logan, WR (1972-73-74-75)
One of the best all-around athletes in CU history, as he was drafted professionally in football, baseball and basketball. Dave was an All-American split end (1975) at CU, and is still fourth all-time in receiving yards and sixth in receptions. He also starred on Sox Walseth's basketball team at forward, but chose football for his career and went on to play nine years in the NFL.

Bill McGlone, G (1923-24-25-26)
Bill McGlone was one of the anchors of a line which paved the way for some of the finest seasons in CU history. An outstanding blocker and defender, his up-front leadership sparked the Buffaloes to a 26-9-2 record between 1923-1926. McGlone was one of the top performers on the 1924 team which went unscored upon in the regular season.

Herb Orvis, DE (1969-70-71)
One of three players at CU to twice earn All-America status (1970 & 1971). He anchored the defense that led CU to a 10-2 record in 1971 and a No. 3 national ranking. Herb went on to play 10 years in the NFL (Detroit and Baltimore).

Mickey Pruitt, SS (1984-85-86-87)
One of the hardest hitters in Colorado history, Mickey would do it with a smile enroute to becoming the third all-time leading tackler at CU. He was a candidate for the Thorpe Award and enjoyed a banner CU career, setting a Buff record for career pass deflections. He was a three-time winner of the Derek Singleton Award, for spirit, enthusiasm and dedication. He is now playing with Chicago in the NFL.

Joe Romig, OG/LB (1959-60-61)
Joe is the only player in CU history to captain two straight teams and win unanimous All-American honors in both seasons. He then won a Rhodes Scholarship and became an outstanding physicist. Romig was a quick, deadly blocker on offense and a linebacking terror who used his great ability, strength and intelligence to dominate a game defensively. His inspirational leadership paced the 1961 Buffaloes to the school's first undisputed Big Eight championship. He is a member of the GTE Academic Hall-of-Fame.

John Stearns, DB/P (1970-71-72)
"Bad Dude," as he came to be known, was one of the most fierce competitors in CU football history. Though he later gained fame as a star catcher with the New York Mets, Stearns is remembered most for making good on a fake punt in the 1971 Bluebonnet Bowl which helped CU to victory and a No. 3 final ranking. He led CU in interceptions in both 1970 and 1971, and garnered all-Big Eight honors in 1972.

Bob Stransky, HB (1955-56-57)
Now a school teacher in Denver, Stransky was a big part of the 1956 team which defeated Clemson in the Orange Bowl. He was the nation's second leading rusher in 1957 and earned All-American honors that season.

Billy Waddy, RB (1973-74-75-76)
Billy opened in a blaze of glory at CU as he set a freshman running record in 1973 and closed as one of the most dangerous return men in the nation. Always a threat to break the big plays, Waddy averaged almost 17 yards every time he touched the ball. He went on to star with the NFL Los Angeles Rams following his CU career.

Gale Weidner, QB (1959-60-61)
His passing and running talents were key factors in CU's burst to the top under Sonny Grandelius. As a sophomore quarterback and safety in 1959, he led the Buffaloes in passing, scoring and interceptions. He had 732 yards and three touchdowns as a junior then led the Buffaloes to the Big Eight championship in 1961.

Byron White, B (1935-36-37)
Byron "Whizzer" White is CU's most renowned graduate, a 1937 All-American then a Rhodes Scholar and professional football great with Pittsburgh and Detroit and, since 1962, a U.S. Supreme Court Justice. White was a brilliant single wing tailback for three seasons under Bunnie Oakes and in his senior year led the country in rushing and scoring and for good measure completed 22 of 48 passes for 314 yards, returned 36 punts for 731 yards and punted for a 43.3 yard average. He did all this in only eight games before starring in the Cotton Bowl game.

Lee Willard, B (1918-19-20-21)
Lee Willard is the only man in CU history to earn 16 letters (football, basketball, baseball and track) in a career. He began his gridiron career as an end then played mostly at halfback before finishing at quararterback. Willard had 9.8 sprinter speed, a fine arm and tremendous tenacity on both offense and defense. His outstanding play in the post-World War I period helped to rejuvenate CU's program.

John Wooten, G (1956-57-58)
Big John Wooten was a pillar of strength for the Buffaloes as he played a key role in CU's march to an Orange Bowl victory during his sophomore season, then won All-America honors as a senior. Wooten was a crushing trap blocker in Dal Ward's single-wing attack as the weak side guard. He was also devastating as he pulled to help lead interference to the strong side. Defensively, he played tackle. Following graduation, John was a long time regular for powerful Cleveland Brown teams and is currently in player personnel with the Dallas Cowboys.

BEHIND THE SCENES

There have been no secret formulas in the birth, development and continued growth of the University of Colorado athletic program. The process was, and continues to be, simple with one basic element: having the right men on hand, in the right place and at the right time.

Call it luck, good fortune, wise selection, whatever, the presence of strong leadership was constant, no less so at the turn of the first century than it was in the beginning.

From that early time, in the fall of 1890 when the first football team was fielded, CU has been blessed with a steady succession of strong visionaries who have guided the school's intercollegiate program consistently and, for the most part, wisely. During the course of any century of any type of human involvement there will be peaks and valleys, times of elation and times of despair.

CU's path was no different than that of any other school. It has, however, always been a leader with the accomplishments of its men on and off the playing fields placing Colorado in the front ranks of the nation's universities. Many men have shared the leadership role and it is not totally fair to single out seven men as those most responsible for CU's record through 10 decades of victories, defeats, turmoil, turbulence and - always - growth.

But a look at the record indicates that the strength, wisdom, energy, foresight and, above all, dedication, places the following men in the front row as CU's outstanding leaders of the first century.

The first was Frederick Gorham Folsom, who took over as football coach in 1895 and quickly developed CU teams into perennial Rocky Mountain powerhouses. Even in those embryonic years, football was the most popular sports attraction for students, alumni and the populace in general.

So it was the football coach to whom university people looked to for leadership. Then, as now. So it was Folsom, a productive activist off the field as well as on, who led the way for the quick development of CU into a regional leader, in both team results and athletic facilities.

Soon after his arrival - in 1898 - a gymnasium was built on campus, in the general area of where Norlin Library now stands. In 1900 a football-track complex was added just south of the gym. A quarter-mile track circled the gridiron which also included a baseball field. A west grandstand seating 1000 was completed in 1901 and the complex was finished a year later with the construction of another 1000-seat grandstand on the east side.

Thus, CU in less than a decade possessed the best coach and the finest facilities in the Rocky Mountain west. The four primary sports on the program - football, baseball, basketball and track - quickly became successful. CU was a leader, practically from the start.

This is not to imply that the CU athletic department was a well-organized, tightly-knit operation in those early times. Many of the sports programs were primarily intramural or club-type affairs. The school did not get its first athletic director until 1903 when Dave Cropp assumed that duty. But it was hard to distinguish Cropp as the director. He was, in reality, a one-man band: coaching football, baseball and track as well as overseeing the department's physical facilities. (There is no record of the school owning a popcorn machine at the time; but had there been one, Cropp undoubtedly would have been at the controls.)

If Folsom was the man who got CU's athletic program going in the beginning, six more stand out as men who kept the momentum moving forward: three in the front ranks of leadership and three more as key behind-the-scenes administrators.

Since 1928, when the school was moving into the more modern portion of its existence, only three men have served as athletic director: Harry Carlson, 1928-65; Eddie Crowder, 1965-84; and Bill Marolt, 1984-present. Each has been involved in periods of dramatic growth.

Carlson's soft-spoken, scholarly demeanor belied his quiet strength. He was known affectionately as "the Dean" because of his professorial approach and because he was actually a dean (of men from 1932-59 and of

HARRY CARLSON

the physical education department from 1926-65.) In addition, he also wore a fourth hat, as the school's most successful baseball coach from 1928-45. Let it be noted that he occupied all four of these major posts for 13 years, from 1932-45.

Carlson's outstanding ability as an administrator was his effectiveness in working with what he liked to call "constituted authority." Never one to rock a boat despite his personal convictions, he always considered his role as one in which he worked in harmony with the school's administration and faculty. Progress often came slower than he, or his underlings, might have wished. But it always seemed to arrive.

Probably his greatest contribution to CU athletics was his efforts in moving the school into the Missouri Valley intercollegiate athletic conference, then the Big Six, later the Big Seven and now the Big Eight. Despite many concerns from many quarters that CU teams would be overmatched in the prestigious midlands league, Carlson worked diligently to overcome local doubts and convince Big Eight authorities that CU was worthy of membership.

The future lies to the east, he constantly emphasized to his associates as early as the mid-1930's when he began scheduling Big Six teams regularly. With the exception of war years 1943-4-5, Big Eight teams have appeared on every CU football schedule since 1934.

Important factors in Carlson's reasoning were the denser populations of the midlands and the constantly improving transportation means to reach these locations. And always present in any athletic director's thoughts are economics. More populations meant more spectators and more money. Not necessarily a mercenary, Carlson nonetheless grasped this fact of athletic life early in his career.

He got an important boost in his quiet campaign from an old CU ally, Nebraska chancellor Dr. Reuben Gustafson, who had served as chemistry professor, then dean of the graduate school and acting president when Robert Stearns went to active air force duty in World War II. Gustafson became chancellor of Nebraska after the war and his support of CU's bid was extremely valuable.

Never one to brag about his achievements publicly, Carlson nevertheless got great pleasure from the immediate success of CU's bold venture into the midwest alliance. And he derived an understandable satisfaction at the silencing of the skeptics by CU teams which finished second twice in football and won a major bowl game, won two basketball championships (with a third-place national finish), golf and tennis championships within the first decade in the Big Eight.

When he finally stepped aside as athletic director in 1965, Carlson continued to serve the university as he was elected to the board of regents in 1966 and served a 6-year term. With that on his record, he had, in 1972, concluded 46 years of continuous service to the university and its programs, a record which is unlikely ever to be broken.

But even before Carlson came another important figure who never wore the title of athletic director but was nevertheless a powerful force in the development of the CU program. He was Walter Franklin, a 4-sport star who stayed on to become graduate manager of athletics in 1921, continuing in that capacity until 1940. As manager of the departmental purse strings, Franklin was a key figure in the day-to-day operation of the department, a director without portfolio until Carlson arrived and second in command afterwards.

Like Carlson, an extremely well-educated man, Franklin earned CU degrees in both chemistry and law and began a long career as a business professor in 1933. In his spare time, he also managed to coach golf (1926-38), boxing (1930-36) and assisted in football

WALTER FRANKLIN

from 1922-30.

After concluding his association with the athletic department in 1940 to become a full-time professor, Franklin retained one last tie to sports by becoming CU's conference faculty representative in 1945.

A whirlwind of energy, constantly involved in student and faculty affairs, he was one of the vital figures in the construction of Folsom Stadium in 1924, the men's gymnasium in 1924 and the CU field house in 1937.

The man who replaced Franklin was another former great CU athlete, William C. (Kayo) Lam. The title was changed to athletic business manager but the responsibilities were basically the same: manage the finances and the physical plant and serve as unofficial assistant athletic director. To say that Lam did this with a unique flair is a massive understatement.

Lam blended perfectly with Carlson. He was flamboyant. Carlson was quiet. Lam flailed away at problems, often overpowering them with sheer energy. Carlson was cerebral. Even their athletic backgrounds were opposite. Carlson had been a crafty pitcher whose assortment of curves earned him a brief stint with the Cincinnati Reds. Lam's explosive football feats earned him All-America mention and made him the first CU gridder ever to play in the Shrine East-West game, at that time the nation's top post-season all-star contest. The two worked excellently together, covering both sides of the street. As might be gathered, Carlson was a dedicated family man. Home and hearth were his haven. Lam's energies extended beyond his working hours, often far into the night. As a college football star

he gained additional prominence as a band leader and dance contest winner. The pair made an excellent team.

Like Franklin before him, Lam was active as a coach, assisting in football and basketball and serving as head wrestling coach. For all his fidgety mannerisms and impulsive personality, Lam was a solid, effective figure in the department for more than three decades. Any evaluation of the school's top administrators would give him a high mark.

Lam continued to serve Carlson's successor at the athletic helm, Eddie Crowder, from 1965-1970, then moved into a full-time position as an associate professor in the men's physical education department, a position which he had occupied in a part-time role for many years.

WILLIAM C. (KAYO) LAM

The finish of the Carlson-Lam team was not an especially fitting one. An athletic bypass had been established in 1959 when CU administrators dealt directly with football coach Sonny Grandelius instead of proceeding through the normal channels. With the resulting loose supervision from the distance, CU was soon enveloped in a recruiting scandal which plummeted the Buffalo football team from first place to seventh in 1962.

Eddie Crowder was brought in to treat the football crisis, returning credibility and winning play in three years. When Carlson retired in 1965, Crowder was a quick, and popular, choice to succeed him as director. Dual athletic director - football coaches were beginning to disappear from the scene at the time but Crowder had apprenticed under one of the nation's masters, Bud Wilkinson of Oklahoma, and was ready for the test.

A tightly-wound package of endless energy and drive, he attacked the coaching and administrative problems with the same intensity with which he had transformed his rather routine physical abilities into becoming an All-American quarterback at Oklahoma. Within five years he had produced dramatic improvements in both CU's football and facilities programs.

EDDIE CROWDER

In fact, no CU athletic director has presided over physical plant improvement of such scope as Crowder. Refuting the fears of traditionalists who fretted that multiple-jobbed men were products of the relatively quiet pasts and unequipped to handle the overwhelming problems of the present, Eddie managed a quick, efficient and impressive transformation.

Consider these accomplishments. Folsom Stadium was expanded by nearly 6,000 seats in 1967. At the same time, a badly-needed team building was added at the stadium's north end. A new outdoor track with an all-weather surface and baseball field were built on east campus. A year later, a 5-story structure was erected above the west stands to house the media and a new booster club which provided the funds to finance the project. Then followed a synthetic surface in the field house to cover the dirt base upon which CU athletes had worked for more than three decades and which transformed the old building into a truly all-purpose facility used extensively for student activities as well as athletic events.

In 1971, artificial turf was added to Folsom Stadium and the stadium renovation was completed in 1976 in a million-dollar project which included concreting the sides of the original bowl, replacing the wooden benches with aluminum ones and adding a new quarter-million dollar scoreboard.

Crowder managed all this while guiding a CU football program which would produce five bowl teams during his 11 seasons as coach. With his resignation as football coach in 1973, he directed his energies to building a new basketball arena. This project resulted in the 8-million dollar Events-Conference Center which opened in 1979.

Unfortunately, Crowder's administrative career, like Carlson's, ended under less than satisfactory conditions. In 1980, departmental deficits nearing one million dollars required the elimination of six sports (men's baseball, wrestling, gymnastics and swimming, and women's gymnastics and swimming.) In fairness to Eddie, more than half of the deficit was created by the required addition of women's programs, force-fed into being by governmental edicts, produced no income. The resulting sudden, and staggering deficit forced Crowder, under the strong insistence of president Arnold Weber, to trim the program. Crowder took most of the heat. Only half the blame was his. He, as director, had failed to hire football coaches who could maintain the quality he had established. Football income declined sharply at the same time as women's athletics emerged. The resulting deficit and the problems created by them soon wearied him of the battle and he resigned, under no duress, in 1984 to enter private business in Boulder.

With his departure, he left still another important contribution to CU athletics in the form of his assistant director, Jon Burianek, the third in the line of background giants which previously included Franklin and Lam.

Burianek, like Franklin a chemistry major at CU, had moved quietly into the athletic department as an hourly student employee for Lam in 1968. His abilities and energies earned him a full-time position as ticket manager in 1970 and he became assistant athletic director for business affairs in 1979. Crowder promoted him to associate director in 1983 and he was an important figure in the transition period following Crowder's departure.

Except for not being an athlete at CU, Burianek was almost a carbon copy of Franklin and Lam. A tireless worker with an outstanding understanding of the entire operation, he was the man nearly everyone turned to in business or physical plant affairs. The primary duty of an athletic director is to work the public side of the street, particularly in fund-raising which had become such an important part of departmental financing by the mid-sixties. This involvement requires an outstanding aide to manage the internal affairs.

Like Lam, Burianek has served two directors well. A totally unsung member of the department, he has been a strong, solidifying member of the CU cast during the final two decades of the

Handling ticket requests became a pleasant problem for the CU ticket office as the first century closed. Associate Athletic Director John Burianek and Assistant Caroline Fenton look over the remaining tickets for the 1989 Nebraska game.

first century. And although relatively unknown to the general public, his value to the department is recognized by every administrator and athletic figure who has worked with him. Burianek is one of the real rocks in the CU athletic foundation as it enters its second century.

The man in charge is Bill Marolt, who became the first CU graduate to serve as athletic director when he succeeded Crowder in 1984. Like his predecessors, he was an outstanding athlete, but in a different sport. Carlson and Crowder were from traditional college backgrounds, baseball and football. Marolt was an All-American and Olympic Alpine skier. If the three men came from different competitive areas, they were similar in personality: none was a colorful public figure in his administrative role, each man preferring to let his actions speak for him.

After an outstanding competitive skiing career (All-American at CU in 1963 and U.S. Olympian in 1964), Marolt burst to prominence as a coach after taking over the ski program in 1969 when his CU team won seven straight NCAA championships from 1972-78. From CU he became director of the U.S. ski team, overseeing a multi-million dollar program which produced the nation's finest Olympic results in 1984 when American skiers won five Alpine medals, three of them gold.

His combined record as a CU and national coach and administrator made him a popular choice to succeed Crowder. Like his predecessors he did not arrive without critics. There were reservations in some quarters that his

ski background had not prepared him for managing an intercollegiate program. Overseeing a ski program, his strength, would be one of the least of his responsibilities in a job which required controlling the time-and-money-devouring sports of football and basketball.

Marolt was the first to acknowledge the disadvantages of his skiing background. But on his credit side were the qualities which had made him an outstanding success as a skier then as a college and national coach: the ability to cope with administrative problems and manage people plus a more than average supply of intelligence, energy, dedication and probably his top intangible, his devotion to his school. A native Coloradoan and CU graduate, he went about the business of assuming control of CU athletics quietly and efficiently.

Although he was in command for only the last six years of the first century, he led a movement which sharply stepped up CU's continuing quest for athletic glory. By his fourth year as director, his efforts had nearly doubled the school's athletic budget to nearly 10 million dollars.

Marolt made what possibly might have been the wisest and most courageous decision of the century when, late in the 1984 season with McCartneys third CU squad standing at 1-7 and headed for a disastrous 1-10 campaign, he gave Mac a contract extension. It wasn't necessarily the most popular move (McCartneys over all record at that point was only 7-22-1) but it gave Mac the breathing room needed to get his program on track. The move paid

BILL MAROLT

immediate dividends. In the following five regular seasons, the McCartney men marched to a 39-19 mark and, amazingly, the Buffaloes had made a dramatic transistion from the basement to the penthouse. Certainly much of the credit was due to McCartneys efforts. But just as certainly Marolts 1984 vote of confidence opened the door for Mac.

Directing a program of this scope is a time-consuming, energy-eating experience. The Bill Marolt of 1990 has learned his lessons well to become an able administrator, a man highly capable of leading CU into its second century. It's not an easy assignment. But CU has always found men to match her mountains. Under the latest, Marolt, the school moved toward the end of the 20th century with confidence and quality, the way it has for the first 100 years.

A Century of Buffalo Records

INDIVIDUAL RECORDS

RUSHING

Net Yards
Quarter — 131, Eric Bieniemy vs. Oregon State in Boulder, Sept. 24, 1988 (on nine carries, fourth quarter).
Half — 206, Charlie Davis vs. Oklahoma State in Boulder, Nov. 13, 1971.
Game — 342, Charlie Davis vs. Oklahoma State in Boulder, Nov. 13, 1971.
Season — 1386, Charlie Davis, 1971.
Career — 2958, Charlie Davis, 1971-1973.

Average Per Game
Season — 140.1 (1121 yards in 8 games), Byron White, 1937.
Career — 89.6 (2,958 yards in 33 games), Charlie Davis, 1971-1973.

Touchdowns
Game — 4, by eight players. Last two; James Mayberry vs. Northwestern in Boulder, Sept. 30, 1978; Bobby Anderson vs. Tulsa in Boulder, Sept. 20, 1969.
Season — 18, Bobby Anderson, 1969; J.J. Flannigan, 1989.
Career — 34, Bobby Anderson, 1967-1969.

Longest Play from Scrimmage
Scoring — 95, Emerson Wilson vs. Kansas State in Boulder, Nov. 20, 1954.
Non-scoring — 70, James Mayberry vs. Oklahoma State in Boulder, Oct. 8, 1977.

Most Yards Gained by a Quarterback
Game — 207 (26 carries), Bobby Anderson vs. Oklahoma State at Stillwater, Nov. 9, 1968.
Season — 1004 (186 carries), Darian Hagan, 1989.
Career — 1,430 (361 carries), Mark Hatcher, 1985-87.

Most 100-Yard Rushing Games
Season — 7, by James Mayberry, 1977 (five home, two road), and Eric Bieniemy, 1988 (four home, three road).
Career — 13, Charlie Davis, 1971-1973.

Most 200-Yard Rushing Games
Season — 1, Carroll Hardy (1954), Bobby Anderson (1968), Charlie Davis (1971), Billy Waddy (1973), James Mayberry (1977), Eric Bieniemy (1988).

Single Season Yards
1,386 Charlie Davis, 1971.
1,299 James Mayberry, 1977.
1,243 Eric Bieniemy, 1988.
1,210 Tony Reed, 1976.
1,187 J.J. Flannigan, 1989.
1,121 Byron White, 1937.
1,097 Bob Stransky, 1957.
1,043 Kayo Lam, 1935
1,004 Darian Hagan, 1989.

PASSING

Completed
Game — 25 by Steve Vogel (51 attempts) vs. Kansas State at Manhattan, Nov. 20, 1982; Steve Vogel (48 attempts) vs. Michigan State in Boulder, Sept. 8, 1985.
Season — 112 (of 222), Bobby Anderson, 1968.
Career — 309 by Steve Vogel, 1981-1984.

Most Yards Gained
Quarter — 176, Randy Essington vs. Texas Tech in Boulder, Sept. 12, 1981.
Half — 273, Randy Essington vs. Texas Tech in Boulder, Sept. 12, 1981.
Game — 361 by Randy Essington vs. Nebraska at Boulder, Oct. 9, 1982.
Season — 1,432, Steve Vogel, 1984.
Career — 3,912, Steve Vogel, 1981-1984.

Most Touchdown Passes Thrown
Game — 3, Paul McClung, vs. Wyoming in Boulder, Oct. 26, 1940; Gale Weidner vs. Kansas in Boulder, Nov. 7, 1959 and vs. Kansas in Boulder, Oct. 7, 1961; Bobby Anderson vs. Kansas State in Boulder, Oct. 19, 1968; Randy Essington vs. Texas Tech in Boulder, Sept. 12, 1981; Steve Vogel vs. Kansas at Boulder, Nov. 13, 1982; Steve Vogel vs. Michigan State in Boulder, Sept. 8, 1985; Steve Vogel vs. Iowa State in Boulder, Oct. 13, 1985.
Season — 12, Steve Vogel, 1983.
Career — 27, Steve Vogel, 1981-1984.

Most Consecutive Games Throwing a Touchdown Pass
6 — Steve Vogel (last three in 1982 and first three in 1983).

Longest Play
Scoring — 90 yards, Marc Walters to Jeff Campbell, vs. Kansas State in Boulder, Nov. 19, 1988.
Non-Scoring — 77 yards, Woody Shelton to Ronnie Johnson, vs. Northwestern at Evanston, Sept. 29, 1951.

Single-Season Yards
1,432 Steve Vogel, 1984.
1,385 Steve Vogel, 1983.
1,341 Bobby Anderson, 1968.
1,282 David Williams, 1975.
1,203 Jeff Knapple, 1977.
1,200 Gale Weidner, 1959.
1,199 Randy Essington, 1981.
1,175 Bernie McCall, 1965.
1,174 Bill Solomon, 1979.
1,126 Ken Johnson, 1971.
1,121 Randy Essington, 1982.
1,101 Gale Weidner, 1960.
1,002 Darian Hagan, 1989.

TOTAL OFFENSE

Yards Gained
Game — 353 (207 rush, 146 pass), Bobby Anderson vs. Oklahoma State at Stillwater, Nov. 9, 1968.
Season — 2129 (788 rush, 1341 pass), Bobby Anderson, 1968.
Career — 4565 (2367 rush, 2198 pass), Bobby Anderson, 1967-1969.

Average Per Game
Season — 212.9 (2129 yards in 10 games), Bobby Anderson, 1968.
Career — 152.2 (4565 yards in 30 games), Bobby Anderson, 1967-1969.

Most Games Gaining 300 Yards or More
Season — 1, Bobby Anderson, 1968; Charlie Davis, 1971; Ken Johnson, 1971; Jim Bratten, 1969; Randy Essington, 1981; Randy Essington, 1982; Craig Keenan, 1984.

Highest Average Per Play
Game (minimum 30 plays) — 10.1, Charlie Davis vs. Oklahoma State in Boulder, Nov. 13, 1971.
Season (minimum 1000 yards) - 7.4 (271 plays, 2006 yards), Darian Hagan, 1989.
Career (minimum 2,000 yards) — 5.5 (538 for 2,958), Charlie Davis, 1971-1973.

RECEIVING

Receptions
Game — 10 (for 142 yards), Ed Reinhardt vs. Michigan State in Boulder, Sept. 8, 1984.
Season — 51 (for 680 yards), Jon Embree, 1984.
Career — 111 (for 1,436 yards), Monte Huber, 1967-1969.

Receptions Per Game
Season — 4.6 (51 receptions in 11 games), Jon Embree, 1984.
Career — 3.7 (111 receptions in 30 games), Monte Huber, 1967-1969.

Yards Gained
Game — 222 (5 receptions), Walter Stanley vs. Texas Tech in Boulder, Sept. 12, 1981.
Season — 680 (51 receptions), Jon Embree, 1984.
Career — 1,436 (111 receptions), Monte Huber, 1967-1969.

Touchdown Passes Caught
Game — 3, Richard Johnson vs. Kansas at Boulder, Nov. 13, 1982.
Season — 8, Gary Knafelc, 1953.
Career — 11, Gary Knafelc, 1952-1953.

Single-Game Reception Bests
10 Ed Reinhardt vs. Michigan State in Boulder, Sept. 8, 1984.
9 Monte Huber vs. California at Berkeley, Sept. 28, 1968.
8 Ken Blair vs. Utah at Salt Lake City, Sept. 22, 1962.
8 Jon Embree vs. UCLA in Boulder, Sept. 29, 1984.
8 Jon Embree vs. Kansas in Boulder, Nov. 3, 1984.
8 John Farler vs. Missouri in Boulder, Nov. 6, 1965.
8 Monte Huber vs. Kansas State at Manhattan, Nov. 18, 1967.
8 Monte Huber vs. Air Force in Boulder, Nov. 23, 1968.

Career Receptions
111 Monte Huber, 1967-69.
91 Dave Hestera, 1981-1983.
86 Lee Rouson, 1981-1984.
80 Jon Embree, 1983-1986.
78 Loy Alexander, 1982-1985.
67 Dave Logan, 1972-1975.
61 J.V. Cain, 1971-1973.
57 Ron Brown, 1981-1985.
52 Chris McLemore, 1982-1983.
51 Don Hasselbeck, 1973-1976.
48 Merwin Hodel, 1949-1951.

PUNT RETURNS

Punt Return Yards
Game — 159 (3 returns), Byron White vs. Utah in Boulder, Nov. 7, 1936.
Season — 587 (47 returns), Byron White, 1937.
Career — 904 (84 returns), Jeff Campbell, 1986-1989.

Punt Return Average
Game — 53.0 (3 returns for 159 yards), Byron White vs. Utah in Boulder, Nov. 7, 1936.
Season — 16.58 (26 returns for 431 yards), Charlie Greer, 1965.

Longest Punt Return
98 — Bob West vs. Colorado College at Colorado Springs, Nov. 18, 1944.

KICKOFF RETURNS

Kickoff Return Yards
Game — 184 (5 returns), Howard Ballage vs. Nebraska in Boulder, Oct. 21, 1978.
Season — 704 (30 returns), Walter Stanley, 1981.
Career — 1198 (51 returns), M.J. Nelson, 1986-1989.

Kickoff Return Average
Game — 53.3 (3 for 160 yards), Walter Stanley vs. Oklahoma in Boulder, Oct. 4, 1980.
Season — 29.4 (18 for 530 yards), Howard Ballage, 1978.
Career — 26.5 (32 for 849 yards), Billy Waddy, 1973-1976.

Kickoff Return Touchdowns
Season - 2, Cliff Branch, 1971.
Career - 2, Cliff Branch (1970-1971), Billy Waddy (1973-1976), Howard Ballage (1976-1978).

Longest Kickoff Return
102 — Byron White vs. Denver at Denver, Nov. 26, 1936 (old record).
100 — Cliff Branch vs. Kansas in Boulder, Nov. 7, 1970; Billy Waddy vs. Kansas State in Boulder, Nov. 22, 1975; Howard Ballage vs. Nebraska in Boulder, Oct. 21, 1978; Walter Stanley vs. Oklahoma in Boulder, Oct. 4, 1980.

ALL-PURPOSE RUNNING

Yards Gained
Game — 353 (342 rushing, 11 receiving), Charlie Davis vs. Oklahoma State in Boulder, Nov. 13, 1981.
Season — 1524 (1386 rushing, 79 receiving, 59 return), Charlie Davis, 1971.
Career — 3164 (2958 rushing, 131 receiving, 75 return), Charlie Davis, 1971-1973.

Highest Average Per Play
Season (1,000 yards minimum) — 20.3 (62 plays for 1261 yards), Cliff Branch, 1971.
Career (1,000 yards per season) — 17.8 (141 plays for 2507 yards), Cliff Branch, 1970-1971.

INTERCEPTIONS

Passes Intercepted
Game — 3, Roy Shepherd vs. Colorado A&M in Boulder, Nov. 29, 1952; Frank Bernardi and Carroll Hardy vs. Utah in Boulder, Nov. 7, 1953; Dick Anderson vs. Oregon at Eugene, Sept. 23, 1967; Rich Bland vs. Air Force in Boulder, Oct. 13, 1973; Victor Scott vs. Oklahoma State at Stillwater, Oct. 16, 1982.
Season — 7, Dick Anderson (1967), and Cullen Bryant (1972).
Career — 16, John Stearns, 1970-1972.

Interception Return Yards
Game — 120 (2 returns), Dick Kearns vs. Denver at Denver, Nov. 24, 1938.
Season — 158 (5 returns), John Stearns, 1971.
Career — 339 (16 returns), John Stearns, 1970-1972.

Longest Interception Return
102 — Dick Kearns vs. Denver in Denver, Nov. 24, 1938.

Interception Return Touchdowns
Game — 2, Victor Scott vs. Oklahoma State at Stillwater, Oct. 16, 1982.
Season — 2, Victor Scott, 1982.
Career — 3, Victor Scott, 1980-1983.

PUNTING

Highest Average Per Punt
Game (5 minimum) — 59.8 (5 for 299), Keith English vs. Oregon State in Boulder, Sept. 24, 1988.
Season (30 minimum) — 48.2 (38 for 1830), Zack Jordan, 1950.
Career (75 minimum) — 44.9 (153 for 6873), Barry Helton, 1984-87.

Longest Punt
84 — Byron White vs. Missouri in Boulder, Oct. 2, 1937 (without roll).

SCORING

Points Scored
Game — 25, Byron White vs. Utah in Boulder, Nov. 7, 1936 (4 TD's, 1 PAT), Howard Cook vs. Arizona at Tucson, Oct. 11, 1958 (4 TD's, 1 PAT).
Season — 122, Byron White, 1937 (16 TDs, 23 PATs, 1 FG).
Career — 212, Bobby Anderson, 1967-1969.

Touchdowns Scored
Game — 4, by nine players, Last two: Bobby Anderson vs. Tulsa in Boulder, Sept. 20, 1969, Richard Johnson vs. Kansas in Boulder, Nov. 13, 1982.
Season — 19, Bobby Anderson, 1969.
Career — 35, Bobby Anderson, 1967-1969.

Points Accounted for
Game — 34, Byron White vs. Denver at Denver, Nov. 25, 1937 (Rushed for two TDs, passed for two, returned interception for one, and converted 4 of 5 PATs).

Field Goals Made
Game — 4, Tom Field vs. Washington State at Spokane, Sept. 18, 1982; Tom Field vs. Oklahoma State at Stillwater, Oct. 16, 1982.
Season — 15 (of 34), Fred Lima, 1972.
Career — 36 (of 55), Tom Field, 1979-83.

Most Consecutive Field Goals Made
8 - Ken Culbertson, 1989.

Longest Field Goal Made
58 — Jerry Hamilton, vs. Iowa State in Ames, Oct. 24, 1981.
57 — Dave DeLine, vs. Nebraska in Boulder, Oct. 25, 1986.
57 — Fred Lima, vs. Iowa State in Boulder, Oct. 14, 1972.

Extra Points Made/Kicking
Game — 8, J.B. Dean vs. Wyoming in Boulder, Sept. 8, 1971; Fred Lima vs. Cincinnati in Boulder, Sept. 16, 1972.
Season — 59, Ken Culbertson, 1989 (of 59).
Career — 86 (of 92), Dave Haney, 1968-1970.

Points Scored by Kicking
Game — 14 (4 FGs, 2 PATs), Fred Lima vs. Kansas in Boulder, Nov. 11, 1972.
Season — 98 (13 FGs, 59 PATs), Ken Culbertson, 1989.
Career — 190 (82 of 86 PAT, 36 of 55 FG), Tom Field, 1979-1983.

Single-Season Points
122 Byron White, 1937.
114 Bob Anderson, 1969.
108 J.J. Flannigan, 1989.
90 Merwin Hodel, 1950.
90 Jim Kelleher, 1976.
84 Charlie Davis, 1972.
80 Fred Lima, 1972.
78 James Mayberry, 1978.
77 Bob Stransky, 1957.

Single-Season Touchdowns
19 Bobby Anderson, 1969.
18 J.J. Flannigan, 1989.
16 Byron White, 1937.
15 Merwin Hodel, 1950.
15 Jim Kelleher, 1976.
14 Charlie Davis, 1972.
13 James Mayberry, 1978.

Career Points
212 Bobby Anderson, 1967-1969.
191 Byron White, 1935-1937.
190 Tom Field, 1979-1983.
168 Merwin Hodel, 1949-1951.
162 J.J. Flannigan, 1987-1989
158 Charlie Davis, 1971-1973.
152 Carroll Hardy, 1952-1955.
150 James Mayberry, 1975-1978.
149 Dave Haney, 1968-1970.
144 John Bayuk, 1954-1956.
138 Terry Kunz, 1972-1975.

Career Touchdowns
35 Bobby Anderson, 1967-1969.
28 Merwin Hodel, 1949-1951.
27 J.J. Flannigan, 1987-1989.
26 Charlie Davis, 1971-1973.
26 Byron White, 1935-1937.
25 James Mayberry, 1975-1978.
24 John Bayuk, 1954-1956.
23 Terry Kunz, 1972-1975.

DEFENSIVE

Total Tackles
Game — 30 (5 UT, 25 AT), Jeff Geiser vs. Kansas State in Boulder, Nov. 24, 1973
Season — 183 (102 UT, 81 AT), Ray Cone, 1982.
Career — 493 (245 UT, 248 AT), Barry Remington, 1982-1986.

Quarterback Sacks
Game — 5 (for 36 yards), Dan McMillen vs. Kansas at Lawrence, Nov. 2, 1985.
Season — 14 (for 86 yards), Dan McMillen, 1985.
Career — 22½ (for 166 yards), Alfred Williams, 1987-1989.

TEAM RECORDS

TOTAL OFFENSE

Yards Gained
Quarter — 337, vs. Oklahoma State in Boulder, Nov. 13, 1971 (2nd).
Half — 512, vs. Oklahoma State in Boulder, Nov. 13, 1971 (1st).
Game — 676 (in 89 plays) vs. Oklahoma State in Boulder, Nov. 13, 1971.
Season — 5201 (in 768 plays), 1989.

Most Touchdowns, Rushing and Passing
Game — 9, vs. Arizona at Tucson, Oct. 11, 1958 (8 rushing, 1 passing).
Season — 59, in 1989.

Highest Average Per Game
Season — 472.8 in 1989 (5201 yards in 11 games).

FIRST DOWNS

First Downs
Game — 39, vs. Northwestern in Boulder, Sept. 30, 1978.
Season — 243, in 1975.

First Downs/Rushing
Game — 35, vs. Northwestern in Boulder, Sept. 30, 1978.
Season — 182 in 1989.

First Downs/Passing
Game — 17, vs. Michigan State in Boulder, Sept. 8, 1984.
Season — 121, in 1984.

RUSHING

Yards Gained
Game — 551 (69 attempts), vs. Arizona in Tucson, Oct. 11, 1958.
Season — 4090 in 1989.

Average Per Game
Season — 371.8 in 1989 (4090 yards in 11 games)

Average Per Rush
Game — 14.28 (36 for 514 yards) vs. Kansas State in Boulder, Nov. 20, 1954.
Season — 6.42 (492 for 3160 yards), 1954.

Touchdowns
Game — 8, vs. Arizona at Tucson, Oct. 11, 1958; vs. Northwestern in Boulder, Sept. 30, 1978.
Season — 54 in 1989.

PASSING

Completions
Game — 26 vs. Kansas State at Manhattan, Nov. 20, 1982.
Season — 191 (of 396 attempts) in 1984.

Yards
Game — 361 vs. Nebraska in Boulder, Oct. 9, 1982.
Season — 2,571, in 1984.

Highest Average Per Game
Season — 233.7, in 1984.

SCORING

Points Scored
Quarter — 35 vs. Iowa State at Ames, Oct. 14, 1989. (2nd)
Half — 45 vs. Iowa State at Ames, Oct. 14, 1989. (1st)
Game — 65, vs. Arizona at Tucson, Oct. 11, 1958.
Season — 452 in 1989.

Touchdowns Scored
Game — 10, vs. Arizona at Tucson, Oct. 11, 1958.
Season — 59 in 1989.

Extra Points Made/Kicking
Game — 8, vs. Wyoming in Boulder, Oct. 26, 1940, vs. Wyoming in Boulder, Sept. 8, 1971; vs. Cincinnati in Boulder, Sept. 16, 1972, vs. Kansas State in Boulder, Nov. 19, 1988; vs. Kansas State at Manhattan, Nov. 18, 1989.
Season — 59 (of 59) in 1989.

Scoring Average
Season — 41.1 in 1989.

INTERCEPTIONS

Interceptions
Game — 7, vs. Utah in Boulder, Nov. 7, 1953.
Season — 22, in 1965.

Interception Return Yards
Game — 188, vs. Nebraska at Lincoln, Oct. 21, 1967.
Season — 368, in 1967.

FUMBLES

Fewest Fumbles Lost
Season — 5, in 1956.

TURNOVERS

Fewest Turnovers
Game — 0, several times.
Season — 11, in 1956.

PUNTING

Average Per Punt
Game — (min. 4) — 61.5 (4 for 266), vs. Air Force in Boulder, Nov. 29, 1958.
Game (min. 6) — 57.2 (6 for 343), vs. Arizona in Boulder, Oct. 21, 1950.
Season — 46.0 (52 punts), in 1985.

TOTAL DEFENSE

Fewest Plays Allowed
Game — 35, vs. Nebraska at Lincoln, Nov. 18, 1961.
Season — 509, in 1946.

Fewest Passing Attempts Allowed
Game — 0, vs. Oklahoma in Boulder, Nov. 15, 1986.
Season — 101, in 1948.

Fewest Completions Allowed
Game — 0 (of 12) Nebraska at Lincoln, Nov. 18, 1961, (of 3, at LSU, Sept. 14, 1974); (of 1) vs. Oklahoma at Norman, Oct. 4, 1975; (of 0) vs. Oklahoma in Boulder, Nov. 15, 1986.
Season — 39 (of 107), in 1947.

Fewest Yards Allowed
Game — 31 (35 plays) vs. Nebraska at Lincoln, Nov. 18, 1961.
Season — 1796, in 1946.

Fewest Rushing Yards Allowed
Game — minus 40 (31 attempts), vs. Wichita State in Boulder, Sept. 27, 1975.
Season — 799 (10 games), in 1946.

Fewest Passing Yards Allowed
Game — 0, vs. Nebraska at Lincoln, Nov. 18, 1961; vs. Oklahoma at Norman, Oct. 4, 1975; vs. Oklahoma in Boulder, Nov. 15, 1986.
Season — 557, in 1960.

Fewest Points Allowed
Game — 0, 218 times.
Season — 13 (10 games), 1924.

Fewest First Downs Allowed
Game — 0, vs. Nebraska at Lincoln, Nov. 18, 1961.
Season — 102, in 1958.

Most Turnovers Forced
Game — 8, Utah in Boulder, Nov. 7, 1953; Iowa State at Ames, Oct. 19, 1985; Iowa State in Boulder, Oct. 29, 1988.
Season — 49 (30 fumbles, 19 interceptions), in 1976.

MISCELLANEOUS

Highest Scoring Game, Colorado and Opponent
124, Colorado (42) vs. Oklahoma (82) in Boulder, Oct. 4, 1980.

Highest Scoring Tie Game, Colorado and Opponent
25-25, Colorado vs. Oklahoma State at Stillwater, Oct. 16, 1982.

Most Consecutive Victories
21 (1908 through 1912).

Most Consecutive Victories at Home
12 (1895 through 1898)

Most Consecutive Victories on the Road
8 (1922 through 1924)

Most Consecutive Losses
10 (1963 through 1964)

Most Consecutive Shutouts
9, in 1924.

Most Consecutive Games Without Being Shutout
84 (1947 through 1955)

Most Players Scoring in One Game
10, vs. Wyoming in Boulder, Oct. 26, 1940 (Touchdowns scored by; Paul McClung (2), Leo Stasica (2), Vern Miller, Vern Lockard, Harold Carver, Leonard Scott, Hugh Gardner, Conversions scored by: Ray Jenkins (3), John Pudlik (3), Bob Barnes and Paul McClung).